A HISTORY OF
THE MYERS & BURNELL CUP

AND OTHER YORK & DISTRICT

CRICKET KNOCK-OUT COMPETITIONS

Paul Thorpe

Q

This book is dedicated to the late Geoff Maidment who first talked to me of our club's deeds in the Myers & Burnell, to the late John Waddington who provided encouragement and help and to Keith Cowl, happily still with us, who, as well as much help, also gave me the clue that helped complete this book.

Also to all the players, past and present, who have taken part in the Myers & Burnell Cup over the years.

For Mum and Dad, thank you.

All profits from this publication will go to the Primary Club, a charity for blind and partially sighted-cricketers.

ISBN 978-1-912728-11-4

Published and printed by
Quacks Books, 7 Grape Lane, York T: 01904 635967
Copyright Paul Thorpe 2019.
No reproduction without permission.

Typeset in Palatino Linotype and Arial.

THIS BOOK IS SPONSORED BY

Gem Construction (York) Ltd
Construction House
James Nicolson Link
York
YO30 4GR

Tel. 01904 696971
reception@gemcs.co.uk
www.gemcs.co.uk

CONTENTS

Acknowledgements

My thanks go to all the people who have given help and information in compiling this history, with apologies for any omissions.

Jackie Ainley
Kevin Ambrosen
Albert Arundale
Nigel Bartram
Dave Batty
Wally Baynes
Bill Bell
Caroline Bilton
Russ Bilton
Dave Blissett
Paul Botting
Mike Burdett
Steve Burdett
Joey Burton
Lee Bradshaw
Peter Bradshaw
Norman Brown
Bill Carter
Simon Cockerill
Harry Collins
Keith Cowl
Alan Clark
Stuart Craven
Philip Crowe
Paul Dearnley
John Deighton
Nigel Durham
Cliff Elleker
Dave Farmer
Alan Fletcher
Dave Flett
Nigel Fowler
Zilla Fraser
David Freeman
Andy Galloway

Alan Gott
Tony Haines
Phil Hall
Trevor Haw
Alex-Jane Hardstaff
Trevor Hardy
Linda Harper
Richard Hobson
Graham Hogben
Keith Houlston
Henry Houseman
Pete Houseman
Gina Huntington
Andy Inns
Ken Johnson
Mick Kenyon
Tony Kerrison
David Langstaff
Howard Lewis
Viv Littlewood
Dave Lockwood
Herbert Lockwood
Jim Love
Ken Magson
Robbie Marchant
Rosie & William Miers
Colin Mole
Joe Moore
Graham Morritt
Paul Mosey
Ann Mowbray
Ann Musgrave
Ian Nicholson
Dennis North

Mary & Mick Oldfield
Hal Parris
Albert Pattison
Alf Patrick
Martin Piercy
Roy Piercy
David Poole
Brian Prest
Neil Reader
Ken Robertson
Clive Robinson
Phil Robshaw
Bill Roddham
Peter Ruddock
Mark Sessions
Geoff Skilbeck
Ken Skilbeck
Les Smith
Neil Smith
Rob Smith
Brian Sprigg
Dave Sykes
Billy Thornton
Elaine Thorpe
Carol Vine
John Waddington
John Wetherill
Dick Whalley
Pat Wood
Daniel Woodhead
Timothy Wynn-Wernink
Des Wyrill
Alwyne Yorke
Charlie Yorke
John Yorke

I would like offer a word of thanks to all the staff at the British Library reading room at Boston Spa, whose help and patience during my researches has been greatly appreciated. I am grateful to Mike Green and GEM Construction for their generous support. Finally I am indebted to Horst Meyer and Katy Midgley at Quacks for their help and guidance in turning my manuscript into this beautifully produced book.

The photos in this book are published with the kind permission of the following; Newsquest Media, Keith Cowl, Alan Fletcher, Philip Crowe, Dave Lockwood, Graham Morritt, Paul Mosey, Nigel Fowler, Trevor Haw, Des Wyrill, Woodhouse Grange C.C., Easingwold C.C., Heworth C.C. and Giles Cookson, whose website www.cardindex.com contains some fascinating images of sport in the York area, including rare photos of both the Bootham Crescent and Wigginton Road grounds.

Introduction

The Myers & Burnell began 100 years ago and quickly became the most prestigious local cricket Cup competition and few who took part in it over the years could have imagined a time when evening Cup cricket would no longer be played. Sadly that time has almost come but I hope this book will serve as a small reminder of what was undoubtedly a "Golden Age" in local club cricket. The book came about as a result of a project to compile an illustrated history of my club Clifton Alliance C.C. in 2017, the year we celebrated 150 years of cricket on our ground. In its early years the team played as the North Riding Mental Hospital, later changing its name to Clifton Hospital, then Clifton Hospital Alliance when the Alliance club moved from the Knavesmire to the Hospital ground. Once the Hospital closed and we bought the ground the name changed for the final time to Clifton Alliance. I was aware that the Hospital side were a force in local cricket, particularly Cup cricket and had heard many tales of our successes in the Myers & Burnell Cup from our late President Geoff Maidment, who had worked at the Hospital and played for both the Hospital side and the Alliance club.

As part of the history I was writing I hoped to include a small section on the Myers & Burnell Cup and I began what I believed would be the fairly simple task of locating the trophy and noting the winners. Little did I realise that the Cup was not only missing but that no one appeared to have a comprehensive list of winners. It also became evident that the missing cup was not even the original and despite finding the original Cup, little information was forthcoming as it had been put on a different base and been used for a different competition. It became apparent that I would have to do some research to find the information I was after; just how addictive and time consuming it would become I was yet to learn. I began by talking to all the clubs and players I could find who had taken part in the competition over the years and started to fill in the blanks. John Waddington, the former Clifton Hospital and Stamford Bridge player, started the ball rolling with his tremendous memory for names, dates and faces and brought me new facts, pictures and cuttings on a weekly basis. Sadly

John passed away before I completed this book and I can only hope that I have done justice to all the information he provided. His enthusiasm was boundless and his encouragement always positive.

I met with and pestered many players and officials, looked through peoples' photos and press cuttings, all of which produced valuable information. Cliff Ellerker of Heworth C.C. kindly gave me access to his wonderful collection of press cuttings going back over fifty years. Keith Cowl from Dringhouses C.C. supplied a number of photos and cuttings and happened to recall having a list of winners which he thought had come from either Peter Vine or Malcolm Huntington, both now no longer with us, and who both covered cricket, amongst other sports, for *The Yorkshire Evening Press*. (The local evening paper has undergone several name changes over the years, starting life as *The York Evening Press* becoming *The Yorkshire Evening Press* and finally simply *The Press*, its current title which for ease I will use throughout) Although he was unable to locate this, Keith had given me the clue that would eventually lead me to a list of winners. Having contacted Carol Vine she kindly gave me access to her late husband's collection of press cuttings, photos and notes for his articles, many of which proved very useful, but none more so than a copy of an article by Malcolm Huntington. In this article from 1977 Malcolm gave some interesting snippets of information on the Myers & Burnell and to my amazement a list of winners from 1919 to 1977, which was a huge step toward completing the list of winners.

It was also around this time I discovered that the British Library at Boston Spa could provide original back copies of *The Press* as well as the *Yorkshire Gazette* and the *Yorkshire Herald* who merged in 1954 to become the *Yorkshire Gazette and Herald*. These publications gave detailed reports and scorecards from 1919 onward and weekly visits to Boston Spa throughout 2017 and 2018 helped me to find most of the missing pieces of the jigsaw. I realised during my research that there appeared to be no comprehensive list of any of the other local cricket cup competitions, so I have added a brief history of some of the main ones with a list of winners and runners-up where known. My thanks for help with this go to all the players and officials at the various local cricket clubs who I hope I have included in my acknowledgements, especially Tony Haines at Acomb C.C., Keith Cowl at Dringhouses C.C., Geoff and Ken Skilbeck at Easingwold C.C., Les Smith at Yapham C.C., Neil Reader at Escrick Park C.C., Dennis North at Stillington C.C. and, last but not least, Phil Hall at Osbaldwick C.C. who not only gave me help with his clubs' records, but also generously shared his genealogical expertise which helped complete names from many other clubs. The statistics were compiled initially from the various local newspapers mentioned and were greatly enhanced thanks to Clifton Alliance C.C., Woodhouse Grange C.C., Easingwold C.C., Heworth C.C., New Earswick C.C., Sheriff Hutton Bridge C.C., EscrickPark C.C., Acomb C.C., Thirsk C.C. and Dringhouses C.C. who all made old score-books available. I owe a debt of gratitude to my lifelong friend Ian Nicholson, who proof read my manuscript, pointed out numerous mistakes and contradictions, corrected my generally appalling grammar and re-wrote many of my rambling sentences, however any remaining mistakes are my responsibilty. Finally my thanks go to my wife Elaine, without whose help I could not have completed this task. Her patience has been truly remarkable and her constant supply of tea has kept me going. Due to time constraints I have been unable to pursue every avenue of enquiry and I make no claim to the information contained in this book being 100% accurate. Memories can be unreliable, many discrepancies were discovered between score-books and press reports and some details have been impossible to obtain. I have endeavoured to present the facts as accurately as possible, but I am certain that errors will have occurred and a glance at some of the lists show the self- evident omissions. My greatest pleasure would be to produce a revised edition with all the missing pieces in place, so I would be delighted to hear from anyone who can fill in any gaps or correct any mistakes.

Paul Thorpe 2019.

Contact me on   Tel. 07743 337803

E-mail pntethorpe@gmail.com

Chapter One

Myers & Burnell: the business.

The Myers & Burnell Cup was the premier cricket cup competition in the York area for many years until 2007, when Woodhouse Grange defeated Clifton Alliance in the very last final. The Cup takes its name from the firm of Myers & Burnell whose managing director John Harold Kaye donated the original Cup in 1919.

The firm were originally coach-builders, who were recorded trading in York as early as 1750. Martin Burnell was head of the company by 1800, being joined in 1829 by Christopher Myers and by 1836 they were operating as Myers & Burnell. The firm had begun with workshops in Peasholme Green but soon expanded and opened another set of premises in Davygate. George Kay, the son of a coachman from Heslington, was apprenticed to the firm by his father in 1870 and after a seven year apprenticeship he quickly rose through the ranks to become Works Manager. Martin Burnell had passed the business on to his son Benjamin who died in 1889 leaving it to his daughter Margaret who was married and living in London. She put it up for sale in early 1890 at which point George Kay in partnership with George Hare and a Mr. Havercroft succeeded in buying the workshops in Peasholme Green for £1,830. The Carriage Shop and Showroom in Davygate were bought by a London firm and rented to the partnership known as Hare, Havercroft and Kay.

The partnership was dissolved by mutual consent in 1902 and the shares of Hare and Havercroft were acquired by George Kaye, who added an "E" to his name at this juncture (his uncle John was already known as Kaye). The following year George bought the rented premises in Davygate and his son John Harold joined the business at the age of 18. In 1911 George, who as the son of a coachman, had spent his working life with coaches and did not view the advent of the motor car with any great enthusiasm, began to take a less active part in the business and allowed John Harold to supervise the transition from carriage building to motor dealers. John went on to become a well known figure in York, serving the City as an Alderman, Sheriff and Lord Mayor. It was John Harold who donated the original Cup in 1919 and until his death in 1957 attended the final as part of the presentation party, his connections allowing him to persuade many well known local dignitaries including Lord Mayors, M.P.'s and businessmen to present the Cup, although occasionally he or members of his family would do the honours.

John Harold was succeeded in the business by his son John Jacques Kaye who sold the Davygate property and moved to Stockhill Garage at the junction of Stamford Bridge Road and Church Balk in Dunnington as a result of the rapid expansion in the business and difficulty of access in the City centre. The firm began as coach-builders who supplied horse drawn carriages to businesses and wealthy private clients and in 1835 they were granted the Royal Warrant to supply coaches to the Duchess of Kent and her daughter Princess Victoria, soon to become Queen, and were still providing cars for Royal occasions in the 1950's. With the advent of the motor car they built bodies to go on the chassis supplied by companies such as Rolls Royce and Daimler. Once motor manufacturers began to assemble complete cars using their own bodies, the firm switched to become a motor dealer and repair garage, becoming the main distributors in the York area for Rolls Royce, Bentley, Rover, Standard Cars, Buick and Overland amongst others.

After the Second World War they also became agents for Ferguson tractors and agricultural machinery. Following the move to Dunnington in 1958 they became exclusively a dealer in agricultural vehicles and equipment, operating as an agent for Massey Ferguson and also running a petrol station and garage on the same site. The petrol station closed in the mid 1960's and the firm were bought out in 1983 by Burells, another Massey dealer from South Yorkshire, who were buying up agencies to expand their own business, so bringing to an end one of York's oldest firms. However many examples of their work can still be seen at vintage motor shows today, including several Rolls Royce models showing off the firm's superb craftsmanship.

Below are a selection of local press adverts for Myers & Burnell.

1919

1946

1923

1955

Chapter Two
Myers & Burnell: the Cup.

Following the First World War the York Cricket Club, then based at Bootham Crescent on the ground now used by York City F.C., held a meeting in early 1919 in the Guildhall to discuss the future of cricket in the City. The meeting was chaired by the Lord Mayor, Alderman Sir W. A. Foster-Todd, and attended by many local cricketers from clubs in the York area. The aims of the meeting were to revive cricket after the War, to strengthen the York Club which had experienced a long period of financial difficulty even before the outbreak of war and to encourage the development of the smaller local clubs. One of the suggestions to come out of the meeting was for a competition to be organised between local cricket clubs, to be called the "York and District Cricket Challenge Cup" and to be run by the York Club. John Kaye had already offered to provide a trophy and following several more meetings Mr. S. M. Toyne, usually known as Sammy, Headmaster at St. Peter's School and the newly elected York C.C. captain, drew up the first set of rules which are reproduced at the end of this chapter. The Cup itself was manufactured by Pearce and Sons who had premises in London, Leicester, Leeds and at 15 Lendal in York. The shop in York was described as a "diamond merchants" and was next to the post office in Lendal and there is still a Jewellery shop at 15 Lendal that continues the business today. The Cup was hallmarked as sterling silver in Birmingham in 1908, with a makers mark for Pearce & Sons and it weighs 30 ounces.

The Cup is engraved as follows;

YORK AND DISTRICT

PRESENTED BY
Messrs MYERS & BURNELL
1919

CRICKET CHALLENGE CUP

John Harold Kaye was a keen sportsman who played golf to a good standard and also played cricket for Crockey Hill well into "his older years" according to his daughter Zilla who also recollects that "if you worked at Myers & Burnell you had to play cricket". The firm did have cricket links before the Kay(e) family became involved and as far back as 1846 they fielded a team of eleven employees against a team from rival coach-builders Kearsley Ltd. John Harold occasionally got up teams to play those of his good friend Dr. Riddolls using the Haxby C.C. pitch on the Ethel Ward playing field where sadly cricket is no longer played, but the pavilion is still standing. During his time running the firm he appointed one of his trusted employees, Fred Blanchard, to organise the Myers & Burnell cricket teams and they continued to field a team until the early 1970's. They played mainly friendlies but did have several seasons in the Evening League in the early 1950's. Their pitch on the Knavesmire, a strip of dubious quality, cut out amongst the football pitches behind the Chase Hotel, was probably the main reason for not continuing in the League, although they did enter the Cup that bore their name on occasion albeit with little success, losing in the second round in 1968 being their best recorded performance.

The following is a transcription of an article published in *The Yorkshire Gazette* in April 1919 giving the rules of the new competition and the first ever draw.

KNOCK-OUT CRICKET.
York and Dristrict Myers-Burnell Challenge Cup.

One of the results of the various cricket meetings which have been held in the city this year is the institution of a cup competition on the knock-out principle. It is felt that owing to daylight saving the cricket loving populace of York would appreciate a competition of this type, provided that it could be arranged to play the games during the long summer evenings. Accordingly the York Cricket Club have placed their ground at liberty for this purpose on Tuesday evenings, and Mr. S. M. Toyne has very kindly granted the use of St. Peter's school ground on Thursday evenings. No less than 20 clubs have entered for the cup, and the preliminary round commences on 27 May.

The Rules of the Competition.

1/ The Cup shall be called "The York and District Myers-Burnell Cricket Challenge Cup". The Cup shall be played for annually and held in trust by the winning club, and returned to the treasurer of the York Club before 1 July in each year. It becomes the property of any club winning it three times.

2/ The York Club will present medals to both teams competing in the final round.

3/ All clubs within ten miles of York Minster shall be eligible to enter the competition at a fee of five shillings for non-affiliated clubs. No entrance fee shall be charged for affiliated clubs. The playing members of each club must reside within five miles of their club ground or headquarters, or must have played in four matches for his club during the present season.

4/ The matches shall be played on the York Club-ground, or on a ground approved by the York Club Committee.

5/ All matches shall be played in the evening, commencing not later than 6.15 p.m., excepting the final, which shall be played on a Saturday afternoon.

6/ The final and semi-final rounds shall be played to a finish, each side having one completed innings, if necessary.

7/ In the previous rounds, the matches shall be decided on a time limit basis. Each side shall be allowed 1½ hours batting, unless the innings be completed in less time, and the side scoring the larger number of runs shall be the winner.

8/ In case of ties or where play has been interrupted by weather conditions so as to prevent a definite decision being arrived at the match shall be replayed.

9/ Not more than 10 minutes shall be allowed between the innings. The incoming and outgoing batsmen must cross on the field of play.

10/ The Umpires shall be appointed by the York Club.

11/ Each club shall send to the Secretary of the York Club a complete list of competing players at least two clear days before the first round of the competition is begun. No professional, nor any player whose name does not appear on this list, is eligible to take part in the competition and no player shall be allowed to play for more than one club in the competition in the same season.

12/ No man who has played three times for the York Council team during the present season shall be eligible to play in this competition. (Players introduced to the Council team from affiliated clubs excepted).

13/ All disputes shall be decided by the committee of the York Club, who shall be the Governing Body of the competition. Protests must be lodged within three days of the match.

An Interesting Innovation.
As will be seen, this provides for a trial of "time limit" cricket, which we believe is an innovation in York. In all the ties except the semi-finals and final, each side will be allowed one and a half hours batting provided the innings is not completed in less than that time, so that spectators at the games should see some good lively cricket. As the name signifies, the cup has been presented by Mr. Kaye, of Messrs. Myers and Burnell, Davygate, and the thanks of all cricketers in the district are due to him for his generosity.

The Draw.
The draw for the preliminary and first rounds of the cup took place on Thursday evening and the following is the result:
Preliminary round- A 27 May, Burton-lane club and Institute v. Poppleton; B 29 May, Rowntrees v. Y.M.C.A.; C 3 June, Civil Service v. York Police; D 5 June, Dringhouses v. Stamford Bridge.
1st round-10 June, Huntington v. Haxby; 12 June, Monkgate P.M. v. Bishopthorpe; 17 June, York Revellers v. winners of D; 19 June, York N.E.R. v. Ricall; 24 June, Heworth v. St. Thomas's: 26 June, winners of C v. winners of A; 1 July, St. Michaels' v. winners of B; 3 July, Osbaldwick v. Old Priory Adult School.
All matches on Tuesdays will take place on the York ground and those on Thursdays at St. Peter's ground.
This list certainly promises very interesting games and it is most difficult to say what team will be the first to have its name engraved on the cup.

Heworth C.C. the first winners in 1919.

Back row; T.Varley (President), William Ware, Unknown, H.Craig, Major S.M.Dowsett, Arthur Smith, H.Herbert or Arthur Nettleton, Claude Anson, Unknown. Front row; H.Herbert or Arthur Nettleton, Charlie Trendall, George Ware, A.G.Simpson, J.W.Wheatley (Captain).

The original Myers & Burnell trophy won outright by York Ramblers in 1928, from 1929 to 1964 used as a cup for Senior School cricket and finally from 1989 to 2007 awarded to the runners-up in the Myers & Burnell.

Chapter Three

Myers & Burnell: the venue and format.

At the inauguration of the competition entry was restricted to clubs within a 10 mile radius of York Minster, this being relaxed at a later date and the first club I can find to compete from outside this area is Yapham C.C. in 1937. Initially the early rounds took place on York Cricket Club's home ground at Bootham Crescent on Tuesday evenings and St. Peter's school ground on Thursday evenings, these early rounds being played on one evening, each side having 1½ hours to bat. The semi-finals were played over two evenings, each side having "one completed innings" and the final, played to the same format, was to be completed on a Saturday afternoon with both the semis and the final to be played at Bootham Crescent.

The Bootham Crescent ground had been the home of the Club since 1881 when Sir Joseph Terry, head of the famous local confectioners and the Club's President, funded their relocation from the Knavesmire, to which they had moved following the building of York's first Railway Station on their previous ground in Toft Green. The use of the St. Peter's ground ceased after the inaugural season and in 1920 the Yorkshire Gentlemen's ground on Wigginton Road and the Rowntrees ground at Mille Crux were used for earlier rounds in addition to Bootham Crescent. From 1921 onwards preliminary rounds were played on the ground of the team "first out of the hat" at the draw and all subsequent games were played at Bootham Crescent.

COUNTY CRICKETERS AT YORK.

A. T. Barber, the new Yorkshire cricket captain, leading the County man out at York on Saturday for their match with the York and District Sixteen, which marked the opening of the York and County season.—Y.G.

From *The Yorkshire Gazette* Saturday 3rd May 1930. A rare photo of the Bootham Crescent ground and pavilion, which was the Myers & Burnell venue from 1919 to 1931.

The format of the competition has varied over the years as the rules were changed and added to on a regular basis and it has proved very difficult to unearth much information other than that which can be gleaned from the scorecards. Up to 1926 the format remained as set out in the 1919 rules, an interesting effect of the rule to allow each team a completed innings in the semi-finals being evident in the 1919 competition. In the first semi-final on 7th August Civil Service were 95 all out and the following evening Heworth amassed 214 for 6 before it became too dark to continue. The second semi-final went a similar way, with Bishopthorpe scoring 133 all out on 12th August and St. Michael-le-Belfry going on to score 174 for 7 the following evening. In 1927 the final became a "time limit" game, each side having 2½ hours to bat with no limit on the number of overs which could be bowled. Acomb were 188 all out off 54 overs in 2 hours 20 minutes and Bootham Park replied with 190 for 8 off 61.4 overs with time almost expired. The earlier rounds and semi-finals remained unchanged from the 1919 rules. The next change came in 1930 when the earlier rounds, although retaining the 1½ hour time limit, were restricted to a maximum of 28 overs, the exact purpose of this change being unclear. There was some speculation at the time, repeated in 1974 by his team mate Alf Aveyard when interviewed by Malcolm Huntington, that the excessively long run up of the North Riding Mental Hospital bowler Ernie Marshall had brought this about. This seems to make little sense as the time limit was retained, meaning Marshall's opponents would still receive fewer overs. In 1933 the final was fixed at 50 overs per side on a Saturday afternoon, the semi-finals to be 40 overs per side over two consecutive evenings and the earlier rounds remained a maximum of 28 overs in 1½ hours to be played on one evening. In 1946 the time limit on the early rounds was abandoned, leaving the format as 50 overs per side in the final, 40 overs per side in the semi-finals and 28 overs per side in the early rounds, this format continuing until 1958 when Woodhouse Grange became the last club to win a Saturday afternoon final.

By this time many clubs were finding the commitment to Saturday afternoon League cricket was making it difficult to play in the final on an August Saturday, so from 1959 onwards all the rounds up to and including the final were fixed as 18 overs per side and for the first time eight ball overs were to be used instead of the usual six. All games were to be played in the evening and the traditional Thursday evening final in late July soon became the highlight of local knock-out cricket. Initially there were no restrictions on the overs that could be bowled by a player, which remained the case until a maximum of five overs per bowler was introduced in 1975. The last change to the format was introduced in 1994, when in an effort to revive the fortunes of the competition the final was moved to a Sunday afternoon, each side having two innings comprising 16 eight ball overs, with a restriction of four overs per bowler in each innings. The earlier rounds were also reduced to 16 eight ball overs with the same four over restriction on bowlers. However it appears from score-books that some clubs were not fully aware of the change and several early round games were still played as 18 over games!

In January 1932 the York Cricket Club, who were actively looking for a new home, decided to move to the ground on Wigginton Road which had been the home of the Yorkshire Gentlemen's Cricket Club since 1864, this being vacant due to the Gentlemen relocating to Escrick Park at the invitation of Lord Wenlock, one of their wealthy members. The lease on the vacant Bootham Crescent was taken up by York City Football Club, who built stands and terraces, some of which survive to this day, and improved the drainage which was poor and a major factor in the Cricket Club's desire for a new ground. The advantage of the move to Wigginton Road was twofold; the ground was much better drained and was also a purpose built Cricket Ground which involved no major work or expenditure for the Club. As an interesting aside, Wigginton Road is the only ground in York to have hosted first class cricket. The game started on 9th June 1890 with Yorkshire winning a three-day Championship match against Kent by eight wickets on the second day. The first ever touring team, the 1868 Australian Aboriginals, also played a two day game at Wigginton Road, where they were beaten by an innings and 51 runs by the Yorkshire Gentlemen.

Following the move to Wigginton Road the preliminary round games were played on the ground of the club "first out of the hat" at the draw and all subsequent games were played at Wigginton Road. In the mid 1960's plans were put in place for a new District Hospital on the Wigginton Road site and York Corporation, who had acquired the land during the Second World War from Bootham Park Hospital, sold the site to the York Hospital Board and then served notice on the Club with little or no warning. (How little has changed in York Council's attitude to sport over the years!) The Club were forced to move again, this time to land provided by the Hospital Board on Shipton Road adjacent to the Clifton Hospital ground, their new ground becoming known as Clifton Park. Initially all games except preliminary rounds were played at the new ground, but from 1976 onward both preliminary and 1st round games were played on the competing clubs' grounds to accommodate the new Isaac Poad Invitation competition. The remaining rounds were played at Clifton Park with the final still being played on a Thursday evening.

By the late 1980's a steady decline in interest in local cricket and particularly evening cup cricket saw fewer clubs able to raise teams, especially when few outside the top half dozen or so sides had a realistic chance of competing, let alone winning, so in 1994 the format changed to the two innings final as previously described. Despite this innovation interest continued to decline and in early 2008 York C.C. chairman Chris Houseman told the *The Press* that the competition would no longer take place, stating "the quality of entry and competition has deteriorated substantially." He went on to say "it might have once attracted thirty or forty teams, now it struggles to get eight". In point of fact for the last five years of the competition there were no real contenders outside the four teams who regularly contested the semi-finals, Acomb, Clifton Alliance, Woodhouse Grange and York. It was a sad end to a competition that once saw the ground on Wigginton Road packed for many games and certainly for the finals, where many spectators arrived up to an hour early to secure a seat. The crowd for the 1948 final between Acomb and Dringhouses was 3,129 and the following year 2,924 saw Clifton CC beat Dringhouses. The Gate money in the 1940's often topped £100, equivalent to around £6,000 in today's terms. After the move to Shipton Road the decline in attendance was bemoaned by many players and supporters alike but nevertheless over 600 attended the 1970 final between Dringhouses and Dunnington and 650 saw Easingwold beat Sheriff Hutton Bridge in 1972. The 1983 final between Acomb and Stamford Bridge was said to have seen a crowd of over 700 and set an attendance record for a final at Shipton Road.

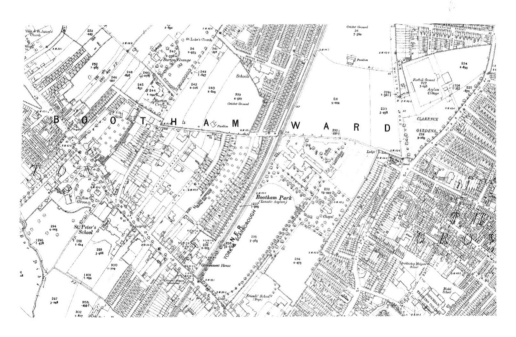

A 1909 map showing the Bootham Crescent ground with the pavilion in the south west corner, the Wigginton Road ground, then used by the Yorkshire Gentlemen's C.C. and the Football ground, the home of York Rugby League club.

Myers Burnell Cup Match. New Earswick v Dringhouses on York Ground. ~ June. 1950.

Back Row.~ **B. Goodhall. C. Coultate. J. Brewer. W. Anderson. N. Coates. K. B. Shaw.**

Front Row.~ **R. Nevison. W. E. Bryan. L. B. Barker. W. Walls (Capt.). H. Freer.**

The winning hit was made by Dringhouses off the last ball of the game.

A photo showing New Earswick on the York C.C. ground in 1950; the game was a 3rd round tie, in effect a quarter-final. The houses on Wigginton Road can be clearly seen in the background.

Stillington cricket team, who last night won the Myers Burnell Cup in an exciting final, beating Civil Service by nine runs. Back row (left to right): N. Morse, J. Wyrill, D. North, R. Midgley, A. Grainger, K. Snell. Front row: D. Spavin, C. Wood, J. Fowler, M. Denton, C. Minton.

The 1964 winners Stillington.

The 1947 winners Clifton C.C. in front of the pavilion at Wigginton Road.
Back row; G.G.Duncombe (Scorer), Arthur Broadhurst, Harold Hornshaw, Jim Pulleyn, Bill Roberts, Robert Henry Tate (Chairman), Cyril Myton.
Front row; Jim Blackburn, Bob Leadley, Herbert Harrison (Vice-Captain), George Edwards, Jack Pulleyn (Captain), Bob Crosby, Harry Craven.

The last final at Wigginton Road in 1966 with Woodhouse Grange captain Nigel Fowler ready to toss the coin with Dringhouses captain Geoff Limbert. Dringhouses went on to win and retained the trophy in 1967 in the first final at Clifton Park.

Chapter Four

Myers & Burnell: the competition.

The competition started in May 1919 with the first ever match taking place at Bootham Crescent between Burton Stone Lane WMC and Poppleton, each side having 1½ hours to bat, with Poppleton emerging victorious. The first final later that summer was won by Heworth, who batted first and "before a large assembly" they beat Saint Michael-le-Belfry by "a handful of runs" (Although some sources suggest that the winning team was Heworth Parish Church, my researches confirm that they did not enter the Myers & Burnell in 1919). The following year York Ramblers had the first of their four victories. In 1921 Dringhouses completed the first of their six wins defeating Escrick Park. York Ramblers won again in 1922.

The 1922 winners York Ramblers.

Only four players in this photo have been identified. F.W. Adamson is 2nd left back row, Harry Moult is 2nd right back row, Sam Buttery is 2nd left seated and the Captain Major Harry Johnson is seated in the centre with the Cup and the team mascot.

Escrick Park had their one and only success in 1923. Rowntrees won the first of their two Cups in 1924 and York City Amateurs had their only success in 1925. North Riding Mental Hospital (later to become Clifton Hospital then Clifton Alliance) defeated Acomb to win the Cup at their first attempt in 1926, and the following year saw another Hospital, Bootham Park, take the Cup. In 1928 the York Ramblers became the first club to win three times and under the rules of the competition were awarded the Cup to keep. The Ramblers were reluctant to accept it, as being a nomadic club at the time they had nowhere to display it. John Kaye, the donor, was keen they should have the cup and stated he would be delighted to provide a replacement. Following a letter to the local newspapers from a spectator at the final suggesting that the cup could be used to encourage local youth cricket, the Ramblers decided to lend the Cup to the York Education Committee to be competed for by "the York Elementary Schools", but would retain ownership of the Cup. A stamped and signed agreement to that effect dated 19th April 1929 is reproduced later in the book, as is a list of the known winners from 1929, when Knavesmire Higher Grade Boys were victorious, to 1964 when St. John's School won the last competition. The agreement stipulated that the Cup be renamed "The York Ramblers Cricket Cup" and be presented to the winning team each year by the Ramblers' president.

John Kaye made good his promise and donated a replacement trophy to be played for under the same rules as the original cup and the Ramblers then went on to win again in 1929, becoming the first club to retain the trophy and the first to register four wins. They were captained that year by Harry Moult who became the first player to appear in four finals. Acomb won in 1930, the first of their six wins. In 1931 the host club won when York Reserves took the trophy, the first of ten wins in the competition which the York club achieved under various guises. 1932 saw the start of a period of total dominance of the competition by the North Riding Mental Hospital, who won four consecutive Cups through to 1935, a unique feat, only York coming close with their three wins in the 2000's. The 1935 Hospital team contained W.I. Churchill (usually known as Ivor) and George A. Harling who set a then record, both appearing in their fifth final while Tommy Robinson and Percy Poole were playing in their fourth and went on to play in nine finals each. Fred Oliver, Harling and George William Appleby ended their careers with seven finals each and Alec Thompson played in six. Alf Aveyard, Joe Littlewood and Ivor Churchill played in ten finals and were still playing in the Myers & Burnell for Clifton Hospital over 30 years later. Ivor would have played in eleven finals had his daughter's wedding not taken place on the day of the 1953 final and he must surely have made more appearances than anybody in the competition. Although it has been impossible to compile a list of career appearances Reg Baines of Clarence C.&I. and Rowntrees, Noel Hare of Escrick Park and York, Norman Pearson of Stamford Bridge and Ken and Geoff Skilbeck of Easingwold all may have come close.

The 1934 runners-up New Earswick reached two other finals in 1953 and 1959, losing in 1953 to the Mental Hospital, by then known as Clifton Hospital and in 1959 to Tadcaster. Following their 1933 win the North Riding Mental Hospital became the first team to win the new trophy three times and under the rules it became their property, John Kaye announcing at the after-match presentation that he would be happy to provide a second replacement. The Hospital graciously accepted the Cup but generously declined to keep it, handing it back to be played for annually with the stipulation of a rule change to prevent any team winning it outright in the future. The Hospital won again in 1935 and their authorities withdrew the team the following year despite protests from their own players and pleas from the organisers and the donor. Tadcaster who were runners-up in 1933 and 1935 took advantage of the Hospital's absence to win in 1936.

A new name appeared on the trophy in 1937, Clifton C.C. defeating Tadcaster in the final. They were to appear a further four times in the next dozen years, being successful in 1942, 1946, 1947 and 1949, in the process becoming the third side to retain the trophy. A "nomadic" team made up of local businessmen and St Peter's School old boys, they played friendly fixtures at the weekends and on Wednesday afternoons, using the School ground in late July and August and playing only away fixtures during the early part of season. In 1938 the North Riding Mental Hospital who had returned to the competition in 1937 were defeated by Tadcaster who were appearing in their fourth consecutive final. Another new name appeared in 1939, when York Zingari, supposedly a nomadic mid-week side, but containing several York first team players won. They were bending the rules to say the least, also winning the Senior Charity Cup in 1939, but many objections were raised with the organizers of both competitions and they were never seen again in local cricket.

THE MYERS-BURNELL CUP

MR. J. H. KAYE presenting the Myers-Burnell Cricket Cup to the captain of Tadcaster, who defeated New Earswick in the final on the York ground, Wigginton-road.

A feature of the *Press, Gazette and Herald* were the sporting cartoons which adorned their pages. This one comes from the Press of August 1940.

1940 saw Tadcaster win again and they also reached the final in 1941 only to lose to York Railway Institute who secured the first of their three wins. Captained by Bob Stather, the team also contained his sixteen year old nephew Peter Morritt who would feature in their last two wins in 1960 and 1961 when they became the fourth team to successfully defend the trophy. Peter's son Graham appeared in two finals for Heworth in 1988 and 1992. In 1943 the Cup was won by the North Riding Mental Hospital playing under the name Clifton Hospital, part of the institution having become a military hospital for recuperating soldiers during the War and it was felt a name change would be appropriate.

After the War, with the creation of the N.H.S, the Hospital reverted to being a civilian mental hospital but the new name was retained and they won again in 1950 and 1953 and then in later years following their merger with the Alliance C.C. went on to win as Clifton Alliance in 1999 and 2001. 1944 saw Acomb take their second Cup to be followed by another win in 1948. A team from the R.A.F. base at Melbourne near Pocklington won in 1945. The winners in 1951 were Ovington C.C. who at the time played no competitive Saturday cricket. Based on the Knavesmire, they played almost exclusively friendlies along with some evening cup cricket and they are still proud to be the only Knavesmire based side to win the Cup. Their opponents in that final were Stamford Bridge C.C. another team who played no league cricket on Saturdays, playing friendlies, evening cup cricket and Wednesday afternoon fixtures. Stamford eventually played in five finals without success

The 1950 winners Clifton Hospital, pictured with replacement Cup which they won outright in 1933.
Back row; Len Freer, Joe McConnon, Mick Smith, Stan Page, Bob Carter snr., Tommy Robinson, Arthur Taylor, Percy Poole, Jimmy Hughes, Fred Oliver.
Front row; Ronnie Freer, Syd Appleyard, Hubert Dryland, Ivor Churchill (Captain), Dr. J. Russell, Alf Aveyard, Joe Littlewood.

The following season 1952 saw Dringhouses' second win, which heralded a long period of dominance for them in local cup cricket. They went on to win a further four times in 1955, 1966, 1967 and 1970 as well as reaching the final in 1962 and 1968 bringing their tally to six wins from twelve final appearances. In addition they had success in both the Senior and Junior Charity competitions, the Acomb Invitation and the Sawkill Cup. They were the last team to win the cup on the

Wigginton Road ground in 1966 and the first to win at Clifton Park in 1967, in the process becoming the fifth team to retain the trophy. Rowntrees who were runners-up in 1952 won their second Cup in 1954 and were runners-up again in 1958 which was their last appearance in a final. The host club won for a second time in 1956, this time as "York an XI" after being runners-up in 1955. Being a Yorkshire League club the rules limited them to no more than two first team players in the Myers & Burnell, hence the name was used to differentiate from their first team. 1957 saw the only win by the Magnets Sports Club from Tadcaster. The year 1958 saw Woodhouse Grange win for the first time. They went on to become one of the most successful local clubs in both League and Cup cricket, as well as having success at regional and national level, culminating in seven Lord's finals, four of which they won. It is somewhat surprising then that their next appearance in a Myers & Burnell final did not come until 1989 when they defeated Acomb. This was the start of five finals in eight years for Woodhouse, winning again in 1990 to become the sixth team to retain the trophy. They won in 1996, were runners-up in 1991, 1994 and 2003 and won the last ever competition in 2007, bringing their total final appearances to ten with five wins. 1959 saw Tadcaster register their last win and as previously mentioned York R.I. were successful for the next two years. Cawood were winners in 1962 beating Dringhouses in the final, a notable achievement for such a small village team. Huntington W.M.C, later to become Huntington C.C, won the Cup in 1963, their first season in the York and District Senior League and went on to win it again in 1965 and 1973.

John Beckett and Norman Pearson of Stamford Bridge go out to open the innings in the 1971 semi-final against Rowntrees. Stamford won the game but went on to lose to "York an XI" in the final.

York R.I. captain Geoff Britton receives the cup from former
Yorkshire captain Billy Sutcliffe after the 1960 final.

Another village side came to the fore in 1964 with Stillington
registering their only win. In 1968 Easingwold recorded the first of
their five wins in nine final appearances beating Dringhouses in the
last over, their other wins coming in 1972, 1974, 1979 and 1982. The
host club won again in 1969, this time playing as York Nomads and
this was followed by another win in 1971, this time under their usual
name of "York an XI". In between Dringhouses had their last win in
1970. Having reached the final for the first time in 1973 and losing to
Huntington W.M.C., Sheriff Hutton Bridge won the Cup in 1975 and
again in 1978. Dunnington put their name on the Cup for the only
time in 1976. "York an XI" won again in 1977, with two more wins
in 1980 and 1987. Sessay won the first of their two Cups in 1981, the
second coming in 1994 in the first of the "two innings" Sunday finals
at Clifton Park. 1983 saw Acomb win again 35 years after their last
triumph and in 1984 Heworth ended an even longer wait, winning
again 64 years after they won the inaugural competition. The mid-
eighties saw three sides from Division two of the Senior League
cause upsets, Crayke beat Sessay in 1985, Osbaldwick beat local rivals
Heworth in 1986 and in 1988 Thorp Arch & Boston Spa also beat
Heworth. Woodhouse Grange then reasserted the supremacy of the
"big guns" with successive wins in 1989 and 1990, just missing out on
making it three in a row in 1991 when Heworth gained victory with

three balls to spare in a closely fought game. Pocklington appearing in their only final upset favourites Heworth to win in 1992, thanks to the batting of Paul Jackson and wickets from part-time bowler Kevin Hinch. Heworth came back to win the following year and also won in 1997 in addition to being runners-up in 1996 and 2002, ending with a total of sixteen final appearances and five wins. Acomb registered their fifth win in 1995. Thirsk, who had never previously reached a final, made three consecutive appearances, winning in 1998 and 2000 and finishing runners-up to Clifton Alliance in 1999. Clifton Alliance went on to win again in 2001 and were runners-up in the last four finals from 2004 to 2007, which coupled with their record in previous incarnations as North Riding Mental Hospital and Clifton Hospital left them with ten wins from eighteen finals. In 2003 Acomb won for the sixth and last time in their twelfth final appearance. York then won three in a row from 2004 to 2006 to become the last team to retain the cup and bring their total to ten wins from fifteen finals. Finally Woodhouse Grange won the last ever Myers & Burnell in 2007, their fifth win from ten final appearances.

1970 winners Dringhouses

DRINGHOUSES C.C.
A. Fountain, R. Patterson, G. Myerscough, A. Bulmer, P. Smales, and A. Stilgoe.

Back row; Alan Fountain, Roly Pattison, George Myerscough, Andy Bulmer, Peter Smales, Tony Stilgoe.
Front row; Alwyne Yorke, Brian Wilson, Keith Cowl (Captain), Dave Burrows, Alan Burrows.

Chapter Five

Centurions, batting performances and big totals.

The first century scored in the competition was in the first ever semi-final, played at Bootham Crescent in August 1919, Arthur Henry Naylor of Saint Michael-le-Belfry scored 101 n.o. in a total of 174 for 7 on the evening of 13th August, Bishopthorpe having being bowled out for 133 on the previous evening.

Naylor was a prolific batsman and "a firm favourite with the York crowds" according to *The Gazette*. He scored 74 n.o. in the final to bring his total runs in the competition for the 1919 season to 266 at an average of 133. The photo shows him in suitable pose for the local newspapers on the Bootham Crescent ground prior to the start of the final.

In 1924 George Curry batting at number four for York Revellers against Henry Leetham & Sons scored 124 n.o. in a 1st round game restricted to 90 minutes per innings. Going in at 11 for 2 he hit 18 fours and one six in 70 minutes, the team total being a record 219 for 7. His individual record score was equalled in 1933 but never beaten. Leethams were all out for 82 and the match aggregate of 301 was also a record.

In 1925 Arthur Nelson Taylor, then 16 years old and later to play for Bootham Park and the successful Clifton Hospital side of the 1940's and 50's, scored 106 for York City Amateurs against Osbaldwick in the semi-final.

The 1926 season saw several scoring records set. In the first semi-final at Bootham Crescent, Acomb set a record team total of 294 for 7 in their innings on the first evening, the wonderfully named Captain Francis Leyland Lyster Fzler Roupell and Alan Dalby the Acomb openers setting a record for any wicket of 121. Roupell went on to score 108 and Osbaldwick could only manage 102 the following evening. A week later this record was well and truly beaten as the North Riding Mental Hospital rattled up 336 for 7 in their semi-final on 3rd August and went on to dismiss Rowntrees for 115 the following evening. The Hospital opener S. Tichener equalled Roupell's 108 and Ivor Churchill scored 105 at number three, which still remains the only instance of two players scoring a century in the same innings and their 2nd wicket stand also set a new record for any wicket, of 196. Ironically when these two teams met in the final it was the lowest scoring in the competition's history, Acomb shot the N.R.M.H. out for 69 inside 24 overs, only to fall 13 runs short themselves. Acomb reached the final again in 1927 when batting first they scored a record for a final of 188 all out off 54 overs with 10 minutes left to bat, only for Bootham Park to win with two balls to spare at 190 for 8. Arthur Taylor missed out on a second century with 92 n.o.; a more detailed account of this game appears in Chapter Eight.

The following year saw York Ramblers beat this total with 244 for 7 off 57 overs when time expired. Despite 90 from Reg Baines, Clarence Club & Institute were bowled out for 211 in the 47th over with 15 minutes left. The Ramblers' score was to remain a record in a final for a further thirty years.

In 1929 Reg Baines was in the runs again scoring an unbeaten 111 out of a total of 186 for 4 in 1½ hours for Clarence Club & Institute at Bootham Crescent in a 1st round tie. York City Amateurs could only manage 118 in reply.

The York City F.C. side that reached the quarter-finals of the 1937-38 F.A.Cup. Extreme left on the back row is Reg Baines, who was a prolific run scorer in the Myers & Burnell for Clarence C&I in the 1920's. He went on to captain Rowntrees, for whom he worked, to victory in 1954 and he was still playing into the 1960's. For York City he was a legend. In three spells with the City he scored 93 goals in 140 appearances and netted a record eight hat-tricks for the club. Second right on the front row is Jack Pinder, another City legend who made 229 appearances and played in three Myers & Burnell finals for Acomb and one for York. To his left is Jimmy Hughes who made 127 appearances and scored 36 goals between 1934 and 1939. A spell in Stalag 5497 during the War effectively ended his football career but on his return he played cricket for Clifton Hospital and Bootham Park, appearing in the Myers & Burnell until the late 1950's. Several other York City players turned out in the competition over the years, including Harry Moult for York Ramblers, Bert Brennen for York Zingari, Clifton C.C., York, Ebor Gogues and Clifton Hospital, Bob Stather for York R.I., John Hawksby, (who also played for Leeds United), for British Sugar, Ian Burden for Clifton Hospital Alliance, Chris Topping for Bubwith and John Sharples for Ovington. Goalkeepers have featured prominently, including Bob Ferguson for York, Tommy Forgan for Terrys, Neil Smallwood for New Earswick and Dunnington and Andy Leaning for Acomb. Most notably of all, one of York City's most popular players, Alf Patrick, played in four finals for Dringhouses, three of them with his brother John.

The St. Peter's Headmaster Sammy Toyne scored an unbeaten 102 for Clifton C.C. against St. Luke's in the preliminary round of 1930.

In 1933 Alf Aveyard scored 116 n.o. for the North Riding Mental Hospital against Northern Command in a preliminary round game played on the Hospital ground. The innings was limited to a maximum of 28 overs or 1½ hours whichever came first. He went one better in the final scoring 124 n.o. in 49 overs against Tadcaster to secure the Hospital's third win. Alf thus became the first and only player to score two centuries in the competition as well as becoming the first centurion in a final. His score equalled George Curry's record and was never beaten in the remaining 74 years of the competition.

Alf Aveyard was a well known local sportsman. As well as cricket he also played football, golf, tennis and table tennis to a good standard, and was a mainstay of the Hospital sides for over thirty years. He is the only player to score two separate hundreds in the Myers & Burnell and his 124 n.o. in the 1933 final is the joint highest score by an individual. He is pictured here with his long time opening partner Joe Littlewood going out to bat for Clifton Hospital in the 1949 Myers & Burnell semi-final against Dringhouses at Wigginton Road. Alf is on the right of the picture.

Tadcaster captain Noel Herbert scored 106 n.o. against Stillington in the 1935 semi-final putting on an unbroken 3rd wicket partnership of 162 with Fred Shearsmith.

Walter Skilbeck of the famous cricketing family scored 112 n.o. in 28 overs for Easingwold against York Corporation in an early round of the 1948 competition.

In a 1955 3rd round game of 28 overs per side Dennis Johnson of Yapham scored 104 n.o. in their victory over the much fancied Clifton

Hospital. Going in number three his innings contained seven sixes and nine fours.

The last ever Saturday final took place in 1958 and Woodhouse Grange, in their first appearance in a final, beat York Ramblers' thirty year old record by scoring 250 for 8 off 50 overs. Their opponents Rowntrees reached 46 for 2 before rain stopped play, the veteran Reg Baines being one of the Rowntrees openers dismissed. The final was completed on the following Monday evening and despite 63 from a young John Bond Rowntrees finished 168 all out after 42.5 overs.

In 1959 Guy Raines of Haxby scored 121 n.o. out of 154 for 5 against Naburn Hospital in the extra preliminary round, Naburn being dismissed for just 52. In the preliminary round proper Pat Wood scored 111 for Stamford Bridge against R.A.F. Rufforth, Stamford's total of 231 for 4 being a record for an 18 eight ball over game that was never beaten. The R.A.F. could only manage 89 but the match aggregate of 320 was a record that stood until 1980.

In 1960 Robbie Marchant scored 103 n.o. for York Railway Institute against Escrick Park as R.I. totalled 189 for 2 and went on to win the game. His innings contained only nine fours, the rest being all run. The team's total was reported in The Press as a record although it was somewhat short of Stamford's total of the previous year. However the 1st wicket stand of 182 by Robbie and his partner Tony Keel was a record and stood until 1984.

The first team to score 150 in an 18 over final were Sheriff Hutton Bridge in 1975. In a rather one sided final they scored 150 for 6 before dismissing Cawood for 47 with more than five overs to spare.

Dunnington improved on this score the following year with their 156 for 6 which proved too much for Huntington W.M.C. in their last final appearance. Terry Weston hit 101 n.o. for Dunnington in the semi-final at Clifton Park against Cawood. Terry's runs came in 78 minutes and included 12 fours, his ton coming up in the final over and with the help of 49 from Pat Wood Dunnington put on 142 for the 1st wicket, finishing on 179 for 3. Cawood, finalists the previous year, ended up 86 all out. Terry, who had only taken up cricket a few years earlier at the age of 28, was the first to score a century in the competition since the York club moved from Wigginton Road in 1967. He will be known by many as proprietor of "Wood n' Things" DIY shop on Tadcaster Road and a successful local wildlife photographer.

It took Sheriff Hutton Bridge only two years to reclaim the record, scoring 162 for 3 in 1978, once again defeating Cawood, with Des Wyrill ending on 98 n.o. Despite putting up a much improved performance Cawood finished on 141 for 7. Des had scored a record 323 runs in the competition that year at an average of 107.66.

Easingwold improved on the Bridge's total in 1982 with 172 for 7 batting first. Heworth replied with a tremendous 158 for 7 in what was decribed as "appalling light". This proved to be the highest scoring 18 over final with Heworth's total being a record for a runner-up.

Yorkshire player Jim Love scored 105 n.o. for Bubwith against Hemingbrough in a 1984 2nd round match, Bubwith making 185 without loss and Hemingbrough finishing on 98 for 8. The opening stand between Love and Neil Readman was a record for any wicket in an 18 over game. Jim became the only player to score a century in the Myers & Burnell and the Isaac Poad, having scored another unbeaten century for Thorp Arch & Boston Spa against Easingwold in the Poad in 1979.

1988 saw Kevin Smith of Pocklington score 105 n.o. against Sheriff Hutton in an early round.

In the 1996 2nd round game between Clifton Alliance and Dringhouses several scoring records were set. Batting first, Clifton scored 191 for 3, a record for a 16 eight ball over game with Scott Bradley and Dave Taylor establishing a record partnership of 144 for the 1st wicket. Dringhouses made a spirited reply and finished on 162 for 4 thanks to opener Chris Evans, whose 105 n.o. from 68 balls included 10 fours and two sixes and was the first century in a 16 over game, the match aggregate of 353 also being a record. Naturally there were some sorry looking bowling figures. Clifton top scorer Bradley went for 48 off his four overs and centurion Evans conceded 58 off his four overs.

Clifton Alliance became the first side to score 200 in a final, racking up 202 for 3 in the 1st innings of the 1999 final against Thirsk, with Australian Ben Higgins scoring only the second century in a final with 114 n.o. followed up with 57 in the 2nd innings to give him a record 171 runs in a final. This took his total in the competition for the season to 328 runs at an average of 118.66, beating Des Wyrill's 21 year old record.

2005 saw Clifton Alliance reach the final once more, Australian Daniel Harris with 305 runs at an average of 101.66 being a major factor. His 108 n.o. against Acomb in the 2nd round was the 23rd and last century ever scored in the competition.

In the penultimate final in 2006 York scored 203 for 3 in their first innings on the way to beating Clifton Alliance.

Mention should be made here of a remarkable 2nd round game in 1980 between Tadcaster and Heworth, which saw several records set and some amazing performances from both sides. Played at Tadcaster the home side batted first and after ten overs were kept to a modest 58 for 2 thanks to some accurate bowling from Jim Collis and Steve Young. Howard Conroy was then joined by Dave Marsh and the pair set about the Heworth change bowlers Pete Machin and Dave Riley, putting on exactly 100 for the 5th wicket. Conroy scored 66 and Marsh finished 44 n.o. and Tadcaster's final total was 176 for 5. Heworth's reply stumbled to 50 for 5 thanks to two wickets each from skipper Terry Downey and Eric Wallis, before Dave Riley and Dave Wood came together and took 53 runs of the next three overs. They continued to score runs so freely that they overtook Tadcaster's score with six balls to spare ending on 179 for 5. Riley ended with 72 n.o. and Wood 60 n.o. in an unbroken 6th wicket partnership of 129. This is the only instance of two 100 run partnerships in any Myers & Burnell game with the aggregate total of 355 runs also setting a record for an 18 over game.

In researching all these scoring feats I came across many low scoring games and some embarrassingly low totals. I have not compiled a list of these for fear of offending anyone, but I can mention the two lowest team totals I have come across as both clubs no longer exist. In a 1962 preliminary round Naburn Hospital visited Sheriff Hutton Bridge and were bowled out for 12, Sid Lusher taking 5 for 5 and Jeff Shipley 3 for 6. The Bridge lost Des Wyrill for 2 and Maurice Woodliffe and Dave Firminger for ducks before Jim Rhodes Junior's 7 n.o. and Harry Goddard's 4 n.o. saw them home. The Naburn score was only one better than Strensall C.C. who entertained Heworth in a 1924 preliminary round. Their ground was on the edge of Strensall Common close to the Army camp and was of a questionable standard. Heworth batted first and scored 55 all out which proved to be a very decent total as Strensall could manage only 11 in reply.

Centurions

Player	Score	Team	Opponents	Year	Round	
George Curry	124*	York Revellers	Henry Leethams	1924	1st round	90 mins
Alf Aveyard	124*	N.R.M.H	Tadcaster	1933	Final	49 overs
Guy Raines	121	Haxby	Naburn Hospital	1959	1st Prelim	18 x 8
Alf Aveyard	116*	N.R.M.H	Northern Command	1933	prelim	28 overs
Ben Higgins	114*	Clifton Alliance	Thirsk	1999	Final	16 x 8
Walter Skilbeck	112*	Easingwold	York Corporation	1948	early rnd	28 overs
Reg Baines	111*	Clarence C.&I.	York City Amateurs	1929	1st round	90 mins
Pat Wood	111	Stamford Bridge	R.A.F. Rufforth	1959	Prelim	18 x 8
Daniel Harris	108*	Clifton Alliance	Acomb	2005	2nd round	16 x 8
Francis Roupell	108	Acomb	Osbaldwick	1926	Semi-final	no limit
S.Tichener	108	N.R.M.H	Rowntrees	1926	Semi-final	no limit
Noel Herbert	106*	Tadcaster	Stillington	1935	Semi-final	40 overs
Arthur Taylor	106	York City Amateurs	Osbaldwick	1925	Semi-final	no limit
Jim Love	105*	Bubwith	Hemingbrough	1984	2nd round	18 x 8
Kevin Smith	105*	Pocklington	Sheriff Hutton	1988	early rnd	18 x 8
Chris Evans	105*	Dringhouses	Clifton Alliance	1996	2nd round	16 x 8
Ivor Churchill	105	N.R.M.H	Rowntrees	1926	Semi-final	no limit
Dennis Johnson	104*	Yapham	Clifton Hospital	1955	3rd round	28 overs
Robbie Marchant	103*	York Railway Inst	Escrick Park	1960	2nd round	18 x 8
Sammy Toyne	102*	Clifton C.C.	St. Luke's	1930	Prelim	28 overs
Arthur Naylor	101*	St. Michael-le-Belfry	Bishopthorpe	1919	Semi-final	no limit
Terry Weston	101*	Dunnington	Cawood	1976	Semi-final	18 x 8

Jack Braime of Woodhouse Grange was credited with having scored a century in the 1950's, according to Malcolm Huntington in *The Press* in 1974, but I have been unable to verify this.

Most runs in a season

Player	Club	Year	Runs	Ave.
Ben Higgins	Clifton Alliance	1999	328	164
Des Wyrill	Sheriff Hutton Bridge	1978	323	107.66
Daniel Harris	Clifton Alliance	2005	305	101.66
Alan Kenworthy	Ebor Gogues	1960	286	286
Arthur Naylor	St.Michael-le-Belfry	1919	266	133
Alf Aveyard	North Riding Mental Hospital	1933	264	66
Darren Reeves	Clifton Alliance	2001	245	49

Kev Smith of Pocklington who scored 105 n.o. in 1988 against Sheriff Hutton, seen here holding the Cup in 1992 after their final victory over Heworth.

Back row; Martyn Nesom, Barry Pearson, Andy Inns, Matthew Atkinson, Richard Foster, Dick Wright.
Front row; Phil Stephenson, Paul Jackson, Kevin Smith (Captain), Steve Lyus, Kevin Hinch.

Ben Higgins of Clifton Alliance became only the second player to score a century in a final in 1999, 66 years after the first. He also holds the record for most runs in a season in the Myers & Burnell. He is pictured here on the left with his regular opening partner Dave Taylor after they had put on an unbroken 301 1st wicket partnership in a York Senior League game.

Partnerships

1919 to 1958

196	2nd	Ivor Churchill & S.Tichener	North Riding M.H.	Rowntrees	1926	Semi-final
162*	3rd	Noel William Herbert & Fred Shearsmith	Tadcaster	Stillington	1935	Semi-final
142	1st	Henry Dalton & O.Shaw	Bootham Park	Ainsty Nomads	1927	Semi-final
133*	3rd	Eddie Cooper & Vic Bedford	Acomb	Dringhouses	1948	Final
133	2nd	John Lawson & Phil Dalby	Dringhouses	Escrick Park	1952	2nd round
124	2nd	Eddie Legard & Joe Triffitt	York Ramblers	Clarence C.&I.	1928	Final
121	1st	Captain Francis Roupell & Alan Dalby	Acomb	Osbaldwick	1926	Semi-final
120	1st	George Watson & Norman Morse	York an XI	Escrick Park	1957	Prelim
116	2nd	Hubert Smith & Dennis Hutchinson	Easingwold	Acomb	1951	2nd round
115	1st	S.Mayo & A.Shaw	Dringhouses	York Banks	1921	2nd round
113*	3rd	R.E.Warner & Henry Lund	York City Amateurs	Layerthorpe A.S.	1920	1st round
112	1st	Ken Steele & G.Morell	Tadcaster	Escrick Park	1933	Prelim
111*	3rd	Hubert Dryland & Ivor Churchill	North Riding M.H.	Dringhouses	1928	1st round
110	5th	Mick Cockerill & John Richardson	York an XI	Tadcaster	1957	Semi-final
109*	1st	Henry Dalton & O.Shaw	Bootham Park	Southlands	1927	1st round
105	1st	Bryan Moor & Reg Baines	Rowntrees	York R.I.	1955	1st round
104	1st	Dick Crowther & Peter Martin	Osbaldwick	York an XI	1954	1st round
100	3rd	John Bond & George Watson	Rowntrees	Woodhouse Grange	1958	Final
99	4th	Eric Kay & Roy S. Nicholson	Acomb	Clifton C.C.	1947	Final
94*	1st	Norman Morse & Mick Cockerill	York an XI	Osbaldwick	1957	1st round
94	3rd	W.Rafton & A.Shaw	Dringhouses	Poppleton	1924	2nd round
93*	1st	H.G.Henderson & Sammy Toyne	Clifton Church Inst.	York Banks	1929	2nd Prelim
90*	1st	S.Mayo & C.Lancaster	Dringhouses	Escrick Park	1921	Final
85	5th	Tom Barton & Charlie Sherwood	Stamford Bridge	Escrick Park	1951	Semi-final
84	3rd	Bill Taylor & G.R.Toes	Clifton C.C.	Ovington	1937	1st round
84	4th	Harold Hornshaw & Arthur Broadhurst	Clifton C.C.	Acomb	1947	Final
83	4th	Harry Moult & Eddie Legard	York Ramblers	Stamford Bridge	1929	2nd round
83	1st	John Bond & George Watson	Rowntrees	Haxby	1958	Prelim
82*	7th	Clive Birdsall & Basil Jewitt	Tadcaster Magnet S.C.	York an XI	1957	2nd round
82	3rd	Captain A.E.Dent & Arthur H. Naylor	St. Michael-le-Belfry	Bishopthorpe	1919	Semi-final
81*	2nd	Lol Cooper & Sid Fisher	Stockton & Hopgrove	R.A.F. Rufforth	1956	1st round
81	5th	Ken Steele & Johnny Munford	Tadcaster	North Riding M.H.	1938	Final
79	4th	Tommy Hobson & Claude W.Thompson	Escrick Park	St. Martin's	1921	2nd round
79	2nd	Norman Pearson & Frank Lindsay	Stamford Bridge	Rowntrees	1957	Prelim
78	7th	Vic Bedford & J.Tremlin	Clifton C.C.	Dringhouses	1929	2nd round
78	1st	Alf Aveyard & Joe Littlewood	North Riding M.H.	Tadcaster	1935	Final
76	1st	George Herbert & J.J.Waterhouse	Rowntrees	Dringhouses	1924	Final
76	1st	Fred Davison & A.Shaw	Dringhouses	Clifton C.C.	1929	2nd round
75	3rd	Percy Poole & Joe McConnon	Clifton Hospital	Clifton C.C.	1950	Final
75	3rd	Dennis Hutchinson & Billy Duck	Easingwold	Dringhouses	1951	3rd round
74	4th	J.Woodward & W.Hair	Tadcaster	New Earswick	1954	1st round
73	2nd	A.Walker & J.N.Blenkin	Poppleton	Dringhouses	1924	2nd round
73	4th	Alf Aveyard & Tommy Robinson	North Riding M.H.	Tadcaster	1933	Final
73	1st	George McClennan & John Falshaw	Ebor Gouges	Stamford Bridge	1957	1st round
72	3rd	R.A.Crookes & D.Fraser	Bootham Park	York Wanderers	1957	2nd round
71	7th	T.Anthony & Major Harry O. Johnson	York Ramblers	Escrick Park	1920	Final
71	3rd	Bob Stather & F.Boyes	Clarence C.& I.	St. Michael-le-Belfry	1928	2nd round
70	1st	F.Akers & F.Cook	Bishopthorpe	St. Michael-le-Belfry	1919	Semi-final
70	4th	R.Pratt & Dr.Morrison	Escrick Park	York Ramblers	1921	Semi-final

1919 to 1958 continued

Score	Wkt.	Players	Team	Opponents	Year	Round
69*	3rd	Ken Lockwood & John Raine	Rowntrees	Bootham Park	1954	1st round
69	2nd	O.Shaw & Arthur Taylor	Bootham Park	Acomb	1927	Final
69	1st	Joe Littlewood & Alf Aveyard	North Riding M.H.	South Bank W.M.C.	1933	Semi-final
68	10th	Lawrence Johnson & Robson	North Riding M.H.	York Ramblers	1928	2nd round
68	2nd	Norman Garland & Sid Hepton	York R.I.	Escrick Park	1956	Prelim
68	2nd	Lewis Barker & Herbert Freer	New Earswick	Clifton Hospital	1953	Final
67	1st	J.Hartley & M.Smith	Clifton C.C.	Haxby	1954	1st round
67	1st	Alf Nicholls & John Pitt	York an XI	Woodhouse Grange	1954	Semi-final
66	1st	John Bond & Reg Baines	Rowntrees	Ebor Gogues	1958	3rd round
66	1st	Alf Aveyard & Len Freer	Clifton Hospital	New Earswick	1958	2nd round
66	3rd	Clive Kay & Alisdair Swann	Woodhouse Grange	Rowntrees	1958	Final
65	2nd	Eddie Legard & Arthur R.Birch	York Ramblers	North Riding M.H.	1928	2nd round
65	2nd	George Shepherdson & Steve Megginson	Woodhouse Grange	Heworth	1958	Semi-final
64	1st	Alf Nichols & Charlie Boddy	York an XI	Easingwold	1954	2nd round
63	10th	W.Steele & A.Thomlinson	Tadcaster	New Earswick	1940	Final
63	2nd	John Shaw & Phil Dalby	Dringhouses	York an XI	1952	Final
62	1st	Eric Cross & Norman Swinden	Tadcaster	Popp. Sugar Factory	1956	Prelim
61	5th	Eddie Cooper & D.Danby	Acomb	Easingwold	1951	2nd round
61	3rd	M.Robson & Trevor Burdett	Sugar Beet Factory	Escrick Park	1952	1st round
61	1st	Stanley Goodyear & Maurice Scoreby	Long Marston	Clifton Hospital	1957	Prelim
61	3rd	Reg Docking & Jimmy Hughes	York Wanderers	Dringhouses	1957	Prelim
61	2nd	John Falshaw & Denzil Webster	Ebor Gogues	Stamford Bridge	1957	1st round
60	2nd	Alf Aveyard & Percy Poole	Clifton Hospital	Clifton C.C.	1950	Final
60	1st	Norman Featherby & G.Thornton	Yapham	Dringhouses	1954	1st round
60	1st	Norman Morse & George Watson	York an XI	York R.I.	1956	2nd round
60	2nd	Tommy Hobson & Steve Megginson	Woodhouse Grange	Long Marston	1958	2nd round

The 1958 Rowntrees team who beat Tadcaster in the 2nd round; they reached the final only to finish runners-up to Woodhouse Grange. Harry Harvey replaced Frank Lindsay in the final.

Back row; Vic Bedford, Ken Lockwood, Reg Baines, Ken Moor (Captain), Frank Lindsay, George Watson.
Front row; M.Watson, Dennis Ramsey, Ted King, John Pitt, John Bond.

1959 to 1993 18 x eight ball over games

Score	Wkt.	Players	Team	Opponents	Year	Round
185*	1st	Jim Love & Neil Readman	Bubwith	Hemingbrough	1984	2nd round
182	1st	Robbie Marchant & Tony Keel	York R.I.	Escrick Park	1960	2nd round
154	1st	Alisdair Swann & Richard Hobson	Woodhouse Grange	Clifton C.C.	1962	Prelim
142	1st	Pat Wood & Terry Weston	Dunnington	Cawood	1976	Semi-final
129*	6th	Dave Riley & Dave Wood	Heworth	Tadcaster	1980	2nd round
122*	1st	Norman Morse & Denis North	Stillington	Rowntrees	1979	1st round
116	1st	Dave Tompkins & Lewis Barker	York an XI	Stillington	1975	1st round
112	1st	Geoff Powell & Tony Moore	Heworth	Naburn Hospital	1964	Prelim
112	1st	Steve Lawrence & Will Robinson	T.A.B.S.	Heworth	1988	Final
108	3rd	Des Wyrill & Brian Shirley	Sheriff Hutton Bridge	Huntington W.M.C	1975	Semi-final
106	3rd	Des Wyrill & Don Pringle	Sheriff Hutton Bridge	Escrick Park	1972	1st round
103	1st	Gerry Grinham & Jim Rhodes Jnr.	Sheriff Hutton Bridge	Popp. Sugar Factory	1961	Prelim
101	1st	Tony Simpson & Derek Pattison	Dringhouses	Cawood	1963	2nd round
101	4th	Eric Wallis & Terry Downey	Tadcaster	York an XI	1971	1st round
100	5th	Howard Conroy & Dave Marsh	Tadcaster	Heworth	1980	2nd round
100	1st	Steve Taylor & Mick Hammerton	Heworth	Acomb	1984	Final
99*	4th	Keith Cowl & Tony Stilgoe	Dringhouses	Easingwold	1970	Semi-final
99*	3rd	Robbie Marchant & Clive Robinson	York an XI	Tadcaster	1977	Final
99	2nd	Alan Kenworthy & Joe Valente	Ebor Gogues	York Ramblers	1960	Semi-final
98*	1st	Gerry Grinham & Jim Rhodes Jnr.	Sheriff Hutton Bridge	Acomb	1962	Prelim
97	4th	Brian Hall & D.Abbott	Cawood	N.M.U.	1967	2nd round
92	4th	Des Wyrill & Wally Craven	Sheriff Hutton Bridge	Stamford Bridge	1978	Semi-final
92	1st	Val Toase & Peter Gilleard	Easingwold	Woodhouse Grange	1982	2nd round
91	1st	Brian Shirley & Des Wyrill	Sheriff Hutton Bridge	Stillington	1973	3rd round
91	1st	Martin Robinson & Denis Sell	Easingwold	Civil Service	1993	1st round
89	4th	Frank Gibson & Maurice Cram	Acomb	York R.I.	1964	Prelim
88	4th	Robbie Marchant & Nigel Henshall	York an XI	Tadcaster	1971	1st round
85*	5th	Dave Simpson & Ian Wilson	Heworth	Cawood	1986	1st round
85	1st	Pat Wood & Sid Fisher	Dunnington	Selby Londesborough	1967	1st round
85	1st	Des Wyrill & Bill Revis	Sheriff Hutton Bridge	Cawood	1978	Final
85	1st	Ike Jackson & Andy Forster	Stockton & Hopgrove	Stamford Bridge	1979	1st round
85	1st	Jack Sinclair & Dave Tompkins	York an XI	Clifton Hospital All.	1981	1st round
84	2nd	Howard Lewis & John Ridley	York R.I.	Rufforth	1971	1st round
84	4th	Bill Reader & Noel Hare	Escrick Park	British Sugar	1974	1st round
84	1st	Andy Thrall & Bob Graves	Acomb	Bilton-in-Ainsty	1984	1st round
83	1st	Val Toase & Stuart Burton	Easingwold	Rowntrees	1974	3rd round
81	1st	Denis North & Norman Morse	Stillington	Dringhouses	1979	2nd round
81	4th	Steve Simpson & Jason Gatus	Heworth	Sheriff Hutton Bridge	1992	1st round
80	3rd	Phil Woodliffe & Clive Clark	Pocklington	Escrick Park	1978	2nd round
80	6th	Steve Precious & Kevin Wilson	Heworth	Stamford Bridge	1984	3rd round
79	1st	Alec Backhouse & Dave Airey	York an XI	Woodhouse Grange	1980	Final
79	2nd	Dick Sykes & Chris Simpson	Acomb	Stamford Bridge	1983	Final
79	2nd	Dave Simpson & Rick Moglia	Heworth	Dunnington	1991	Semi-final
77	1st	Val Toase & Peter Gilleard	Easingwold	Stillington	1962	1st round
77	1st	Mal Caddie & Kevin Wilson	Heworth	Stockton & Hopgrove	1987	Prelim
77	1st	Graham Dawson & Andrew Dawson	Crayke	Acomb	1989	2nd round
76*	2nd	George Myerscough & Alwyne Yorke	Dringhouses	Civil Service	1970	2nd round
76	2nd	Bill Bell & Dennis Hutchinson	Easingwold	Dringhouses	1970	Semi-final
75	1st	Derek Pattison & Ray Varney	Dringhouses	Woodhouse Grange	1966	Final
74	1st	Des Wyrill & Bill Revis	Sheriff Hutton Bridge	Cawood	1975	Final

1959 to 1993 18 x eight ball over games continued

74	1st	Chris Simpson & Bob Graves	Acomb	Sessay	1984	Semi-final
73	2nd	Don Blake & Brian Pudsey	Clifton C.C.	Acomb	1966	2nd round
72*	4th	John Lawson & Don Paver	Dringhouses	New Earswick	1962	Semi-final
72	2nd	Brian Pudsey & Wally Baynes	Huntington	Stockton & Hopgrove	1976	Prelim
72	2nd	Keith Cowl & Ian Storey	Dringhouses	Stillington	1979	2nd round
72	3rd	Andy Gilleard & Jon Wright	Crayke	Easingwold	1985	Semi-final
70	1st	Wally Baynes & Trevor Markham	Huntington W.M.C	Acomb	1976	2nd round
69	2nd	George Myerscough & John Gibb	York Ramblers	Tadcaster	1960	1st round
69	2nd	Briggs & Lancaster	Bilton-in-Ainsty	Tadcaster	1959	Prelim
69	1st	Mal Caddie & Dave Simpson	Heworth	Rowntrees	1987	3rd round
68	1st	Joe Shaw & Alf Nichols	Heworth	Bilton-in-Ainsty	1961	1st round
68	1st	Bill Revis & Brian Shirley	Sheriff Hutton Bridge	T.A.B.S.	1975	1st round
68	1st	John Flintoff & Dave Harrison	Sessay	Acomb	1981	Final
67	1st	Andy Gilleard & Dennis Hutchinson	Crayke	Sessay	1985	Final
66	5th	Alisdair Swann & Robert Atkin	Woodhouse Grange	Osbaldwick	1966	1st round
66	6th	Norman Pearson & Roy Lawson	Stamford Bridge	T.A.B.S.	1971	2nd round
66	1st	Dave Tute & Tony Hinder	Acomb	Sheriff Hutton Bridge	1976	1st round
66	3rd	Dick Sykes & Joey Burton	Acomb	Heworth	1986	2nd round
65	1st	Val Toase & Jeff Robinson	Easingwold	Stockton & Hopgrove	1974	2nd round
64	1st	Steve Taylor & Mick Hammerton	Heworth	Civil Service	1984	Semi-final
63	2nd	Guy Shuttleworth & Phil Dalby	York Wanderers	Minster Choir O.B.	1964	1st round
63	1st	Norman Pearson & John Beckett	Stamford Bridge	Rowntrees	1971	Semi-final
63	1st	Ian McKenzie & Barry Emmott	Tadcater	Clifton Hospital All.	1980	1st round
62	1st	Pete Knapton & G.Jackson	Dringhouses	Terrys	1961	1st round
62	4th	Eric Wallis & Terry Downey	Tadcaster	Escrick Park	1967	1st round
62	2nd	Brian Shirley & Bill Revis	Sheriff Hutton Bridge	Civil Service	1973	Semi-final
62	1st	Eddie Howcroft & Dave Gibson	Cawood	Sheriff Hutton Bridge	1975	Final
61*	1st	Irvine Rudd & Malcolm Wilson	Escrick Park	Dunnington	1960	Prelim
61	1st	Robbie Marchant & Tony Keel	York R.I.	Dringhouses	1960	Semi-final
61	1st	Joe Shaw & Alf Nichols	Heworth	Bilton-in-Ainsty	1961	1st round
61	2nd	Dave Simpson & Rick Moglia	Heworth	Woodhouse Grange	1991	final
60	6th	Steve Johnson & Kev Davidson	Woodhouse Grange	Rowntrees	1975	1st round
60	2nd	Dave Gibson & Brian Hall	Cawood	Woodhouse Grange	1975	Semi-final
60	5th	Martin Robinson & Geoff Skilbeck	Easingwold	Heworth	1982	Final
60	5th	Ian Wilson & Steve Precious	Heworth	Woodhouse Grange	1984	1st round

1994 to 2007 16 x eight ball overs

Score	Wkt.	Players	Team	Opponents	Year	Round
144	1st	Scott Bradley & Dave Taylor	Clifton Alliance	Dringhouses	1996	2nd round
142*	1st	Daniel Harris & Dave Taylor	Clifton Alliance	Woodhouse Grange	2005	Semi-final
130	3rd	Stephen Piercy & Andrew Kay	York	Clifton Alliance	2004	Final 1st inn
114	4th	Tommy Banks & Martyn Piercy	Easingwold	Woodhouse Grange	2006	1st round
113*	1st	Simon Hill & James Postill	Clifton Alliance	Ovington	1999	1st round
111	1st	Sanjay Rodrigo & Andy Tute	Acomb	Woodhouse Grange	2003	Final 1st inn
118*	1st	Dave Simpson & Jonathan Bean	Heworth	Civil Service	1994	3rd round
107	3rd	Adam Clark & Mick Pickering	Clifton Hospital All.	Huntington	1994	2nd round
106	2nd	Ben Higgins & John Hunter	Clifton Alliance	Easingwold	1999	3rd round
105	1st	Lincoln McCrae & Andrew Hawke	Thirsk	Dringhouses	2000	1st round
102*	4th	Paul Mosey & Mike Burdett	Woodhouse Grange	Sessay	1994	Final 1st inn
102	1st	Jonathan Bean & Nick Hadfield	Woodhouse Grange	Stamford Bridge	2003	2nd round

1994 to 2007 16 x eight ball overs continued

101	2nd	Darren Reeves & Simon Dwyer	Clifton Alliance	Acomb	2001	Final 4th inn
100*	2nd	Dave Simpson & Shahid Khan	Heworth	Clifton Alliance	2002	Semi-final
97	2nd	Ben Higgins & John Hunter	Clifton Alliance	Thirsk	1999	Final 1st inn
96*	4th	Duncan Snell & Jason English	York	Clifton Alliance	2006	Final 2nd inn
96	2nd	Dave Taylor & Adam Clark	Clifton Hospital All.	Osbaldwick	1994	1st round
94	2nd	Daniel Harris & Chris Malthouse	Clifton Alliance	Acomb	2005	2nd round
93*	1st	Lorenzo Ingram & James Postill	Clifton Alliance	Sessay	2004	1st round
90	1st	Sanjay Rodrigo & Andy Tute	Acomb	Clifton Alliance	2003	2nd round
87	1st	James Postill & Darren Reeves	Clifton Alliance	Osbaldwick	2001	2nd round
86	1st	Steve Jackson & Rich Carew	Osbaldwick	Heworth	2002	Final 2nd inn
85	4th	Harwood Williams & Steve Simpson	Dunnington	Clifton Hospital All.	1995	2nd round
85	2nd	Simon Corley & James Postill	Clifton Alliance	York	2001	1st round
84	1st	Dave Thomas & Graham Dawson	Crayke	Woodhouse Grange	1994	1st round
83	1st	Rob Taylor & Matthew Stokes	Clifton Alliance	Stamford Bridge	1997	1st round
83	2nd	Johnny Stevens & Steve Mouncey	Stamford Bridge	Clifton Alliance	1997	1st round
83	2nd	Neil Stephenson & Des Wyrill	Thirsk	Dringhouses	1997	1st round
83	2nd	Darren Reeves & Simon Dwyer	Clifton Alliance	Acomb	2001	Final 2nd inn
81	3rd	Neil Stephenson & John Harper	Thirsk	Clifton Alliance	1999	Final 2nd inn
80	6th	Martyn Piercy & Dan Copeland	Easingwold	Thirsk	2000	Final 3rd inn
77	1st	Dave Taylor & Lorenzo Ingram	Clifton Alliance	Stamford Bridge	2004	Semi-final
75	4th	Dave Simpson & Michael Brooke	Heworth	Osbaldwick	2002	Final 3rd inn
73	1st	Dave Taylor & Ben Higgins	Clifton Alliance	Acomb	1999	Semi-final
73	2nd	Travis Borlace & John Gilham	Clifton Alliance	Heworth	2002	Semi-final
70	1st	Andy Freeman & Andy Hall	Huntington	Clifton Hospital All.	1994	2nd round
69	2nd	Lorenzo Ingram & John Myers	Clifton Alliance	Heworth	2004	2nd round
68	1st	Dave Taylor & James Postill	Clifton Alliance	Easingwold	2002	1st round
68	2nd	Daniel Harris & Richard Musgrave	Clifton Alliance	York	2005	Final 2nd inn
66	1st	Kieran Powar & Paul Mosey	Heworth	Easingwold	1997	Final 1st inn
65	1st	Nick Fisher & Dave Simpson	Heworth	Clifton Alliance	2000	1st round
65	4th	James Postill & John Myers	Clifton Alliance	York	2004	Final 3rd inn
63	3rd	G.Yeoward & N.Manners	Dunnington	Thirsk	2000	Semi-final
62	2nd	Rob Taylor & John Hunter	Clifton Alliance	Selby Londesborough	1997	1st round
61	6th	Tommy Darnell & Dan Copeland	Easingwold	Osbaldwick	1998	1st round
61	2nd	Dave Taylor & John Hunter	Clifton Hospital All.	Woodhouse Grange	1994	3rd round
61	1st	Harwood Williams & Dave Simpson	Dunnington	Clifton Hospital All.	1995	2nd round
61	1st	Sanjay Rodrigo & Andy Tute	Acomb	Woodhouse Grange	2003	Final 3rd inn
61	2nd	Darius Slabbert & Richard Bowling	Heworth	Clifton Alliance	2004	2nd round

The 1999 Clifton Alliance side pictured here with the Myers & Burnell Cup on the left, the Senior League Trophy centre and the Acomb Invitation on the right.
Back row; James Postill, Paul Clary, John Hunter, Mick Knowles, Darren Barton, Rob Taylor.
Front row; Mick Pickering, Dave Russell, Duncan Naylor (Captain), Ben Higgins, Simon Dwyer, Dave Taylor. Rob Taylor and Paul Clary did not play in the final while Jon Bladen who did is missing from this photo.

Progressive team totals in finals over the years.

Completed innings finals

1919	Heworth	146 a.o.	v St. Michael-le-Belfry
1920	York Ramblers	146 a.o.	v Escrick Park
1923	Escrick Park	160 a.o.	v Dringhouses
1927	Acomb	188 a.o.	v Bootham Park
1927	Bootham Park	198 - 8	v Acomb
1928	York Ramblers	244 - 7	v Clarence C. & I.

In 1924 York Revellers scored 219-7 against Henry Leethams & Sons in a 1st round game in one and half hours.

In 1926 Acomb scored 294-7 against Osbaldwick in the first semi-final and in the second semi-final North Riding Mental Hospital scored 336-7 against Rowntrees.

50 overs finals

1933	North Riding M.H.	236 a.o.	v Tadcaster
1958	Woodhouse Grange	250 - 8	v Rowntrees

In 1957 Ebor Gogues scored 192-8 against Stamford Bridge in a 1st round game of 28 six ball overs per side.

18 over finals

1959	Tadcaster	90 - 2	v New Earswick
1960	York Railway Inst.	103 - 7	v Ebor Gogues
1962	Cawood	110 - 6	v Dringhouses
1967	Dringhouses	121 - 8	v Heworth
1969	York Nomads	139 - 3	v Easingwold
1971	York an XI	142 - 6	v Stamford Bridge
1972	Easingwold	143 - 5	v Sheriff Hutton Bridge
1975	Sheriff Hutton Bridge	150 - 6	v Cawood
1976	Dunnington	156 - 6	v Huntington W.M.C.
1978	Sheriff Hutton Bridge	162 - 3	v Cawood
1982	Easingwold	172 - 3	v Heworth

In 1959 Stamford Bridge scored 231-4 against R.A.F. Rufforth in the prelim round
In 1980 Tadcaster scored 176-5 and Heworth replied with 179-5 in the 2nd round.

2 innings finals

1994	Sessay	287	v Woodhouse Grange
1999	Clifton Alliance	351	v Thirsk
2005	York	368	v Clifton Alliance

In 1996 Clifton Alliance scored 191 for 3 against Ovington in a 16 eight ball over 2nd round game.

Progressive aggregate totals in finals over the years.

Completed innings finals

1919	Heworth v St. Michael-le-Belfry	288
1928	York Ramblers v Clarence C. & I.	455

In 1924 York Revellers v Henry Leetham & Sons totalled 301 in a 1st round game of one and a half hours per side and in the 2nd round Poppleton versus Dringhouses totalled 335 under the same conditions.
In 1926 Acomb v Osbaldwick totalled 396 in the first semi-final and in the second semi-final North Riding Mental Hospital v Rowntrees totalled 451.

50 overs finals

1933	North Riding M.H. v Rowntrees	414
1934	North Riding M.H. v New Earswick	423
1947	Clifton C.C. v Acomb	463

In 1957 Ebor Gogues v Stamford Bridge totalled 316 in a 28 six ball over 1st round.

18 over finals

1959	Tadcaster v New Earswick	179
1960	York Railway Inst. v Ebor Gogues	205
1962	Cawood v Dringhouses	216
1969	York Nomads v Easingwold	274
1976	Dunnington v Huntington W.M.C.	274
1978	Sheriff Hutton Bridge v Cawood	303
1982	Easingwold v Heworth	330

In 1959 Stamford Bridge v R.A.F. Rufforth totalled 320 in an 18 x 8 ball prelim.
In 1980 Tadcaster v Heworth totalled 355 in an 18 eight ball over 2nd round.

2 innings finals

1994	Sessay v Woodhouse Grange	571
1999	Clifton Alliance v Thirsk	609
2005	York v Clifton Alliance	661

In 1996 Clifton Alliance v Dringhouses totalled 353 in a 16 eight ball over 2nd round game.

The 1936 Tadcaster team pictured with the Myers & Burnell Cup and the York & Distict Senior League Trophy.
Back row: J.A. Grimston (Umpire), Fred Shearsmith, Ernie Stubbs, Ken Steele, J.Clifford, Alf Whitelock, Johnny Munford, N.Ryder (Secretary), W.Hickson (Scorer). Front Row: D.Pickering, George Shearsmith, Noel Herbert (Capt.), Norman Swinden, H.Metcalfe. J.Clifford did not play in the Myers & Burnell final and C.Dixon who did is missing fom this photo.

The 1965 Huntington W.M.C team pictured here with the Sawkill Cup also won the Myers & Burnell.
Back row: Peter Glassby, Fred Storr, Ian Reed, Brian Baines, Lenny Watson.
Front row: Robert Sedgwick, Derek Haw, Dennis Bunce, Derek Magson, Frank Gibson, Kenny Stamp. Kneeling: Sid Hepton and John Skilbeck.
Baines, Sedgwick, Haw and Stamp did not play in the Myers & Burnell final. Mick Storr, Jim Collis and Peter Foster who all did are missing from this photo.

Chapter Six
Bowling Performances.

1919 saw some notable bowling feats in the inaugural competition. The first game ever played was a preliminary round between Poppleton and Burton Stone Lane and it produced a brilliant performance from Samuel Snowball Elmer of Poppleton, who took eight wickets to help dismiss Burton Stone Lane for exactly 100. Only 36 from Sergeant Sowerby and 24 extras gave some respectability to the total and Poppleton won easily. The 1st round game between Heworth and St. Thomas's saw Harry Moult take 7 for 64 in a Heworth total of 162 for 8. William Ware then took five wickets as St. Thomas's were dismissed for 100. Harry Moult and four of his St. Thomas's team-mates went on to win the cup the following year with York Ramblers. In another 1st round game Embleton of Old Priory Adult School took five wickets in dismissing Osbaldwick for 135, but the total proved too much and Old Priory were 82 all out. Henry Dalton the Osbaldwick leg-break bowler took three wickets; a modest start for a player who was to become the pre-eminent bowler in the competition for the next ten years. In the 2nd round William Ware was once again in the wickets, taking a further six as Heworth put out Huntington for 92. In the semi-finals Arthur Smith took five wickets for Heworth as they beat Civil Service and Jack Sweeting took six wickets for St. Michael-le-Belfry to help them to beat Bishopthorpe. Heworth won an exciting final against St. Michael-le-Belfry, Ware taking a further three wickets to bring his seasons total to at least 15, a record for the competition that would stand until 1925.

1920 saw several useful performances. In the 2nd round Gerald Simpson took 7 for 13 for York Ramblers to help dismiss Civil Service for 51, the Ramblers going on to a ten wicket win. J. Chatterton took 7 for 41 to see St. Michael-le-Belfry to an easy win over Heworth Parish Church and Henry Dalton took 7 for 35 with his leg-breaks for Osbaldwick who defeated Acomb 2nd XI. Osbaldwick faced Escrick Park in the 3rd round and were dismissed for 40 thanks to Edwin Reader who took 7 for 11. J. Douthwaite then took 8 for 29 for Osbaldwick only to see Escrick narrowly win. In the final Jimmy Duck of York Ramblers had figures of 6 for 21 from 11 overs to help bowl out Escrick Park for 69 and secure his side's victory.

In the 1921 1st round William Gatenby took 7 for 21 for St. Martin's against York N.E.R. who were all out for 54, St. Martin's winning comfortably for the loss of two wickets. In another 1st round game G. Eliff took 7 for 25 for York Banks to defeat St. Michael-le- Belfry and in the next round Billy Wilkinson of Dringhouses had identical figures against York Banks to see his side on the way to the final.

George Herbert took 8 for 28 for Rowntrees in the 1922 2nd round to dismiss Escrick Park for 95. Trees then struggled, losing seven wickets before scoring the winning runs. In the final Harry Moult, now playing for York Ramblers, finished with 6 for 39 from 10 overs in dismissing South Bank W.M.C. for 109, all his victims being clean bowled. Jack Prest then responded with 5 for 48 from 14 overs, but the Ramblers scraped a win at 113 for 9. A more detailed account can be found in Chapter Eight.

Lacy of Heworth took 7 wickets against York Wanderers in a 1923 1st round game in a losing cause. In the 2nd round Dringhouses captain Billy Wilkinson took 7 for 27 in dismissing York Revellers for 93 and in response off-spinner George Curry took 5 for 30, but Dringhouses won by four wickets. In another 2nd round game Shuttleworth of Stamford Bridge took 7 for 18, six of which were clean bowled and the other lbw, to help his side beat South Bank W.M.C. Ray Ellar helped Escrick Park to the final with 7 for 30 against Sheriff Hutton in the preliminary round and 7 for 22 against York Wanderers in the 1st round. The final saw two more impressive bowling feats. E. Shaw for Dringhouses coming on as second change took 6 for 19 from 14 overs, six of which were maidens, but Escrick Park still managed to score 160 thanks to 41 from the Reverend Roger Franklen Cardale who opened the innings, 32 from number three Edwin Reader and an amazing 40 extras. Dringhouses then had no answer to the Reverend Cardale who also opened the bowling and took 7 for 33 from 9.2 overs as Dringhouses were skittled for 74 in 18.2 overs.

In 1924 Newey of York "B" took 7 for 29 to help defeat Clifton Church Institute in the preliminary round. A. Walker of Poppleton took 7 for 29 to put St. Michael-le-Belfry out for 50 in the 1st round, Poppleton winning for the loss of two wickets. In the final Dringhouses were runners-up again as Arthur Brassey took five wickets for Rowntrees, Dringhouses being bowled out for 106 chasing a total of 159.

1925 saw R. Harrison take 7 for 21 for Monkgate Primitive Methodists to see Osbaldwick dismissed for 41 in their preliminary round, which proved more than sufficient as Monkgate were shot out for 15, C. Wriglesworth taking 5 for 3 and Henry Dalton 5 for 7. Three outstanding efforts in the 1st round saw F. Pearson of Sheriff Hutton take 8 for 15 to see his side to victory over New Central W.M.C., Dick Lund of York City Amateurs take 7 for 10 against Dringhouses and Harry Jefferson of Haxby 7 for 17 against Rowntrees. In the 2nd round Arnold Wood of Sheriff Hutton took 8 for 54, including a hat-trick, against Haxby and J. Singleton of York Civil Service took 7 for 16 against Clarence C.&I. only for both to end up on the losing side. In the semi-final Harry Cordukes took 8 for 30 to help Haxby defeat Clarence C.&I. and secure a place in the final where they met York City Amateurs. Haxby batting first were 94 all out, Joe Triffitt the City Amateurs opening bowler taking 7 for 57 from 15 overs, three of which were maidens. In addition he took a catch to dismiss the last man, the Amateurs winning easily, finishing at 100 for 1.

In the 1926 2nd round Herbert Freestone took 8 for 23 with his occasional left arm spin to see North Riding Mental Hospital dismiss Stamford Bridge for 49 and the Hospital had a comfortable 10 wicket win to book a place in the semi-finals. Henry Dalton of Osbaldwick went one better to see his side to the semi-finals, his 9 for 18 against York Ramblers remaining a record for the competition for another 28 years. Dalton went on to take six wickets in the first semi-final but despite this Acomb racked up a record breaking 295 for 7 on the first evening. Dalton's 29 wickets at 4.48 each established a new record for the competition. Osbaldwick were bowled out for 102 the following evening with A. Wray taking 6 for 19 and S. Strange 4 for 32. A week later in the second semi-final the North Riding Mental Hospital beat Acomb's new record, scoring 336 for 7 against Rowntrees on the first evening. The following night Rowntrees were blown away by F. Slater who took 8 for 29, ably assisted by wicketkeeper S. Tichener, who caught two and stumped one of Slater's victims, as Rowntrees were dismissed for 115. When the teams met in the final North Riding Mental Hospital were bowled out for 69 by Acomb, S. Strange the opening bowler doing the damage with 12 overs 1 maiden 6 for 36. F. Slater the Hospital opener then went one better with figures of 7 for 19 from 10.3 overs, three of which were maidens, to see Acomb fall 13 runs short. All his victims were clean bowled and his tally for the year's competition had risen to 28 wickets at an average of 5.32.

The North Riding Mental Hospital team with the Cup in 1926.

Back row; Walter Spence (Umpire),W.Reeves, George Sprigg, "Tiny"Amos, William Craven, Charles McQuade, Thomas Bertram (Umpire).
Front row; F.Slater, Hubert Dryland, Dr. William Fraser, William Hill, S.Tichener.
Seated; Ivor Churchill, Herbert Freestone (Captain), George Alfred Harling.

1927 saw Henry Dalton playing for Bootham Park Hospital where he worked as a clerk. He opened the batting scoring 166 runs at an average of 55.33, but it was thanks to his bowling that Bootham Park won the Cup. He took seven wickets in the preliminary round against the Royal Army Medical Corps and 9 for 42 in the semi-final against Ainsty Nomads. They met Acomb in the final who posted a very useful total of 188 all out, despite the efforts of Dalton who bowled unchanged to take 6 for 62 from 27 overs, with seven maidens, bringing his tally of wickets to 34 for the competition a record that would stand for another 24 years. Despite this imposing target Bootham Park won with two balls to spare. A full account of the 1926 and 1927 finals can be found in Chapter Eight.

Bootham Park and Terrys tied their 1928 preliminary round, the first replay being interrupted by rain and the second replay was easily won by Bootham Park, with Henry Dalton inevitably in the wickets, taking 8 for 10. 1928 also saw perhaps the most unusual bowling feat in the history of the Myers & Burnell. Sammy Toyne, the St. Peter's School Headmaster who had been responsible for drafting the original rules in 1919, took 8 for 30 for Clifton Church Institute against New Earswick in the 1st round and still ended on the losing side. The remarkable thing was that he was bowling "slow lobs", a style thought to have died out following the retirement of George Simpson-Hayward of Worcestershire and England, around 1920. The following year playing for Clifton C.C. he took 5 for 20 against Dringhouses also bowling "lobs" and there was some suggestion that he only reverted to this style of bowling when wickets were desperately needed, presumably bowling in a more orthodox overarm fashion in normal circumstances. Whatever the case, Sammy is one of the few bowlers of the pre-war era whose bowling style we know something about and he also became one of the select band of Myers & Burnell centurions in 1930. In the 1928 2nd round S. Husband of the York Banks took 8 for 53 against York Revellers who scored 117. The Banks seemed to be out of the game until Husband hit a brisk unbeaten 63 to secure them a semi-final place. The 1928 winners York Ramblers and runners-up Clarence C.&I. both reached the final on the back of consistent performances from their two main bowlers. For Clarence who played five games Reg Baines took 23 wickets at an average of 10.69 and H. Scaife took 15 wickets at 12.8. For the Ramblers who had a bye in the preliminary round, so only played four games, Cecil William Hamilton took 19 wickets at 9.7 and Harry Moult took 13 wickets at 12.

Billy Wilkinson of Dringhouses took 8 for 44 in a 1929 1st round game as his side defeated Terrys. York Ramblers reached the final once again, bowling Clifton C.C. out for 171 in 51.5 overs. Harry Moult took 5 for 33 from 22 overs, with four maidens, and the Ramblers won in 38 overs finishing at 185 for 8. 1929 saw the last appearance of Henry Dalton in the Myers & Burnell. In the 1st preliminary round he took 6 for 10 against St Clement's followed by 7 for 35 in the 2nd preliminary round against the North Riding Mental Hospital, 7 for 28 in the 1st round against Haxby and finally 4 for 50 as they were put out in the 2nd round by Acomb. This brought his total of wickets in the eleven years he took part to at least 172, a remarkable figure never to be bettered.

The 1931 final saw Jim D'Arcy take 6 for 45 in dismissing York Reserves for 124, but this total proved too much for York Station Staff as Tommy White took 5 for 24 for the Reserves, to see the Staff all out for 75.

In the 1932 final four bowlers took five wickets each, Ray Ellar having figures of 14 overs 1 maiden 5 for 49 and Jack Elmhirst 16.5 overs 3 maidens 5 for for 61 as Escrick Park bowled out the North Riding Mental Hospital for 160. In reply Ivor Churchill had figures of 12.2 overs 2 maidens 5 for 34 and Ernie Marshall, the Hospital gardener, 12 overs 0 maidens 5 for 42 as Escrick were put out for 127.

The 1933 final saw the North Riding Mental Hospital victorious again. Despite 6 for 60 from Tadcaster's Alf Whitelock the Hospital scored 236 which proved too much for Tadcaster who were all out for 178.

In 1935 J. Clifford of Tadcaster had the remarkable figures of 7 for 7, from seven overs two of which were maidens, as South Bank were dismissed for 73 in the 2nd round. The final was a repeat of the 1933 final with Tadcaster being dismissed for 125, George Appleby taking 5 for 18, before the Hospital cruised to victory at 127 for 3.

The 1936 final produced one of most remarkable spells of bowling ever seen in the Myers & Burnell. Tadcaster batted first and scored 164 all out with Tommy White, previously a finalist with York Reserves and now playing for the Railway Institute, taking 5 for 70 from 19 overs with three maidens. R.I. were then completely destroyed by Ernie Stubbs, a Detective Sergeant in the West Yorkshire Police stationed in Tadcaster. In 8.1 overs of which seven were maidens he took 8 for 1, his only run being conceded in his 8th over when a snick was missed in the slips. He took wickets with the last two balls of the same over and completed his hat-trick to win the game with the first ball of his next over, as R.I. were all out for 42 in 16.1 overs. He had already taken 7 for 30 in the preliminary round against Acomb.

Next year Tadcaster were once again in the final. Batting first they were dismissed for 64 by Clifton C.C, G.R. Toes with 16 overs 4 maidens 6 for 32 doing the damage. Clifton won inside 20 overs finishing on 70 for 5; this time Stubbs could not save Tadcaster but he did take 4 for 24. Earlier in the competition Osbaldwick had bowled York Revellers out for just 35 runs in the preliminary round, Fred Scott taking 8 for 13. Osbaldwick, after several early set backs, won at 37 for 5 with Scott top scoring with 19 n.o. Osbaldwick met Sand Hutton in the next round and were bowled out for 57 by the brothers Len and Ronnie Freer, Ronnie then going on to score 43 n.o. to give Sand Hutton a 10 wicket win. The Freer brothers went on to play for Clifton Hospital, both featuring in the 1950 final and Len in the 1953 final. In another preliminary round Lovitt of New Earswick took 7 for 43 in their victory over L.N.E.R. Institute and in the 1st round Jim Blackburn of Clifton C.C. took seven wickets to help defeat Ovington.

In 1938 A. Teale of City of York Police took 7 for 50 in a preliminary round but was on the losing side against eventual finalists North Riding Mental Hospital. Their opponents in the final were old rivals Tadcaster, the third time the sides had contested the final in six years. Tadcaster were 175 all out batting first, Bob Carter Snr. taking 5 for 65 from 10 overs. The much feared Hospital batting line-up failed for once and could only manage 107, the ever reliable Ernie Stubbs taking 4 for 24 from 14.3 overs to end the game. In an exciting 1st round game earlier that year W.F. Cox of York City Amateurs took 7 for 26 to see Poppleton 65 all out. The Amateurs were well placed at 57 for 5 but Leadley was then clean bowled for a duck and the last four batsmen were run out for the addition of only four runs to give Poppleton an unlikely victory.

Roy Nicholson took seven wickets in a losing cause for York Reserves against York Zingari in the 1939 2nd round. Nicholson would have been familiar with his opponents as Zingari fielded several York 1st XI players, in what was essentially a "made up" team full of what would be termed "ringers" today. Zingari went on to reach the final where they met Acomb, who were dismissed for 113, with Frank Richardson taking 5 for 49. Zingari struggled against J. Thompson who took 5 for 42 before they won with seven wickets down, Zingari also won the Senior Charity the same year.

In a 1940 1st round game F. Scott of York Corporation Highways (probably Fred Scott of Osbaldwick) took 7 for 23 to dismiss York "A" for 57 and see his side to a comfortable win. In the final Ernie Stubbs, now captain of Tadcaster, saw them to another win. Tadcaster were 140 all out and in reply New Earswick were dismissed for 81, with Stubbs inevitably doing the damage. Opening the bowling he finished with figures of 11.3 overs 2 maidens 6 for 27, giving him 22 wickets in four final appearances.

The following year Tadcaster, again under the captaincy of Stubbs, reached the final, this time losing out to York Railway Institute. R.I. batted first and although Stubbs failed to take a wicket his opening partner John Marriott took 7 for 59 as R.I. finished 164 all out. Tadcaster could only muster 68 all out in 20 overs with R. Brown proving "very difficult to play", taking 5 for 20 from 10 overs.

The 1941 winners York Railway Institue.

Back row; S.Jackson (Secretary), Harry Brazier, N.Ogden, D.Shaw, Jim Blackburn, G.R.Smith, Peter Morritt, A.S.Asquith.
Front row; G.Ingleby, Frank Baker, Bob Stather, Jack Birch, R.Brown.

In 1942 Clifton C.C. once again won the cup, bowling out Clifton Hospital for 146 thanks to R. Horwell who took 6 for 51. After a good start Clifton lost several cheap wickets but finally crossed the line at 147 for 7. In a 1942 1st round game George Long of Easingwold took 5 for 61 to help his side defeat Tadcaster.

Clifton C.C. again made the final in 1944, when Acomb scored 154 for 9 a total that might have been much larger had it not been for the Clifton skipper Jack Pulleyn who brought himself on as third change and took 5 for 17 from eight overs, three of which were maidens. Despite this the score was out of reach as Acomb's opening bowlers Matt Oates and Alan Dalby took just 30.5 overs to see Clifton 82 all out. Oates had figures of 15 overs 1 maiden 5 for 39 and Dalby 15.5 overs 3 maidens 4 for 37.

1945 saw possibly the two strongest sides ever to take part in the competition reach the final. R.A.F. Melbourne were dismissed for 146, Syd Appleyard taking 5 for 24 for Clifton Hospital. A "very quick and accurate" opening spell by Jamaican fast bowler C.R. Knight yielded only 11 runs but the Hospital openers kept their wickets intact and it was the first change bowler who turned the game for the R.A.F side. Flying Officer John Quarmby, later to play for York Nondescripts after the war, dismissed both openers and went on to finish with 6 for 26 to leave the Hospital 15 runs short of victory. A more detailed account can be found in Chapter Eight.

The following year Clifton C.C. were bowled out in the final for 121 by York Railway Institute, Cyril Audaer taking 5 for 26, only to see his side dismissed for 83.

The 1949 final saw Clifton C.C. captain Herbert Harrison take 6 for 40 from 14.2 overs to help dismiss Dringhouses for 102 and win the game by 42 runs.

In their 1951 2nd round game Easingwold beat Acomb thanks to 5 for 62 from Gordon Paragreen. In the semi-final Dennis Hutchinson took 5 for 38 from 12 overs for Easingwold but Ovington passed Easingwold's total of 81 for the loss of seven wickets. The final then saw two remarkable bowling performances. Jack Allison of Stamford Bridge took 7 for 46 from 20 overs to see Ovington all out for 110. Derek Ainley then took 9 for 40 from 16.2 overs, the best figures ever in a final, to leave Stamford 6 runs short. Derek Ainley's performances throughout the 1951 competition set a record that that was never bettered. Forty one entrants meant an extra preliminary round was required so Ovington played six games in total, his figures were as follows;

		overs	maidens	runs	wickets	average
1st Prelim round	v New Earswick	12.1	2	33	4	8.25
2nd Prelim round	v Magnets Sports Club	8.3	2	11	7	1.57
1st round	v York Ramblers	11	1	28	7	4
2nd round	v Bishopthorpe	10	2	28	5	5.6
Semi-final	v Easingwold	9.4	1	29	4	7.25
Final	v Stamford Bridge	16.2	2	40	9	4.44
	Total	67.4	10	169	36	4.69

A full account of the 1951 final can be found in Chapter Eight.

The 1951 Ovington side before the semi-final.

Back row; Gerry Pragnell, Peter Mowbray, Ken Newton, Brian Hanson, Derek Ainley, Jack Haxby.
Front row; Rev.David Bodycombe, Geoff Limbert, Ted Coulson, G.Wright, Stan Bell.
Missing is Brian Boyes who replaced the Reverend Bodycombe in the final.

The 1952 final was postponed due to the weather and played over two evenings as a 40 over per side game. Dringhouses batted first and were all out for 182 off the penultimate ball, Geoff Wilkinson taking 5 for 35 for "York an XI". York were restricted to 129 for 9 off their 40 overs, Stan Hayton finishing with figures of 20 overs 4 maidens 5 for 49.

In a 1954 preliminary round Osbaldwick pulled off a major shock in eliminating the holders Clifton Hospital, with a team containing several players who were to become club legends at Osbaldwick including brothers Ian and Phil Moxon, Dick Crowther and Stuart Myers. Osbaldwick could only manage 102 for 9 in their 28 overs, which seemed an inadequate total against such an experienced side, but Ronnie Wilson with 5 for 30, three wickets for Martin and two smart run-outs saw Osbaldwick to a deserved win by the comfortable margin of 45 runs. In another 1954 preliminary round between "York an XI" and Heslington, York batted first and made 111 for 9 in a game reduced to 24 overs, Brown taking 5 for 52 for Heslington. Geoff Wilkinson then made a piece of Myers & Burnell history. In 7.1 overs four of which were maidens he took all 10 wickets for only nine runs to see Heslington crash to 32 all out , the first and only time a bowler has taken all 10 wickets in the competition. His figures also included an all clean bowled hat-trick. York went on to reach the final, Wilkinson taking only a single wicket as Rowntrees won an enthralling game in unusual fashion; a more detailed report can be found in Chapter Eight. Rowntrees reached the final with the help of some consistent bowling from Ted King who ended up with 18 wickets from the four games they played, his best being 7 for 39 in the 1st round against Bootham Park. Stan Hayton took seven wickets including a hat-trick as Dringhouses beat Yapham in the 1st round. In another 1st round game between Easingwold and Stockton & Hopgrove, Easingwold finished on 110 for 9 thanks to Ron Atkinson taking 6 for 44 in 14 overs. Stockton were all out for 74 thanks mainly to Clarrie Smith taking 5 for 29 from 12 overs two of which were maidens. Also in the 1st round Fred Sherwood took 7 for 40 for Stamford Bridge to see York Police 83 all out in reply to Stamford's 121 for 8.

The following year, 1955, Fred took 8 for 48 against Haxby in the preliminary round to see them finish on 102 for 9 in 28 overs, Stamford winning with an over to spare despite Duncan Steel taking all five wickets to fall for 39 runs. In the next round Fred took 7 for 21 to restrict Dringhouses to 49 for 9 in a game reduced to 25 overs. Despite losing opener Frank Lindsay for a duck, Norman Pearson and his father Wally scored the required runs without further mishaps. Stamford went out to Rowntrees in the 2nd round despite another remarkable performance from Sherwood. Rowntrees scored 134 for 9, Fred taking 8 for 60 from his 14 overs and Stamford fell short with 127 for 5. In only three games Fred had taken 23 wickets at 5.6. Only seven other bowlers have exceeded 20 wickets in a season and all took between four and six games to achieve the feat. In the preliminary round A. Postlethwaite of Civil Service took 7 for 13 as Ovington were bowled out for 19 chasing 104 to win. The next round saw Civil Service face York Ramblers, John Binnie taking 7 for 54 for the Ramblers as Civil Service totalled 126 but his efforts were in vain as his side were 86 all out.

P. Brown of York Ramblers took 7 for 48 in the 1956 preliminary round in their win over Scarcroft. In another preliminary round Jim Collis of "York an XI" took 7 for 28 in an innings of 128 for 8 as Easingwold chased York's 147 for 8. Ron Atkinson of Stockton and Hopgrove took 7 for 41 in a 1st round game as Naburn Hospital were beaten easily. Colin Gell of York R.I. took 7 for 15 as Clifton C.C. were dismissed for 82 in a 1st round game and R.I. made hard work of their task, overhauling that total for the loss of seven wickets in the 23rd over. Stamford Bridge made even harder work of a small total set by Civil service in the 2nd round. Fred Sherwood took 7 for 32 and Terry Barker 3 for 35 as Civil Service struggled to 68 and Stamford then lost eight wickets before finally winning in the 27th over.

In a 1957 preliminary round Cyril Mason of Tadcaster took eight wickets in their win over the National Glass Works and he took a total of 13 wickets in the competition at an average of 7.15. In the 2nd round Tadcaster dismissed Easingwold for 74 thanks to a fine piece of bowling by 17 year old Barry Firn, the Tadcaster Grammar School captain, who took five wickets for 13 runs, including a hat-trick, in just 3.1 overs. Tadcaster went on to a comfortable seven wicket win to secure a semi-final place against local rivals Magnets Sports Club which they subsequently lost. In the 1st round Bill Ogden of Acomb took 7 for 29 to help defeat York R.I. In the 2nd round they met Ebor Gogues who posted a modest 111 for 9 thanks to Tommy Bamford taking 5 for

52. However Ian Hallas then returned the remarkable figures of 8.3 overs 4 maidens 5 wickets for 7 runs and Denzil Webster, later to play for Acomb for many years, took 4 for 37 to see Acomb all out for 48. The 1957 final was Magnets Sports Club's only appearance. The game had been postponed several times and was eventually played on the evenings of the 26th and 27th August. With the evenings drawing in it was agreed to reduce the innings to 35 overs per side. Magnets batted first against Ebor Gogues, a team of local schoolteachers and they were bowled out for a very useful 155 in 34 overs. Ian Hallas, who had been the outstanding Gogues bowler during the competition, taking 14 wickets at 8.71, bowled throughout the innings to take 5 for 60. The following evening Ebor Gogues were dismissed for 129 in the final over, Cyril Conroy coming on as second change and taking 6 for 38 from 11 overs to win the Cup for Magnets.

In the 1st preliminary round in 1958 John Binnie took York Ramblers to an unlikely victory. Having been bowled out by the holders Tadcaster Magnets for only 88, his 7 for 36 helped see Magnets finish all out 17 runs short. In the preliminary round proper Brian Hanson of Ovington took 7 for 5 as Copmanthorpe were all out for just 21, Dave Sherwood and Geoff Limbert having little difficulty in knocking the runs off without loss. In the 1st round Eric "Biddy" Wilson of Dunnington took 6 for 26 to help restrict New Earswick to 93 all out, but for New Earswick Dick Wilks was on fire; in 9.3 overs of which 5 were maidens he took 7 for 5 runs to see Dunnington 37 all out. In the semi-final John Pitt took 7 for 51 with his off-breaks as New Earswick could only manage 98 against Rowntrees who knocked the runs off the following evening. The final was the last 50 over final and Woodhouse Grange ran up an impressive 250 for 8 against Rowntrees despite a marathon bowling spell from John Pitt who bowled unchanged for 25 overs taking 5 for 110. The total proved too much for Rowntrees who were 160 all out. Pitt finished the year's competition with 20 wickets at 12.25.

The following year all games were played under the new format, each side having 18 eight ball overs with both innings to be played on the same evening. There were some useful performances in the preliminary round. Bob Carter Snr. took six wickets in restricting Haxby to 88 for 9, but Duncan Steel then responded with 6 for 24 to see Clifton Hospital all out for 39. Price of Ebor Gogues took 7 for 26 to see Acomb out for 61, setting up an easy nine wicket win for his side, Geoff Hornby of

Dunnington took 7 for 14 in dismissing Scarcroft for 39 and Jim Collis took 6 for 40 for Huntington W.M.C. in their win over Ovington. Peter Armstrong took 6 for 48 for Civil Service to help restrict Clifton C.C. to 97 all out, and Civil Service were indebted to Dave Early for a quick-fire 59 as they struggled to get over the line at 98 for 7. But the most remarkable bowling of feat of the preliminary round belongs to Colin Gell of Ardua, whose side had scored 109 for 5 against Osbaldwick. With four overs to go Osbaldwick were 89 for 4. Gell then struck in the 15th over taking four wickets in four balls in a maiden. Eleven runs came from the 16th over leaving 10 runs to win off the last two. Four runs came off the next over for the loss of the ninth wicket and with the first ball of the last over Gell took the final wicket to seal an unlikely victory. He had taken five wickets in six balls without conceding a run to finish with figures of 7 for 40. W. Morley of Tadcaster bowled consistently throughout the competition, his 15 wickets at 7.4 being a decisive factor in his side lifting the Cup. He took 5 for 46 against Bilton-in-Ainsty, 5 for 35 against Dringhouses and 5 for 30 against New Earswick in the final. His tally may in fact have been higher as there is no record of one of Tadcaster's early rounds or their semi-final. Dick Wilks of New Earswick took 10 wickets at 13.7 to help his side to the final and as with Morley there appear to be no records of two of New Earswick's games. In a series of low scoring games Noel Hare of Escrick Park almost single handedly took his side to the semi-final where they lost to eventual runners-up New Earswick. His record of 25 wickets in this first season of the new format was never bettered, his figures being as follows;

		overs	maidens	runs	wickets	average
Preliminary round	v Minster Choir Old Boys	8.3	3	14	8	1.75
1st round	v Retreat	6	0	31	3	10.33
2nd round	v Yapham	8	0	30	7	4.29
3rd round	v York Ramblers	9	0	48	4	12
Semi-final	v New Earswick	9	0	41	3	13.66
	Total	40.3	3	164	25	6.56

In the final Tadcaster met New Earswick who batted first and were dismissed for 89 off the last ball of the innings, W. Morley taking 5 for 30 from nine overs and Sam Lawrence 5 for 33 from seven overs. Tadcaster made light work of the task, reaching 90 for 2 in the 14th over.

1960 saw Clive Hendry of York R.I. take 6 for 38 from nine overs against Escrick Park in a 1st round game and followed this with 6 for 36 in a 2nd round cliffhanger against "York an XI" for whom John Temple took 7 for 35 to bowl R.I. out for 91. Hendry's efforts though saw his side win as York finished on 90 for 8, their 8th wicket falling as Bob Crosby attempted a single to tie the game and was run out. R.I. reached the final which they won in amazing fashion thanks once again to Hendry's 6 for 42 from nine overs in dismissing Ebor Gogues; a more detailed account can be found in Chapter Eight. Hendry, who missed both the tied semi-final against Dringhouses and the replay, took 18 wickets in three games at an average of 6.44. Charlie Hutchinson took 6 for 55 with his left-arm medium pace for Stillington in the 1960 2nd round to see York Ramblers all out for 111. In very poor light the pace of Philip Crowe with 6 for 35 and his partner Mick Payne with 3 for 34 were too much for Stillington and they ended on 84 all out. Ramblers were knocked out in the semi-final by Ebor Gogues who scored 167 for 5 and Joe Valente then took 6 for 43 as Ramblers could only muster 109 all out.

In a 1961 preliminary round Trevor Craven of Yapham took 7 for 35 as Terrys were restricted to 94 all out, the top scorer for Terrys being York City goalkeeper Tommy Forgan with 23. Yapham were then dismissed for 81 as Pete Timler and P. Mortimer shared the wickets. In the next round Roly Pattison took 7 for 10 from 5.1 overs as Dringhouses dismissed Terrys for just 32 chasing 107 for 5. In the 1st round Alan Shipley of Sheriff Hutton Bridge took 7 for 38 against New Earswick who finished on 78 all out and Bridge won by eight wickets. In the 2nd round Wilf Jackson took 7 for 36 to see York R.I. into the semi-final with a comfortable win over Acomb. Terry Precious took 6 for 22 for Heworth to dismiss Tadcaster Magnets for 56 in the semi-final after Heworth had scored 124 for 3. The other semi-final between York R.I. and York Ramblers saw one of the great recovery acts in the Myers & Burnell. Tony Keel (3 for 47), Clive Hendry (4 for 37) and three run-outs restricted the Ramblers to 92 all out, a total that owed much to a patient 28 from top scorer George Myerscough. R.I. were then reduced to 18 for 8 after eight overs, Mick Payne with five wickets and K. Leadley with three appearing unplayable. Skipper John Bradley then added 41 with number nine Ken Marshall before Bradley was bowled in the 14th over. Marshall then took control. Farming the strike he added 35 of the 37 runs that saw them to an unlikely win with two balls to spare, number 10 Clive Hendry ending 2 n.o. and Marshall 55 n.o. Another thrilling final followed, again featuring Ken Marshall and Clive Hendry. Heworth were dismissed for 71 off the last ball of their innings, Hendry finishing with 5 for 39 from nine overs. R.I. appeared to be heading for a comfortable win, needing four runs off the last over with five wickets in hand. Singles were taken from Dave Wilson's first two balls, the next three were dots one of which clean bowled Peter Morritt. The new man in, wicketkeeper Terry Adams, took a single off the sixth, the seventh was another dot before Ken Marshall once again saved his side with a scrambled single off the last ball to give R.I. the narrowest of wins.

In the 1962 preliminary round Alan Shipley took 7 for 27 to see Acomb all out for 97, Gerry Grinham and Jim Rhodes Jnr. taking Sheriff Hutton Bridge to a 10 wicket win. In another preliminary round Bilton-in-Ainsty were shot out for 38 by Civil Service, Alan Barker taking 6 for 16 and Duncan Steel 4 for 16, their team winning easily for the loss of a single wicket. In the 1st round John Teale took 6 for 31 against Woodhouse Grange to give "York an XI" a narrow victory; chasing 110 for 7 Woodhouse finished on 107 for 9. Stamford Bridge could only manage 60 for 9 against York Ramblers in the 1st round, but Jeff Bellamy took 7 for 36 to dismiss the Ramblers for just 47. The 1962 final saw another last ball thriller. Pete Braithwaite took 6 for 39 from nine overs for Cawood, in their first final appearance, to dismiss Dringhouses for 106 off the final ball of their innings. Cawood then took it to the wire. Needing six to win off the final over, the scores were tied as they took a single from a dropped catch off the penultimate ball. Brian Hall then coolly hit a four through the packed in-field to give Cawood victory at 110 for 6. Braithwaite had been outstanding for Cawood, having taken 6 for 45 against Tadcaster Magnets in the 2nd round and 6 for 34 against Civil Service in the semi-final, to end the competition with 18 wickets at 6.55. He possibly took more, but there is no record of Cawood's 1st round game.

Despite only scoring 67 for 6 Yapham beat Escrick Park in the 1963 1st round thanks to Trevor Craven who had figures of 9 overs 5 maidens 6 for 11 to see Escrick all out for 54, P. Carling taking the other four wickets for 35 runs. Alan Barker with 6 for 36 and Duncan Steel with 4 for 26 bowled Bootham Park out for 66 in a 1st round game, leaving Civil Service a seemingly straightforward target. G. Thacker had other ideas however taking 6 for 21, and Civil Service scraped home with the last pair at the wicket. Another 1st round game saw York Ramblers score 120 all out against Acomb, Denzil Webster taking 6 for 50. Unfortunately for Acomb P. Hulbert responded with 6 for 21 and they collapsed to 51 all out. In the 2nd round Roly Pattison of Dringhouses took 6 for 33 to dismiss Cawood for 65 in reply to 163 for 2. In another 2nd round game Ian Reed had 7 for 54 as Yapham could only manage 99 for 8, Huntington W.M.C. replying with 101 for 4. In the semi-finals Alan Barker of Civil Service took 6 for 50 in a losing cause against Huntington W.M.C. and Tony Keel took 6 for 49 for York R.I. as they beat Dringhouses. The final saw yet another last over finish. R.I. batted first against Huntington W.M.C. and despite 32 from Robbie Marchant and 10 extras, the only double figure scores, they were all out for 83. Ian Reed and wicketkeeper Frank Gibson did the damage, Reed taking 7 for 31, three of his victims being caught by Gibson and one stumped. Huntington were then made to struggle for their win at 85 for 6, Lenny Watson steering them home in the last over to finish with 25 not out.

In 1964 the preliminary round saw several outstanding bowling feats. Heworth scored 147 for 2 against Bootham Park thanks to a 1st wicket partnership of 112 by Geoff Powell and Tony Moore. Moore then took 8 for 6 and Robert Toes 2 for 17 as Bootham were swept away for 24, all the batsmen being clean bowled. Mick Storr took 6 for 18 as Naburn Hospital were 57 all out in reply to 101 from Huntington W.M.C. Barham of Clifton C.C. took 8 for 39 as his side beat "York an XI". Barry Westerman of Tadcaster took 8 for 24 which included four wickets in five balls as Long Marston were dismissed for 70 chasing a total of 142 for 8. Tony Stilgoe took 6 for 17 for Dringhouses as Terrys were bowled out for 40, but his side then found themselves 25 for 7 before they managed to win losing just one more wicket. Clifton Hospital scored 107 for 6 against Ovington thanks to 66 n.o. from West Indian Keith Medford and Ovington were then all out for 77 thanks to the Hospital's veteran opening bat Alf Aveyard taking 7 for 32. In the 2nd round Duncan Steel of Civil Service took 8 for 17 against Minster Choir Old Boys as they were 39 all out in pursuit of 116 to win, all his victims being clean bowled. In another 2nd round game Colin Minton took 6 for 33 for Stillington to beat Clifton C.C. and put his side into the semi-final. In the final Duncan Steel of Civil Service took 7 for 23 from his nine over spell, while in the 2nd innings Malcolm

Denton took 6 for 26 from his nine overs to help Stillington to victory, very much against the odds. A more detailed account can be found in Chapter Eight.

In the 1965 1st round Bower of Tadcaster Magnets took 6 for 31 as Thorp Arch & Boston Spa closed on 120 for 9. Magnets were then made to work hard for their win, finishing on 123 for 6 in the final over, Barry Shann taking 5 for 53 for T.A.B.S. Huntington W.M.C. were once again in the final in 1965, but this time Ian Reed could only manage one wicket before Jim Collis taking 5 for 24 and Fred Storr with 4 for 29 put "York an XI" out for 95, Guy Raines 34 and Noel Hare 15 being the only double figure scorers. Huntington won comfortably at 98 for 5 in 13.2 overs.

In the 1st round in 1966 there were several significant bowling feats. Peter Suffield of York R.I. took 6 for 43 to restrict Easingwold to 124 for 8 in pursuit of R.I.'s total of 140 for 5, John Stillborn took 6 for 22 to see New Earswick defeat Escrick Park and Brian Hough of Acomb took 7 for 26 to put Dunnington out for just 65. Acomb lost five wickets in passing the total with less than two overs left. Acomb met Clifton C.C. in the 2nd round and could only manage 111 for 9, John Whittle taking 7 for 35 with Clifton winning easily by 8 wickets. Terry Fountain took 6 for 34 for Woodhouse Grange in a comfortable win over Osbaldwick in the 1st round. Chasing the Woodhouse total of 161 for 8, Osbaldwick could only manage 72 all out in 13 overs, Stuart Myers being the only double figure scorer with 18. In the next round Woodhouse disposed of Rufforth for 80, thanks to 6 for 48 from Paul Lewis and despite losing three wickets won very quickly. Tony Stilgoe with 6 for 15 and Roly Pattison with 4 for 26 set Dringhouses on the path to the final dismissing Sheriff Hutton Bridge for a mere 46, a total that would have been much smaller without a last wicket partnership of 28 from Chris Tate and Geoff Shipley. Dringhouses were made to struggle and lost five wickets before reaching the required total in the penultimate over, Shipley taking four of the wickets for just 17 runs.

Dringhouses met Woodhouse in the final and restricted them to 102 for 7, Roly Pattison taking 4 for 54 to give him 10 wickets in the competition at 9.9 and Tony Stilgoe took 1 for 36 to finish with 15 wickets at 8.47. Derek Pattison and Ray Varney then took the game away from Woodhouse with an opening stand of 75 and Dringhouses won at 105 for 3 with three overs to spare.

In the 1967 preliminary round A. Cooper took 6 for 23 for Bootham Park to beat Ovington, who were 55 all out attempting to score 70 for victory. In the preliminary round game at New Earswick the home side were 65 all out as Ken Hayton took 7 for 25 for Melbourne but John Stillborn then took 6 for 12 as Melbourne were dismissed for just 47. The 1967 final saw Tony Moore and Tony Stilgoe bowl Dringhouses to victory over Heworth. Chasing 122 to win Heworth managed only 69 all out thanks to 6 for 23 from 7.4 overs by Moore and 4 for 42 from eight overs by Stilgoe.

A formidable opening attack, Tony Moore and Tony Stilgoe bowled Dringhouses to victory in 1967. The photo below shows Stilgoe in his follow through, bowling for Dringhouses against Sheriff Hutton Bridge in a Myers & Burnell game at Clifton Park in the 1970's. Des Wyrill guides the ball wide of wicketkeeper Keith Cowl and Geoff Rollinson at 1st slip.

In 1968 another great opening pair bowled their side to victory. Easingwold won the Cup thanks to the efforts of Ken Skilbeck who took 20 wickets at 8.2 in the competition with a best of 7 for 17 against York R.I. in the 2nd round and Colin Minton who took 18 wickets at 10.39 with a best of 6 for 22 against Magnets in the 3rd round. No other bowler got a look in, as Ken and Colin bowled unchanged in every round. In a 1968 1st round Tony Moore, now playing for Heworth took 7 for 19 to help dismiss Rowntrees for 49 as they chased Heworth's 118 for 8. He also took 3 for 19 in a losing cause in the next round giving him 10 wickets at 3.8 in the two games he played.

In the 1969 preliminary round Heworth bowled Yapham out for 85 thanks to 6 for 30 from Robert Toes, Heworth going on to win for the loss of two wickets. In the 1st round Geoff Skilbeck took 6 for 35 for Easingwold in a comfortable win over Cawood. York Nomads, the eventual winners, dismissed Escrick Park for just 30 in their 1st round game, John Teale taking 6 for 8 from six overs and Tony Temple 3 for 19, York going on to win by 10 wickets. In the semi-final York tied with Civil Service and Tony Temple took a hat-trick in the replay to see his side into the final where they had a comfortable win, thanks to an unbeaten 53 from Robbie Marchant.

In the 1970 1st round Noel Hare took 6 for 57 for Escrick Park against Sheriff Hutton Bridge who were all out for 107, but Escrick could only manage 75 for 6 in reply. In the final Tony Stilgoe contributed to another Dringhouses victory, his 4 for 41 from 8.1 overs helped to see Dunnington dismissed for 102, this time ably supported by Roly Pattison with 3 for 39 from seven overs. Dringhouses made hard work of their task, only 28 from skipper Keith Cowl and 27 n.o. from Alan Fountain seeing them home with four balls to spare and six wickets down.

In a 1971 preliminary round between Heworth and Bilton-in-Ainsty, Heworth batting first were well placed at 86 without loss off 13 overs before Syd Meads came on to take 3 for 19 from three overs to restrict Heworth to 124 for 6. This proved to be more than enough as Ian Reed finished with figures of 7 overs 0 maidens 7 for 19 and Ken Johnson 6 overs 2 maidens 3 for 17 to see Bilton all out for 32. In the 1st round Heworth scored 145 for 5 against Dringhouses thanks to a fine 46 n.o. from Jerry Dunnington. Dringhouses were then dismissed for 80 in 16 overs, Mick Barrett finishing with 8 for 40 from eight overs and Ian Reed taking 2 for 34 from his eight overs at the other end. Mick

Oldfield took 6 for 51 as Dunnington were bowled out for 135 in the 1st round but Sheriff Hutton Bridge could only manage 103 for 9 in reply as Brian Kelly took 6 for 40 and Brian Stacey 3 for 29. In another 1st round game Bernard Shaw took 7 for 58 for Rowntrees to see Acomb finish on 119 for 9, Rowntrees winning comfortably for the loss of four wickets. In the semi-final Heworth met "York an XI" who they bowled out for 104 with only Robbie Marchant (25) and Barry Temple (22) putting up much resistance as Ian Reed took 5 for 25 and Mick Barrett 4 for 39. Phil Crookes then took 5 for 27 from eight overs to see Heworth all out for 84 and put his team into the final where they had a comfortable win over Stamford Bridge, who had much the worse of the conditions, having to bat in very poor light.

In the 1972 final the Skilbeck brothers, Ken and Geoff, bowled Easingwold to victory against local rivals Sheriff Hutton Bridge with 3 for 43 and 3 for 30 respectively, this being the culmination of a great competition for them. Apart from 5.5 overs in the 1st round they bowled unchanged for the rest of the competition. Ken took 16 wickets at 9.25, only to be eclipsed by younger brother Geoff who took 22 at a remarkable 7.09. Ken's best figures were 4 for 6 from five overs against British Sugar in the 1st round, while Geoff's best was 6 for 30 to dismiss Civil Service for 73 in the semi-final, this after Easingwold had only managed 86 batting first, with Peter Robinson taking 6 for 23 from eight overs. In the previous round Thorp Arch & Boston Spa were restricted to 85 for 8 thanks to 5 for 50 from Geoff (one of his victims being Yorkshire's Jim Love), two wickets from Ken and a run out. T.A.B.S. pushed Easingwold all the way, Barry Westerman taking 5 for 36 from 8.7 overs, but 31 n.o. from Geoff at number nine saw them win with nine balls left and eight wickets down.

In the 1973 preliminary round Easingwold had an easy win against Rufforth who were blown away for only 22, Ken Skilbeck taking 7 for 10 from 5.3 overs. In the semi-final Civil Service were dismissed for just 38 chasing Sheriff Hutton Bridge's 139 for 7, Des Wyrill taking 6 for 18 from eight overs and Roy Piercy 3 for 10 from five overs.

Easingwold won the Cup again in 1974 after being bowled out for 86 by Heworth, due mainly to Colin Armstrong who took 5 for 32 in 7.5 overs. They then shot out Heworth for only 48, Jerry Dunnington top scoring with a mere 10. The damage was done by Colin Minton with 6 for 27 from 7.3 overs, ably supported by Ken Skilbeck who took 4 for 20 from seven overs. A more detailed account of this game can be found in Chapter Eight. On the way to the final Ken took 5 for 23 from six overs against Huntington W.M.C. in the 1st round and 5 for 3 from four overs two of which were maidens, against Stockton & Hopgrove in the 2nd round. Stockton lost their first five wickets without scoring a run and ended up 27 all out. In the 3rd round it was brother Geoff's turn, taking 5 for 44 from 7.2 overs to see Rowntrees all out for 75. In the five games Easingwold played in the 1974 competition their opponents totalled just 310 runs and lost 48 wickets with only Stamford Bridge who scored 105 for 8 in the semi-final managing to amass three figures and avoid being bowled out.

The Easingwold team who won the 1968 Myers & Burnell.

Back row: Norman Allen (Umpire), Jeff Robinson, Colin Minton, Ken Skilbeck, Bill Bell,Geoff Skilbeck, Peter King, Gilbert Taylor (Scorer)
Front row: Peter Gilleard, Stuart Burton, Dennis Hutchinson (Capt.), Val Toase, Colin Raper.
The Skilbeck brothers Ken and Geoff bowled them to victory in 1972. Colin Minton teamed up with Ken in the 1968, 1974 and 1979 wins. These three between them took at least 230 wickets in the Myers & Burnell and probably in excess of 250, as full records for several years have proved impossible to locate. Ken took 110 in the 18 seasons between 1968 and 1986, Geoff 51 and Colin 70, although there are incomplete or no records for at least eight of these seasons, and Ken and Colin also played in the Myers & Burnell prior to 1968.

The rule change in 1975 restricting bowlers to a maximum of five overs each greatly reduced the chance of a "five for", so I now include as many instances of a bowler taking four or more wickets as I can trace, although this is necessarily not a complete list.

Mike Stothard of Woodhouse Grange took 4 for 25 including a hat-trick in the 1st round as his side beat Dringhouses. In another 1st round game Colin Minton took 4 for 28 for Easingwold as Sheriff Hutton Bridge closed on 106 for 7, Easingwold being all out four runs short of victory. The reduction to five overs per bowler didn't bother Dave Gibson of Cawood, who in the 1975 semi-final against Woodhouse Grange took a remarkable 7 for 21 from his five overs as well as scoring 40 runs to see his side into the final where they lost to Sheriff Hutton Bridge.

In the 1976 1st round Tony Haines took 4 for 19 for Acomb to help restrict Sheriff Hutton to 102 for 7. Acomb were made to fight hard. With the score on 100 for 9 and two balls to go, 17 year old Dick Sykes came out to join Denzil Webster. Sykes took a single from his first ball, then Webster launched the last ball high into the outfield towards a waiting fielder. They took a single to tie the scores, the catch that would have won the game for Sheriff Hutton was dropped and they came back for the winning run. In another 1st round game Sheriff Hutton Bridge were all out for 84 against York Ramblers, Bill Revis top scoring with 54 and Tony Keel taking 4 for 23. In reply the Ramblers finished on 62 for 9, thanks to 4 for 27 from Mick Oldfield, Keel top scoring with 28. Chasing Dunnington's huge total of 179 for 3 in the first semi-final, Cawood were dismissed for just 87, with Ian Wilkinson taking 5 for 22. This put his team into the final in which they batted first and made a useful 156 for 6. Their opponents, Huntington W.M.C, were well placed at 87 for 3 after 10 overs, but Robin Smith coming on second change took 6 for 18 from a mere 3.6 overs to see Huntington dismissed for 118.

1977 saw "York an XI" defeat Tadcaster in the final. Tadcaster were bowled out for 104 despite 52 from Howard Conroy, their last six wickets falling for just 24 runs, thanks to three run-outs and Dave Wreglesworth with 4 for 8 from just 2.6 overs. An unbroken third wicket stand of 99 by brothers-in-law Robbie Marchant and Clive Robinson saw York to an eight wicket win with more than two overs to spare.

The next year Sheriff Hutton Bridge once again met Cawood in the final in which they scored 162 for 3 from their 18 overs. Des Wyrill and Bill Revis put on 85 for the first wicket, with Wyrill going on to finish unbeaten on 98 . Cawood made a bold reply ending on 141 for 7, Dennis Shipley taking 4 for 32 from his five overs.

In a 1979 1st round game Steve Young took 5 for 17 from five overs to see Heworth knock out Clifton Hospital Alliance who could only muster 78 for 9. Heworth won for the loss of four wickets but took 16 overs to reach their target.

Eric Wallis took 6 for 16 in 4.2 overs for Tadcaster to see his side dismiss Clifton Hospital Alliance for 62 in a 1980 1st round game and Ian McKenzie and Barry Emmott then knocked off the runs without loss. In another 1st round game Dave Smith took 4 for 46 from five overs for the Glassworks in a losing cause against Easingwold, who beat Stockton and Hopgrove in the next round with Ken Skilbeck taking 4 for 21 from four overs. Easingwold were knocked out in the third round by the eventual runners-up Woodhouse Grange. In the semi-final Jim Collis of Heworth had the remarkable figures of 5 overs 2 maidens 3 for 6 , despite which he was on the losing side to "York an XI" who went on to beat Woodhouse in the final.

In a thrilling 1981 1st round game Civil Service's Dave Pepper, whose five overs cost only 11 runs for two wickets, and Bob Steane coming on second change to take 6 for 15 from four overs saw Easingwold finish on 85 for 9. An early wicket each for Colin Minton, Ken Skilbeck and Martin Robinson didn't seem to bother Civil Service, but then two run-outs slowed things up and at 78 for 5 they looked home and dry before Robinson took three more to finish with 4 for 19 from five overs, leaving the game tied with an over to go and two wickets remaining. Colin Minton was brought back for the final over and had Peter Robison caught by Val Toase off his first ball. Steve Whale survived the second, but was caught by Toase off the third to end the game. This was something Easingwold were becoming accustomed to; having tied with Dringhouses in the Isaac Poad the previous week, they won that replay two days later but were easily beaten by Civil Service in the Myers & Burnell replay. The 1981 final was dominated by Sessay captain John Flintoff who took wickets with the third and fourth balls of his first over to leave Acomb struggling. He finished with 4 for 26 from five overs and Acomb's total of 128 for 7 never looked enough.

So it proved, as 81 n.o. from Flintoff saw his side to victory in 16 overs for the loss of a single wicket.

In 1982 York R.I. were bowled out for 70 in the 1st round by Heworth, opening bowler Stan Butler taking 4 for 13 from five overs and Ian Reed 4 for 12 from three overs coming on as first change. Dick Leadley with 5 for 6 from five overs reduced Heworth to 23 for 5 after ten overs but Heworth just managed a win at 73 for 7 thanks to a 7th wicket stand of 39 between Ken Johnson and Colin Markham. In their 1st round game Easingwold beat Stockton & Hopgrove and once again Ken Skilbeck had Stockton struggling, taking 4 for 8 from his allotted five overs, ably backed up by Martin Robinson with 3 for 9 from five overs.

The following year Easingwold met Woodhouse Grange in the 1st round but despite John Kneal taking 4 for 27 from five overs Woodhouse went on to win. Acomb appeared in the final again in 1983 and this time they were victorious thanks to Tony Haines. Stamford Bridge were set 149 to win and ended on 122 for 8 with Haines bowling a miserly spell of five overs taking four wickets for a mere 17 runs.

In the 1984 2nd round Dave Pepper had the remarkable figures of 5 overs 1 maiden 4 for 5 for Civil Service who restricted Dunnington to 78 for 8. Civil Service won the game but lost five wickets in the process.

In the 1985 1st round Heworth met Clifton Hospital Alliance and the Hospital were dismissed for 78 with Trevor Walton taking 4 for 17 from his five overs. Heworth won with four overs to spare but lost six wickets in the process. In the 2nd round against Acomb, Heworth chasing only 84 thanks to Graham Cooper's 4 for 16 from 3.6 overs, had a scare as Mick Robinson took 4 for 13 from five overs, but scraped home at 86 for 8. In the 3rd round Heworth dismissed "York an XI" for 91, with Cooper again in the wickets taking 5 for 20 from five overs and Jonathan Simpson top scoring for York with 33. This proved sufficient as Heworth ended on 86 for 9 in 18 overs thanks to 3 for 20 from Simpson, 3 for 28 from John Herbert and a five over spell from Geoff Coe which conceded only eight runs for one wicket. In another 3rd round clash Paul Spofforth of Dunnington took 4 for 27 from three overs in a tied game against Easingwold, who won the replay, but were beaten in the semi-final by eventual winners Crayke.

In a 1986 1st round game Ian Burden took 4 for 33 from four overs for Clifton Hospital to help restrict Easingwold to 109 for 9, which proved to be enough as the Hospital collapsed to 54 all out in the face of 4 for 8 from five overs from Ken Skilbeck and 3 for 20 from Alan Robinson. In another 1st round game, reduced to 16 overs, Cawood batted first against Heworth and after nine overs they were 71 for 2 but the introduction of Ian Reed, (4 overs 4 for 22) and Graham Cooper (3 overs 3 for 19) saw them finish 104 for 9. Heworth looked to be lost at 23 for 4 after seven overs, with Eric Gibson taking 3 for 12 from four overs and Nigel Bartram 1 for 14 from three overs, but an unbroken 5th wicket stand of 83 between Dave Simpson (35 n.o.) and Ian Wilson (52 n.o.) saw Heworth home. In the semi-final Steve Precious took 4 for 24 from five overs to help defeat Pocklington and put Heworth into the final, where Jon Simpson of Osbaldwick took 4 for 31 from five overs to see Heworth all out for 124 chasing 135 for 6.

In the 1987 semi-final Nigel Briggs took 4 for 33 from five overs to see Heworth into the final at the expense of Sheriff Hutton Bridge.

In the 1989 semi-final Steve Precious helped Dunnington dismiss Acomb for 118, taking 5 for 22 from 4.7 overs. Mike Robinson then took 5 for 10 from just three overs to see Dunnington collapse from 53 for 3 with six overs left, to be all out for 82 with two overs to go. In the final Brian Stow produced one of the most economical spells in the history of the Myers & Burnell only for his side Acomb to lose. Woodhouse Grange were chasing a modest total of 105 for victory, thanks to a couple of wickets from Mike Newhouse and three run-outs. After dismissing opener Stuart Craven cheaply, (the only Woodhouse wicket to fall), Stow made Woodhouse fight all the way finishing with figures of 5 overs 3 maidens 1 for 4 to earn him the Man of the Match award. Woodhouse won with two overs to spare thanks to a patient 67 n.o. from Paul Mosey.

1990 saw a tight finish in the final. Heworth were dismissed for 95 off the last ball of their innings thanks to Mike Newhouse, who came on as second change for Woodhouse Grange and took 5 for 22 from four overs. Against tight bowling from Pete Machin and Steve Simpson Woodhouse then struggled to 26 for 4 from the first 10 overs, before 42 n.o. from Steve Johnson steered them to victory off the last ball of the game, despite three catches for wicketkeeper Paul Miles.

In a 1991 1st round game Dan Copeland took 4 for 24 from five overs for Sessay who lost after Trevor Walton had taken 4 for 20 from 4.1 overs for Heworth.

In the 1993 1st round game between Clifton Hospital and Heworth Martin Sigsworth took 4 for 15 from four overs to see Heworth through to the next round. In the semi-final against Dunnington Steve Simpson took 6 for 37 from four overs to help Heworth into the final where they beat Easingwold in a thrilling game, a more detailed account of which can be found in Chapter Eight.

1994 saw the introduction of the two innings final played on a Sunday afternoon, each side having two innings of 16 eight ball overs with a restriction of four overs per bowler per innings. The earlier rounds were also reduced to the 16 over format with four overs maximum per bowler, although it appears some clubs were unaware of the change and continued to play 18 overs per side in the early rounds for at least a couple of years. In a 1994 1st round game Dave Heartshorne took 4 for 23 from four overs to help Clifton Hospital Alliance beat Osbaldwick. In a 2nd round game in which Heworth defeated Acomb, Heworth batted first and despite 4 for 34 from Acomb's Rich Clayton they scored 161 for 7. Acomb were then bowled out for 153 with Martin Sigsworth taking 4 for 32 from four overs. In the next round, the quarter final stage, Heworth dismissed Civil Service for 116 with Steve Simpson taking 7 for 32 from his four overs. An unbroken 1st wicket stand of 118 between Simpson's Brother Dave and Jonathan Bean saw Heworth to an easy win. In another quarter-final Roger Johnston of Woodhouse Grange took 5 for 15 off only 2.7 overs to see his side to a comfortable win over Clifton Hospital Alliance who collapsed from 61 for 1 to 100 all out chasing 158.

In a 1st round game in 1995 Andy Galloway coming on third change took 4 for 28 from four overs for Easingwold against Pocklington who finished with a useful 135 for 8, but Easingwold won with four wickets down off the last ball thanks to 19 n.o. from Galloway himself.

In a 1996 2nd round game in which Heworth had scored 132 for 3, their opponents Crayke seemed in control after a great start at 54 without loss, but they quickly slid to 92 all out thanks chiefly to the leg-spin of Mark Bell whose four overs cost only 15 runs for the loss of four wickets. In another 2nd round game, chasing Clifton Alliance's 162 for 8, Sessay were bowled out for 110 thanks to 5 for 16 from just

3.7 overs from Scott Bradley. The first outstanding bowling feat in a final following the change to the two innings format came later the same year and it was quite remarkable. Chasing a fairly modest target of 125 set by Woodhouse Grange, Heworth were well placed in the 4th innings at 74 for 2 with seven overs left. Seventeen year old Paul Mouncey then took 6 for 26 in four overs to leave Heworth 11 runs short with nine wickets down.

Paul Redshaw took 4 for 31 from four overs to help Easingwold put out Woodhouse Grange in the 1997 1st round and in the 3rd round Dan Copeland took 4 for 37 from four overs to help them beat Acomb and book a semi-final place against Stamford Bridge, who they beat to set up a final against Heworth. Heworth defeated Civil Service in the 3rd round, Martin Sigsworth taking 5 for 31 from four overs and they then reached the final at the expense of Dunnington who could only manage 101 for 9 off their 16 overs in the semi-final mainly due to Trevor Walton taking 4 for 10 from four overs. Heworth went on to win for the loss of just two wickets. In the final Easingwold were restricted to 85 for 8 in their 1st innings thanks once again to Walton who took 4 for 23 from four overs. Heworth went on to win a close game, Mark Lynch hitting a four off the penultimate ball to see his side home at 93 for 7 in the 4th innings.

In 1998 after a typically tight opening spell from Steve Machen who took 3 for 8 from four overs, Dave Kettlestring came on to take 4 for 15 off 3.1 overs to see Osbaldwick beat Woodhouse Grange in the 1st round. In the 1st round game between Clifton Alliance and Dringhouses Scott Bradley took 5 for 15 from four overs to see Clifton through to the semi-final where they met Easingwold. Chasing a modest target of 101 to win Easingwold fell five runs short thanks to three wickets in the last over from Darren Barton who finished with 4 for 38 from four overs. In the final Thirsk had a comfortable win over Clifton, Barry Petty taking 2 for 17 from four overs in the Alliance's 1st innings and a remarkable 3 for 9 from four overs in their 2nd innings.

In a 1999 1st round game between Ovington and Clifton Alliance, Ovington seemed fairly well set at 89 for 2 with seven overs to go but the introduction of Jon Bladen saw a dramatic reversal as he took the next six wickets to fall to see Ovington close on 111 for 8. His last over was a quite remarkable five wicket maiden which went .w.ww.ww to see him end with figures of 4 overs 1 maiden 6 for 21. Simon Hill and

James Postill both scored unbeaten 50's to see Clifton to a 10 wicket win.

In 2000 Andrew Hawke took 4 for 22 from four overs for Thirsk against Dringhouses in the first round and 4 for 40 from four overs against Dunnington in the semi-final. Steve Precious then took 5 for 33 from four overs for Dunnington but it wasn't enough to prevent Thirsk going through to the final. Thirsk beat Easingwold in the final, Lincoln McCrae taking three wickets in the 1st innings and two in the 2nd. Coincidentally, Jason Sargent bowling for Easingwold also took three wickets in the 1st innings and two in the 2nd.

In a 1st round match in 2001 Sessay were set 138 to win by Woodhouse Grange but were dismissed for just 82 thanks mainly to Sajid Ali who took 5 for 5 from three overs including a hat-trick, the 15th and last in the history of the competition. In the 2nd round game between Clifton Alliance and Osbaldwick Mick Knowles took 4 for 32 from four overs to restrict Osbaldwick to 138 for 8 in pursuit of 172 to win. Knowles took another four wickets in the semi-final to see Heworth all out for 106 chasing 139 to win, his figures being 4 for 29 in four overs. Clifton won the final against Acomb despite Andy Tute taking 5 for 26 from four overs in Clifton's 1st innings.

In a 2002 1st round game Mick Pickering took 4 for 26 from four overs to see Clifton Alliance beat Thirsk. In the 1st round game between Osbaldwick and Dringhouses, the visitors were handily placed at 64 for 1 with eight overs to go when skipper Steve Young brought himself on as second change. In just three overs he took 5 for 11 to see Dringhouses end on 81 for 8. Osbaldwick passed the total with four wickets down and more than two overs to spare. In the final Osbaldwick beat Heworth on run rate after rain stopped play. Gawaine Hogg took six wickets in the match, 3 for 31 from four overs in Heworth's 1st innings and in their 2nd innings he had figures of 3 for 24 from three overs before the game came to a premature end.

Luke Wells took 4 for 32 from four overs in the 2003 1st round to help Clifton Alliance defeat Easingwold but Clifton went out to Acomb in the next round as Sanjay Rodrigo took 5 for 19 from 3.7 overs in a 51 run victory.

In the 2004 1st round Darius Slabbert took 4 for 25 from four overs to help Heworth beat Acomb. Clifton Alliance reached the 2004 final, in large part thanks to the West Indian Lorenzo Ingram, who shared in two big opening partnerships in the 1st round and the semi-final and also a substantial 2nd wicket partnership in the 2nd round, but his bowling was the key. He took 14 wickets in three games and a further four in the final his record being as follows;

		overs	maidens	runs	wickets	average
1st round	v Sessay	4	0	20	4	5
2nd round	v Heworth	3.2	0	24	6	4
Semi-final	v Stamford Bridge	4	0	30	4	7.5
Final 1st innings	v York	3	0	39	1	39
Final 3rd innings	v York	4	0	22	3	7.33
	Total	18.2	0	135	18	7.5

Despite his efforts the final was won by York, Riley O'Neill taking 4 for 36 from four overs to dismiss Clifton for 124 in their 1st innings, he added a further wicket in their 2nd innings to give him five in the match.

The following year Lorenzo returned to the Senior League this time with Stamford Bridge. In the 1st round game between his new club and Clifton Alliance he took no pity on his former team-mates taking 4 for 28 from his four overs to see them all out for 117. At 60 for 2 Stamford seemed well placed to win but tight bowling and three run-outs left them needing 10 to win off the last over. Off-spinner Alex Renton held his nerve and Stamford ended on 116 for 5. Clifton progressed to the final only to be beaten again by York despite 4 for 31 from four overs for John Hunter in the 3rd innings.

In 2006 Danny Grainger of Easingwold took 4 for 18 from four overs to restrict Woodhouse Grange to 126 for 8 and see his side win their 1st round game. In the final Mark Bell took 4 for 29 from 3.4 overs to see Clifton Alliance all out for 99 in their 2nd innings leaving York needing only 46 to win, which they achieved with relative ease.

The 2001 winners Clifton Alliance.

Back row: Darren Barton, John Hunter, Richard Hunter, Simon Corley, Michael Knowles.
Front row: Dave Russell, Darren Reeves, James Postill, Simon Dwyer, Duncan Naylor (Capt.), Dave Taylor.

Outstanding bowling performances

	Player	Team	Opponents	Year	Round
10 for 9	Geoff Wilkinson	York an XI	Heslington	1954	Prelim round
9 for 18	Henry Dalton	Osbaldwick	York Ramblers	1926	2nd round
9 for 40	Derek Ainley	Ovington	Stamford Bridge	1951	Final
9 for 42	Henry Dalton	Bootham Park	Ainsty Nomads	1927	Semi-final
8 for 1	Ernie Stubbs	Tadcaster	York Railway Institute	1936	Final
8 for 10	Henry Dalton	Bootham Park	Terrys	1928	Prelim round
8 for 13	Fred Scott	Osbaldwick	York Revellers	1937	1st round
8 for 15	F.Pearson	Sheriff Hutton	New Central W.M.C.	1925	1st round
8 for 23	Herbert Freestone	North Riding M.H.	Stamford Bridge	1926	2nd round
8 for 28	George Herbert	Rowntrees	Escrick Park	1922	2nd round
8 for 29	J.Douthwaite	Osbaldwick	Escrick Park	1920	3rd round
8 for 29	F.Slater	North Riding M.H.	Rowntrees	1926	Semi-final
8 for 30	Harry Cordukes	Haxby	Clarence C. & I.	1925	Semi-final
8 for 30	Sammy Toyne	Clifton Church Institute	New Earswick	1928	1st round
8 for 35	Henry Dalton	Bootham Park	North Riding M.H.	1929	2ndPrelim
8 for 44	Billy Wilkinson	Dringhouses	Terrys	1929	1st round
8 for 48	Fred Sherwood	Stamford Bridge	Haxby	1955	Prelim round
8 for 54	Arnold Wood	Sheriff Hutton	Haxby	1925	2nd round
8 for 53	S.Husband	York Banks	York Revellers	1928	2nd round
8 for 60	Fred Sherwood	Stamford Bridge	Rowntrees	1955	2nd round
8 wkts*	Samuel S. Elmer	Poppleton	Burton Stone Lane	1919	Prelim round
8 wkts*	Cyril Mason	Tadcaster	National Glass Works	1957	Prelim round
7 for 5	Brian Hanson	Ovington	Copmanthorpe	1958	Prelim round
7 for 5	Dick Wilks	New Earswick	Dunnington	1958	1st round
7 for 7	J.Clifford	Tadcaster	South Bank W.M.C.	1935	2nd round
7 for 10	Dick Lund	York City Amateurs	Dringhouses	1925	1st round
7 for 11	Edwin Reader	Escrick Park	Osbaldwick	1920	3rd round
7 for 11	Derek Ainley	Ovington	Magnets S.C.	1951	2nd Prelim
7 for 13	Gerald Simpson	York Ramblers	Civil Service	1920	3rd round
7 for 13	A.Postlethwaite	Civil Service	Ovington	1955	Prelim round
7 for 15	Colin Gell	York Railway Institute	Clifton C.C.	1956	1st round
7 for 16	J.Singleton	York Civil Service	Clarence C. & I.	1925	2nd round
7 for 17	Harry Jefferson	Haxby	Rowntrees	1925	Prelim round
7 for 18	Shuttleworth	Stamford Bridge	South Bank W.M.C.	1923	2nd round
7 for 19	F.Slater	North Riding M.H.	Acomb	1926	Final
7 for 21	William Gatenby	St. Martin's	York N.E.R.	1921	1st round
7 for 21	R.Harrison	Monkgate Primitive Meths.	Osbaldwick	1925	Prelim round
7 for 21	Fred Sherwood	Stamford Bridge	Dringhouses	1955	1st round
7 for 22	Ray Ellar	Escrick Park	York Wanderers	1923	1st round
7 for 23	Fred Scott	York Corporation H/ways	York "A"	1940	1st round
7 for 25	G.Eliff	York Banks	St. Michael-le-Belfry	1921	1st round
7 for 25	Billy Wilkinson	Dringhouses	York Banks	1921	2nd round
7 for 26	W.F.Cox	York City Amateurs	Poppleton	1938	1st round
7 for 27	Billy Wilkinson	Dringhouses	York Revellers	1923	2nd round
7 for 28	Henry Dalton	Bootham Park	Haxby	1929	1st round
7 for 28	Derek Ainley	Ovington	York Ramblers	1951	1st prelim
7 for 28	Jim Collis	York an XI	Easingwold	1956	Prelim round
7for 29	Newey	York "B"	Clifton Church Institute	1924	Prelim round
7 for 29	A.Walker	Poppleton	St. Michael-le-Belfry	1924	1st round

1919 to 1958 continued

7 for 29	Bill Ogden	Acomb	York R.I.	1957	1st round
7 for 30	Ray Ellar	Escrick Park	Sheriff Hutton	1923	Prelim round
7 for 30	Ernie Stubbs	Tadcaster	Acomb	1936	Prelim round
7 for 32	Fred Sherwood	Stamford Bridge	Civil Service	1956	2nd round
7 for 33	Rev.Roger F.Cardale	Escrick Park	Dringhouses	1923	Final
7 for 35	Henry Dalton	Osbaldwick	Acomb II	1920	2nd round
7 for 36	John Binnie	York Ramblers	Tadcaster Magnets	1958	1ˢ Prelim
7 for 39	Ted King	Rowntrees	Bootham Park	1954	1st round
7 for 40	Fred Sherwood	Stamford Bridge	York Police	1954	1st round
7 for 41	J.Chatterton	St. Michael-le-Belfry	Heworth	1920	2nd round
7 for 41	Ron Atkinson	Stockton & Hopgrove	Naburn Hospital	1956	1st round
7 for 43	Lovitt	New Earswick	L.N.E.R. Institute	1937	Prelim round
7 for 46	Jack Allison	Stamford Bridge	Ovington	1951	Final
7 for 48	P.Brown	York Ramblers	Scarcroft	1956	Prelim round
7 for 50	A.Teale	City of York Police	North Riding M.H.	1938	Prelim round
7 for 51	John Pitt	Rowntrees	New Earswick	1958	Semi-final
7 for 54	John Binnie	York Ramblers	Civil Service	1955	1st round
7 for 57	Joe Triffitt	York City Amateurs	Haxby	1925	Final
7 for 59	John Marriott	Tadcaster	York Railway Institute	1941	Final
7 for 64	Harry Moult	St. Thomas's	Heworth	1919	1st round
7 wkts*	Lacy	Heworth	York Wanderers	1923	1st round
7 wkts*	Henry Dalton	Bootham Park	R.A.M.C.	1927	Prelim round
7 wkts*	Henry Dalton	Bootham Park	Retreat	1930	Prelim round
7 wkts*	Jim S. Blackburn	Clifton C.C.	Ovington	1937	1st round
7 wkts*	Roy Nicholson	York Reserves	York Zingari	1939	2nd round
7 wkts*	Stan Hayton	Dringhouses	Yapham	1954	1st round

* denotes no bowling analysis

1959 to 1974 18 x eight ball overs no restrictions on bowlers

	Player	Team	Opponents	Year	Round
8 for 6	Tony Moore	Heworth	Bootham Park	1964	Prelim round
8 for 14	Noel Hare	Escrick Park	Minster Choir Old Boys	1959	Prelim round
8 for 17	Duncan Steel	Civil Service	Minster Choir Old Boys	1964	2nd round
8 for 24	Barry Westerman	Tadcaster	Long Marston	1964	Prelim round
8 for 39	Barham	Clifton C.C.	York an XI	1964	Prelim round
8 for 40	Mick Barrett	Heworth	Dringhouses	1971	1st round
7 for 10	Roly Pattison	Dringhouses	Terrys	1961	1st round
7 for 10	Ken Skilbeck	Easingwold	Rufforth	1973	Prelim round
7 for 14	Geoff Hornby	Dunnington	Scarcroft	1959	Prelim round
7 for 19	Tony Moore	Heworth	Rowntrees	1968	1st round
7 for 19	Ian Reed	Heworth	Bilton-in-Ainsty	1971	Prelim round
7 for 17	Ken Skilbeck	Easingwold	York Railway Institute	1968	2nd round
7 for 23	Duncan Steel	Civil Service	Stillington	1964	Final
7 for 25	Ken Hayton	Melbourne	New Earswick	1967	Prelim round
7 for 26	Price	Ebor Gogues	Acomb	1959	Prelim round
7 for 26	Brian Hough	Acomb	Dunnington	1966	1st round
7 for 27	Alan Shipley	Sheriff Hutton Bridge	Acomb	1962	Prelim round
7 for 30	Noel Hare	Escrick Park	Yapham	1959	2nd round
7 for 31	Ian Reed	Huntington W.M.C.	York Railway Institute	1963	Final
7 for 32	Wilf Jackson	York Railway Institute	Acomb	1961	2nd round
7 for 32	Alf Aveyard	Clifton Hospital	Ovington	1964	Prelim round
7 for 35	John Temple	York an XI	York Railway Institute	1960	2nd round
7 for 35	Trevor Craven	Yapham	Terrys	1961	Prelim round
7 for 35	John Whittle	Clifton C.C.	Acomb	1966	2nd round
7 for 36	Jeff Bellamy	Stamford Bridge	York Ramblers	1962	1st round
7 for 38	Alan Shipley	Sheriff Hutton Bridge	New Earswick	1961	1st round
7 for 40	Colin Gell	Ardua	Osbaldwick	1959	Prelim round
7 for 54	Ian Reed	Huntington W.M.C.	Yapham	1963	2nd round
7 for 58	Bernard Shaw	Rowntrees	Acomb	1971	1st round
6 for 8	John Teale	York Nomads	Escrick Park	1969	1st round
6 for 11	Trevor Craven	Yapham	Escrick Park	1963	1st round
6 for 12	John Stillborn	New Earswick	Melbourne	1967	Prelim round
6 for 15	Tony Stilgoe	Dringhouses	Sheriff Hutton Bridge	1966	1st round
6 for 16	Alan Barker	Civil Service	Bilton-in-Ainsty	1962	Prelim round
6 for 17	Tony Stilgoe	Dringhouses	Terrys	1964	Prelim round
6 for 18	Mick Storr	Huntington W.M.C.	Naburn Hospital	1964	Prelim round
6 for 21	G.Thacker	Bootham Park	Civil Service	1963	1st round
6 for 22	Terry Precious	Heworth	Tadcaster Magnets	1961	Semi-final
6 for 22	John Stillborn	New Earswick	Escrick Park	1966	1st round
6 for 22	Colin Minton	Easingwold	Magnets	1968	3rd round
6 for 23	A.Cooper	Bootham Park	Ovington	1967	Prelim round
6 for 23	Tony Moore	Dringhouses	Heworth	1967	Final
6 for 23	Peter Robinson	Civil Service	Easingwold	1972	Semi-final
6 for 24	Duncan Steel	Haxby	Clifton Hospital	1959	Prelim round
6 for 26	Malcolm Denton	Stillington	Civil Service	1964	Final
6 for 27	Colin Minton	Easingwold	Heworth	1974	Final
6 for 30	Robert Toes	Heworth	Yapham	1969	Prelim round
6 for 30	Geoff Skilbeck	Easingwold	Civil Service	1972	Semi-final
6 for 31	John Teale	York an XI	Woodhouse Grange	1962	1st round
6 for 31	Bower	Tadcaster Magnets	T.A.B.S.	1965	1st round

6 for 33	Roly Pattison	Dringhouses	Cawood	1963	2nd round
6 for 33	Colin Minton	Stillington	Clifton C.C.	1964	2nd round
6 for 34	Pete Braithwaite	Cawood	Civil Service	1962	Semi-final
6 for 34	Terry Fountain	Woodhouse Grange	Osbaldwick	1966	1st round
6 for 35	Philip Crowe	York Ramblers	Stillington	1960	2nd round
6 for 35	Geoff Skilbeck	Easingwold	Cawood	1969	1st round
6 for 36	Clive Hendry	York Railway Institute	York an XI	1960	2nd round
6 for 36	Alan Barker	Civil Service	Bootham Park	1963	1st round
6 for 38	Clive Hendry	York Railway Institute	Escrick Park	1960	1st round
6 for 39	Pete Braithwaite	Cawood	Dringhouses	1962	Final
6 for 40	Jim Collis	Huntington W.M.C.	Ovington	1959	Prelim round
6 for 40	Brian Kelly	Dunnington	Sheriff Hutton Bridge	1971	1st round
6 for 42	Clive Hendry	York Railway Institute	Ebor Gogues	1960	Final
6 for 43	Joe Valente	Ebor Gogues	York Ramblers	1960	Semi-final
6 for 43	Peter Suffield	York Railway Institute	Easingwold	1966	1st round
6 for 45	Pete Braithwaite	Cawood	Tadcaster Magnets	1962	2nd round
6 for 48	Armstrong	Civil Service	Clifton C.C.	1959	Prelim round
6 for 48	Paul Lewis	Woodhouse Grange	Rufforth	1966	1st round
6 for 49	Tony Keel	York Railway Institute	Dringhouses	1963	Semi-final
6 for 50	Denzil Webster	Acomb	York Ramblers	1963	1st round
6 for 50	Alan Barker	Civil Service	Huntington W.M.C.	1963	Semi-final
6 for 51	Mick Oldfield	Sheriff Hutton Bridge	Dunnington	1971	1st round
6 for 55	Charlie Hutchinson	Stillington	York Ramblers	1960	2nd round
6 for 57	Noel Hare	Escrick Park	Sheriff Hutton Bridge	1970	1st round
6 wkts*	Bob Carter Snr.	Clifton Hospital	Haxby	1959	Prelim round

Sheriff Hutton Bridge appeared in four finals in the 1970's. This photo was taken between innings at Shipton Road in an early round against Civil Service in 1973. They went on to reach the Final only to lose in a low scoring game with Huntington W.M.C.
Back row; Sid Lusher, Mick Willis, Mick Oldfield, Denis Shipley, Keith Snell, Roy Piercy.
Front row; Bill Revis, Brian Poole, Don Pringle (Captain), Albert Pattison, Des Wyrill.

1975 to 1993 18 x eight ball overs maximum 5 overs per bowler

	Player	Team	Opponents	Year	Round
7 for 21	Dave Gibson	Cawood	Woodhouse Grange	1975	Semi-final
6 for 15	Bob Steane	Civil Service	Easingwold	1981	1st round
6 for 16	Eric Wallis	Tadcaster	Clifton Hospital Alliance	1980	1st round
6 for 18	Robin Smith	Dunnington	Huntington W.M.C.	1976	Final
6 for 37	Steve Simpson	Heworth	Dunnington	1993	Semi-final
5 for 6	Dick Leadley	York Railway Institute	Heworth	1982	1st round
5 for 10	Mike Robinson	Acomb	Dunnington	1989	Semi-final
5 for 17	Steve Young	Heworth	Clifton Hospital Alliance	1979	Prelim round
5 for 20	Graham Cooper	Heworth	York an XI	1985	3rd round
5 for 22	Ian Wilkinson	Dunnington	Cawood	1979	Semi-final
5 for 22	Steve Precious	Dunnington	Acomb	1989	Semi-final
5 for 22	Mike Newhouse	Woodhouse Grange	Heworth	1990	Final
4 for 5	Dave Pepper	Civil Service	Dunnington	1984	2nd round
4 for 8	Dave Wreglesworth	York an XI	Tadcaster	1977	Final
4 for 8	Ken Skilbeck	Easingwold	Sheriff Hutton Bridge	1982	1st round
4 for 8	Ken Skilbeck	Easingwold	Clifton Hospital Alliance	1986	1st round
4 for 12	Ian Reed	Heworth	York Railway Institute	1982	1st round
4 for 13	Stan Butler	Heworth	York Railway Institute	1982	1st round
4 for 13	Mike Robinson	Acomb	Heworth	1985	2nd round
4 for 15	Martin Sigsworth	Heworth	Clifton Hospital	1993	1st round
4 for 16	Tony Haines	Acomb	Sheriff Hutton Bridge	1976	1st round
4 for 16	Graham Cooper	Heworth	Acomb	1985	2nd round
4 for 17	Tony Haines	Acomb	Stamford Bridge	1983	Final
4 for 17	Trevor Walton	Heworth	Clifton Hospital Alliance	1985	1st round
4 for 19	Tony Haines	Acomb	Sheriff Hutton	1976	1st round
4 for 19	Martin Robinson	Easingwold	Civil Service	1981	1st round
4 for 21	Ken Skilbeck	Easingwold	Stockton and Hopgrove	1980	3rd round
4 for 22	Graham Cooper	Heworth	Cawood	1986	1st round
4 for 23	Tony Keel	York Ramblers	Sheriff Hutton Bridge	1976	1st round
4 for 24	Steve Precious	Heworth	Pocklington	1986	Semi-final
4 for 24	Dan Copeland	Sessay	Heworth	1991	1st round
4 for 25	Mike Stothard	Woodhouse Grange	Dringhouses	1975	1st round
4 for 26	John Flintoff	Sessay	Acomb	1981	Final
4 for 27	Mick Oldfield	Sheriff Hutton Bridge	York Ramblers	1976	1st round
4 for 27	John Kneal	Easingwold	Woodhouse Grange	1983	1st round
4 for 27	Paul Spofforth	Dunnington	Easingwold	1985	3rd round
4 for 28	Colin Minton	Easingwold	Sheriff Hutton Bridge	1975	1st round
4 for 31	Jon Simpson	Osbaldwick	Heworth	1986	Final
4 for 32	Dennis Shipley	Sheriff Hutton Bridge	Cawood	1978	Final
4 for 33	Ian Burden	Clifton Hospital Alliance	Easingwold	1986	1st round
4 for 33	Nigel Briggs	Heworth	Sheriff Hutton Bridge	1987	Semi-final
4 for 46	Dave Smith	Glassworks	Easingwold	1980	1st round

1994 to 2007 16 x eight ball overs maximum 4 overs per bowler

	Player	Team	Opponents	Year	Round
7 for 32	Steve Simpson	Heworth	Civil Service	1994	3rd round
6 for 21	Jon Bladen	Clifton Alliance	Ovington	1999	1st round
6 for 24	Lorenzo Ingram	Clifton Alliance	Heworth	2004	2nd round
6 for 26	Paul Mouncey	Woodhouse Grange	Heworth	1996	Final 4th inns
5 for 5	Sajid Ali	Woodhouse Grange	Sessay	2001	1st round
5 for 11	Steve Young	Osbaldwick	Dringhouses	2002	1st round
5 for 15	Roger Johnston	Woodhouse Grange	Clifton Hospital Alliance	1994	3rd round
5 for 15	Scott Bradley	Clifton Alliance	Dringhouses	1998	1st round
5 for 16	Scott Bradley	Clifton Alliance	Sessay	1996	2nd round
5 for 19	Sanjay Rodrigo	Acomb	Clifton Alliance	2003	2nd round
5 for 26	Andy Tute	Acomb	Clifton Alliance	2001	Final 1st inns
5 for 33	Steve Precious	Dunnington	Thirsk	200	Semi-final
5 for 31	Martin Sigsworth	Heworth	Civil Service	1997	3rd round
4 for 10	Trevor Walton	Heworth	Dunnington	1997	Semi-final
4 for 15	Mark Bell	Heworth	Crayke	1996	2nd round
4 for 15	Dave Kettlestring	Osbaldwick	Woodhouse Grange	1998	1st round
4 for 18	Danny Grainger	Easingwold	Woodhouse Grange	2006	1st round
4 for 20	Lorenzo Ingram	Clifton Alliance	Sessay	2004	1st round
4 for 22	Andrew Hawke	Thirsk	Dringhouses	2000	1st round
4 for 23	Dave Heartshorne	Clifton Hospital Alliance	Osbaldwick	1994	1st round
4 for 23	Trevor Walton	Heworth	Easingwold	1997	Final 1st inns
4 for 25	Darius Slabbert	Heworth	Acomb	2004	1st round
4 for 26	Mick Pickering	Clifton Alliance	Thirsk	2002	1st round
4 for 28	Andy Galloway	Easingwold	Pocklington	1995	1st round
4 for 28	Lorenzo Ingram	Stamford Bridge	Clifton Alliance	2005	1st round
4 for 29	Mick Knowles	Clifton Alliance	Heworth	2001	Semi-final
4 for 29	Mark Bell	York	Clifton Alliance	2006	Final 3rd inns
4 for 30	Lorenzo Ingram	Clifton Alliance	Stamford Bridge	2004	Semi-final
4 for 31	Paul Redshaw	Easingwold	Woodhouse Grange	1997	1st round
4 for 31	John Hunter	Clifton Alliance	York	2005	Final 3rd inns
4 for 32	Martin Sigsworth	Heworth	Acomb	1994	2nd round
4 for 32	Mick Knowles	Clifton Alliance	Osbaldwick	2001	2nd round
4 for 32	Luke Wells	Clifton Alliance	Easingwold	2003	1st round
4 for 34	Rich Clayton	Acomb	Heworth	1994	2nd round
4 for 36	Riley O'Neill	York	Clifton Alliance	2004	Final 1st inns
4 for 37	Dan Copeland	Easingwold	Acomb	1997	3rd round
4 for 38	Darren Barton	Clifton Alliance	Easingwold	1998	Semi-final
4 for 40	Andrew Hawke	Thirsk	Dunnington	2000	Semi-final

Hat-tricks

Player	Team	Opponents	Year	Round
W.Walker	Poppleton	Civil Service	1919	1st round
George Curry	York Revellers	Dringhouses	1923	2nd round
A.Shaw	Dringhouses	Heworth	1924	1st round
Arnold Wood	Sheriff Hutton	Haxby	1925	2nd round
Mancy	St. Clement's	York Banks	1928	1st round
Ernie Stubbs	Tadcaster	York R.I.	1936	Final
Ivor Churchill	North Riding M.H.	Sand Hutton	1938	Semi-final
Geoff Wilkinson	York an XI	Heslington	1954	Prelim round
Stan Hayton	Dringhouses	Yapham	1954	1st round
Cyril Mason	Tadcaster	Askham Bryan	1954	1st round
Barry Firn	Tadcaster	Easingwold	1957	2nd round
Colin Gell*	Ardua	Osbaldwick	1959	Prelim round
Tony Temple	York Nomads	Civil Service	1969	Semi-final
Mike Stothard	Woodhouse Grange	Dringhouses	1975	1st round
Sajid Ali	Woodhouse Grange	Sessay	2001	1st round

* Gell took 5 wickets in 6 balls, including 4 wickets in 4 balls for match figures of 7 for 40.

Most wickets in a season 1919 to 1958

Player	Team	Ov	M	Runs	Wkts	Ave	Year
Derek Ainley	Ovington	67.4	10	169	36	4.69	1951
Henry Dalton	Bootham Park			c190	34	5.58	1927
Henry Dalton	Osbaldwick			c130	29	4.48	1926
F.Slater	North Riding M.H.			149	28	5.32	1926
Henry Dalton	Bootham Park			c125	25	5	1929
Reg Baines	Clarence C. & I.			246	23	10.69	1928
Fred Sherwood	Stamford Bridge	41	0	129	23	5.6	1955
Henry Dalton	Osbaldwick			c110	20	5.5	1925
Dick Lund	York City Amateurs			c150	20	7.5	1925
John Pitt	Rowntrees	68.3	7	245	20	12.25	1958
Edwin Reader	Escrick Park			103	19	5.42	1920
Cecil Hamilton	York Ramblers			185	19	9.74	1928
Bob Carter Snr.	North Riding M.H.			c182	19	9.58	1938
Ted King	Rowntrees	60.1	9	147	18	8.17	1954
Fred Sherwood	Stamford Bridge			101	18	5.61	1956
Ray Ellar	Escrick Park			81	17	4.76	1923
Ivor Churchill	North Riding M.H.			c159	17	9.35	1933
Geoff Wilkinson	York an XI	42.1	6	105	16	6.56	1954
William Ware	Heworth				15*		1919
Edwin Reader	Escrick Park			c168	15	11.2	1921
H.Scaife	Clarence C. & I.			192	15	12.8	1928
Ernie Stubbs	Tadcaster			c31	15	2.06	1936
Noel Hare	Escrick Park	45.4	6	159	15	10.6	1951
Henry Dalton	Osbaldwick			84	14	6	1920
Ray Ellar	Escrick Park			82	14	5.86	1921
Harry Moult	York Ramblers			c86	14	6.14	1922
George Herbert	Rowntrees			c122	14	8.71	1923
Herbert Freestone	North Riding M.H.			c126	14	9	1926
Ian Hallas	Ebor Gogues			122	14	8.71	1957
Rev. Roger Cardale	Escrick Park			c108	13	8.31	1923
C.Wrigelsworth	Osbaldwick			80	13	6.15	1925
Harry Moult	York Ramblers			156	13	12	1928
Alec Thompson	North Riding M.H.			c174	13	13.38	1938
Terry Barker	Stamford Bridge			155	13	11.92	1956
Cyril Mason	Tadcaster			c93	13	7.15	1957
Henry Dalton	Osbaldwick			c106	12	8.83	1924
Henry Dalton	Osbaldwick			c70	12	5.83	1928
J.Clifford	Tadcaster			c83	12	6.92	1935
Ernie Sanders	Escrick Park	19.5	2	80	12	6.66	1935
Jim Blackburn	Clifton C.C.			c111	12	9.25	1937
Jack E. Sweeting	St. Michael-le-Belfry				12*		1919
John Marriott	Tadcaster			74	12	6.16	1941
Ian Hallas	Ebor Gogues			111	11	10.09	1957
Luke C. Dennison	Escrick Park			47	10	4.7	1920
Henry Dalton	Osbaldwick			c75	10	7.5	1923
Derek Nicholson	Woodhouse Grange	27.5	7	77	10	7.7	1958

c before the Runs indicates exact figures were not available for all the games so an estimate has been made from the scorecard details. * after the Wickets indicates no figures other than wickets taken were given for any games.

Most wickets in a season 1959 to 2007

Player	Team	Ov	M	Runs	Wkts	Ave	Year
Noel Hare	Escrick Park	40.3	3	164	25	6.56	1959
Tony Moore	Dringhouses			181	22	8.23	1967
Geoff Skilbeck	Easingwold	37.6	3	156	22	7.09	1972
Ken Skilbeck	Easingwold	42.9	5	164	20	8.2	1968
Clive Hendry	York Railway Institute	27	1	116	18	6.44	1960
Pete Braithwaite	Cawood	26	0	118	18	6.55	1962
Ian Reed	Huntington W.M.C.			129	18	7.17	1963
Colin Minton	Stillington			149	18	8.28	1964
Tony Stilgoe	Dringhouses			219	18	12.17	1967
Colin Minton	Easingwold	41.1	2	187	18	10.39	1968
Peter Machin	Heworth	35		82	18	4.55	1990
Lorenzo Ingram	Clifton Alliance	18.2	0	135	18	7.5	2004
Roly Pattison	Dringhouses			166	17	9.76	1963
Ian Reed	Heworth			107	17	6.29	1971
Terry Precious	Heworth	30.6	0	137	16	8.56	1961
Duncan Steel	Civil Service			151	16	9.43	1969
Ken Skilbeck	Easingwold	40	2	148	16	9.25	1972
Ken Skilbeck	Easingwold	24	2	68	16	4.25	1974
W.Morley	Tadcaster			111	15	7.4	1959
Tony Moore	Heworth	34.3	3	123	15	8.2	1961
Tony Keel	York Railway Institute			112	15	7.47	1963
Duncan Steel	Civil Service			40	15	2.67	1964
Tony Stilgoe	Dringhouses			127	15	8.47	1966
Colin Armstrong	Heworth			174	15	11.6	1967
Duncan Steel	Civil Service			81	14	5.79	1962
Malcolm Denton	Stillington			121	14	8.64	1964
Steve Simpson	Heworth	22	0	129	14	9.21	1993
Fred Storr	Huntington W.M.C.			111	13	8.54	1964
Tony Stilgoe	Clifton C.C.			125	13	9.62	1968
Steve Young	Heworth	25	1	204	13	15.7	1984
Roly Pattison	Dringhouses			49	12	4.08	1961
Alan Barker	Civil Service			86	12	7.17	1963
Mick Storr	Huntington W.M.C.			128	12	10.67	1965
Mick Barrett	Heworth			79	12	6.58	1971
Bernard Shaw	Rowntrees			155	12	12.92	1971
Des Wyrill	Sheriff Hutton Bridge	19	2	75	12	6.25	1973
Dave Gibson	Cawood			80	12	6.67	1975
Wilf Jackson	York Railway Institute	16	2	60	11	5.45	1961
Alan Barker	Civil Service			46	11	4.18	1962
Tony Stilgoe	Dringhouses			160	11	14.55	1963
John Whittle	Clifton C.C.			73	11	6.64	1966
Geoff Skilbeck	Easingwold	18	2	74	11	6.72	1974
Ken Skilbeck	Easingwold	14.3	0	65	11	5.9	1973
Colin Minton	Easingwold			120	11	10.91	1979
Neil Armstrong	Heworth	19	2	98	11	8.9	1984
Mick Pickering	Clifton Alliance	24	1	142	11	12.09	1999
Mick Knowles	Clifton Alliance	14	0	123	11	11.18	2001
Dick Wilks	New Earswick			c137	10	13.7	1959
Roly Pattison	Dringhouses			99	10	9.9	1966

Most wickets in a season 1959 to 2007 continued

Robert Toes	Heworth			113	10	11.3	1967
Tony Moore	Heworth			38	10	3.8	1968
Alan Greenwood	Rowntrees			62	10	6.2	1971
Peter West	Stamford Bridge			163	10	16.3	1971
Martin Robinson	Easingwold	20	2	86	10	8.6	1982
Graham Cooper	Heworth	11.6	1	56	10	5.6	1985
Mike Robinson	Acomb	13	0	80	10	8	1989
Martin Sigsworth	Heworth	21	1	129	10	12.9	1993
Martin Sigsworth	Heworth	16	0	107	10	10.7	1997

Most wickets in a career

Player	Team	Career	Wkts.
Henry Dalton	Osbaldwick & Bootham Park	1919 to 1929	172
Ken Skilbeck	Easingwold & York	1968 to 1986	110
Noel Hare	Escrick Park & York	1951 to 1973	109
Ian Reed	Huntington W.M.C. & Heworth	1963 to 1985	77
Duncan Steel	Haxby & Civil Service	1959 to 1969	76
Colin Minton	Stillington & Easingwold	1964 to 1981	70
Tony Stilgoe	Dringhouses & Clifton C.C.	1963 to 1979	62
Tony Moore	Heworth & Dringhouses	1961 to 1969	60
Fred Sherwood	Stamford Bridge	1954 to 1956	52
Geoff Skilbeck	Easingwold & York	1969 to 1983	51
Roly Pattison	Dringhouses	1962 to 1968	50
Clive Hendry	York Railway Institute	1957 to 1963	38
Alan Barker	Civil Service	1962 to 1966	33
Tony Keel	York R.I. & York Ramblers	1960 to 1976	33

All these totals are the minimum wickets taken in a career as it has proved impossible to find records of every game for individual players. The dates given indicate the first and the last years for which records have been found.

Chapter Seven

Miscellaneous.

Wicketkeepers.

Some great wicketkeepers have played in the Myers & Burnell over the years. Older readers may remember Tommy Robinson, Arthur Taylor, Vic Bedford, Ted Outhwaite and Gerry Pragnell. Gerry kept wicket for Ovington in the 1950's and stood up to everyone, a remarkable feat on the Knavesmire wickets of those days. It was said that the reason he stood up was that his eyesight was not good and standing up was his best chance of seeing the ball, but whatever the reason he missed very little and he prevented the batsman standing out of his crease to the quicker bowlers. His skill and bravery were certainly appreciated by Derek Ainley who took a record 36 wickets when they won the cup in 1951. Later came some great characters such as Brian Wilson, Brian Shirley, Billy Carter and Dave Rippon, the latter being known to many for his exploits with York and Batley Rugby League clubs. In the more modern era Nigel Durham, Dick Sykes, Paul Miles and Mike Burdett stand out, but of all the keepers I have seen or played against none made it look quite so easy as the late Brian Shirley. He would be top of my personal list, just ahead of Paul Miles who as well as being a brilliant keeper always seemed to score runs when it really mattered, quite often against my own club! Unfortunately trying to unearth wicket-keeping records has proved more difficult than either batting or bowling records, so I will make my apologies now for any omissions.

The first wicketkeeper to get a mention was Robert W. Thompson of Civil Service who took four catches or possibly five, against Poppleton in a 1919 1st round game and he also contributed a useful 36 before having to retire hurt as his side won an exciting contest with the last pair at the wicket.

In the 1926 semi-final between the North Riding Mental Hospital and Rowntrees the Hospital keeper S. Tichener took two catches and a stumping off the bowling of F. Slater who took 8 for 29 to see his side into the final.

Arthur Nelson Taylor kept wicket and opened the batting for York City Amateurs and Bootham Hospital before moving to the North Riding Mental Hospital in 1938. In the 3rd round that year against Acomb he took four stumpings and in the final he took two catches and a stumping in a losing cause against Tadcaster. Earlier that year A.S. Daniel of Yapham took three stumpings off the bowling of W. Greenheld who took 6 wickets against the North Riding Mental Hospital in the 1st round.

In 1954 Vic Bedford, the former York wicketkeeper who had previously played in the Myers & Burnell for Clifton C.C., York Zingari and Acomb, was playing for his employers Rowntrees. He took three catches and a stumping against Bootham Park in the 1st round, a stumping in the 2nd round against Stamford Bridge, two catches and a stumping in the semi-final against Tadcaster and a stumping in the final against "York an XI" to give him nine victims in the season, a record that was only beaten in 1993 by Paul Miles of Heworth.

In 1959 Hall, the Bilton-in-Ainsty wicketkeeper, was responsible for five dismissals off the bowling of Richardson who took 6 for 46 against Tadcaster in the preliminary round, but despite this Tadcaster went on to win.

The next record we have of another keeper claiming three or more victims is Frank Gibson of Huntington W.M.C. In 1963, he took three catches and a stumping, all off the bowling of Ian Reed to deny York Railway Institute victory in the final.

In 1975 Brian Shirley took three stumpings and one catch against Cawood to see Sheriff Hutton Bridge to their first final win.

The late Brian Shirley was one of the best wicketkeepers ever to play in the Myers & Burnell, as well as being a very good bat. He is pictured here, sometime in the mid 1960's, with his good friend and team-mate Des Wyrill during their time with Sheriff Hutton Bridge.

Fred Cowling of Easingwold took four catches in the 1979 final against Stamford Bridge to help his side win.

Nigel Durham playing for Thorp Arch & Boston Spa had a significant part in their only Myers & Burnell success in 1988. Chasing 132 for victory Heworth were effectively put out of the game by a combination of the T.A.B.S. opening spin attack of Stephen Booth and Steve Lawrence and a brilliant display of keeping by Durham. Heworth were restricted to 50 for 5 after 10 overs, with Booth having the remarkable figures of 5 overs 2 maidens 2 for 8 and Lawrence 5 overs 0 maidens 3 for 37 and Durham having taken two catches and a stumping. Heworth never recovered and fell 22 runs short.

1990 saw Paul Miles take three catches for Heworth in a losing cause in the final against Woodhouse Grange.

Paul Miles played a big part in Heworth's success in 1993. In their 1st round game against Clifton Hospital he took three stumpings and a catch, in the semi-final he took three more stumpings and in the final he had two stumpings and a catch as they beat Easingwold. His tally for the competition that year was 13 dismissals made up of eight stumpings and five catches, a record for a wicketkeeper.

The 2001 final saw probably the finest and certainly the most versatile all round performance in the long history of the competition. Darren Reeves, the Clifton Alliance Australian overseas player, opened the batting in both innings and scored 40 in the first and 61 in the second, helping set Acomb a target of 166 to win. Keeping wicket in Acomb's first innings he took one catch and two stumpings, then in their second he emerged from behind the stumps and took 2 for 25 from two overs in addition to taking three catches in the outfield to leave Acomb 23 runs short.

In 2005 York beat Clifton Alliance in the final with both teams' wicketkeepers making significant contributions. Clifton's keeper Chris Malthouse stumped five victims in the match, four in York's first innings and one in their second, in addition to top scoring in Clifton's second innings. For the victors Nigel Durham took two stumpings and a catch in Clifton's second innings.

In a repeat of the final the following year York were victorious once more, Durham again taking two stumpings and a catch in Clifton's second innings.

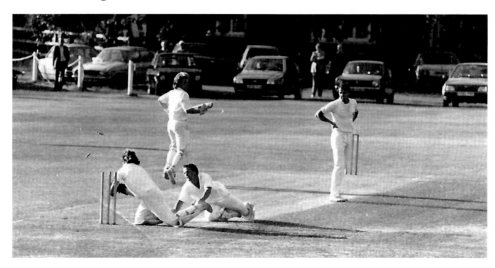

Paul Miles was one of the most successful wicketkeepers to play in the Myers & Burnell. He played in six finals and set a record of 13 dismissals (eight stumpings and five catches) in the 1993 competition. His career total is in excess of 40 but accurate figures are not available for all years. Here he completes one of three run-outs for Heworth against Osbaldwick in the 1986 final, his victims being both opening batsmen, brothers Chris (shown above failing to make his ground) and Mick Hammerton, and Jon Simpson. Osbaldwick made 135 for 6 and Heworth fell 12 runs short as Dave Rippon the Osbaldwick keeper also completed three run-outs.

Family connections.

There are and always have been many family connections in local cricket and the Myers & Burnell is no exception. There have been too many fathers and sons, brothers, uncles and cousins to name them all, but here are a few of the more interesting ones.

The Skilbecks of Easingwold actually began in Escrick. Arthur Skilbeck worked on the Escrick Park estate and played in the 1923 final for Escrick Park and his son Walter who also worked for the Estate as a joiner moved to Easingwold in the early 1900's. He established the family business and began to play for Easingwold in 1907. His sons Walter Jnr. and Frank also played for Easingwold while George, their brother, became professional at nearby Sessay. Frank's sons Ken, Geoff and Dave all played for Easingwold, with Ken and Geoff also playing for York. Ken and Geoff's sons, Paul and Richard both played for Easingwold and it is quite possible that one or more of the family played in every competition from 1920 until at least 2000.

Another long association with the Myers & Burnell began and ended at Escrick. Brothers Edwin and Joe Reader played alongside Arthur Skilbeck in the 1923 final and appeared in two more finals together, while Edwin's son Bill became a fixture in the Escrick Park side from 1939 until 1997 and was joined by his son Neil in the 1970's.

As mentioned previously there have been many fathers and sons who played together in the competition, but in 1987 Tony Simpson played with sons Dave and Steve in the final for Heworth, the only instance I can find of a father and two sons in the same team.

Players appearing in six or more finals.

The following is a list of all the players who have played in six or more finals, with their team and the years they appeared. Players marked with an asterisk reached finals with more than one club and the club named is the one with whom they made their first appearance. Ivor Churchill would have played in 11 finals had his daughter's wedding not taken place on the day of the 1953 final.

Ivor +A2:D33Churchill	10	North Riding Mental Hospital	1926, 32, 33, 34, 35, 38, 42, 43, 45 & 50.
Alf Aveyard	10	North Riding Mental Hospital	1932, 33, 34, 35, 38, 42, 43, 45, 50 & 53.
Joe Littlewood	10	North Riding Mental Hospital	1932, 33, 34, 35, 38, 42, 43, 45, 50 & 53.
Tommy Robinson	9	North Riding Mental Hospital	1932, 33, 34, 35, 42, 43, 45, 50 & 53.
Percy Poole	9	North Riding Mental Hospital	1932, 33, 34, 35, 42, 43, 45, 50 & 53.
Vic Bedford*	8	Clifton C.C.	1929, 37, 39, 44, 47, 48, 54 & 58.
Des Wyrill*	8	Sheriff Hutton Bridge	1972, 73, 75, 78, 93, 98, 99 & 2000.
Dave Simpson*	8	Heworth	1986, 87, 88, 90, 91, 92, 95 & 2002.
Paul Mosey*	8	Heworth	1986, 89, 90, 91, 94, 96, 97 & 2002.
Trevor Walton	8	Heworth	1987, 88, 90, 91, 92, 93, 96 & 97.
George A. Harling	7	North Riding Mental Hospital	1926, 32, 34, 35, 38, 43 & 45.
George W. Appleby	7	North Riding Mental Hospital	1932, 33, 34, 35, 38, 42 & 45.
Fred Oliver	7	North Riding Mental Hospital	1932, 33, 34, 35, 38, 42 & 53.
Fred W. Shearsmith	7	Tadcaster	1933, 35, 36, 37, 38, 40 & 41.
George Shearsmith	7	Tadcaster	1933, 35, 36, 37, 38, 40 & 41.
Jim S. Blackburn*	7	Clifton C.C.	1937, 41, 44, 46, 47, 49 & 50.
Ken Skilbeck	7	Easingwold	1968, 69, 72, 74, 77, 79 & 82.
Geoff Skilbeck	7	Easingwold	1968, 69, 72, 74, 79, 82 & 93.
Dick Sykes	7	Acomb	1981, 83, 84, 89, 95, 2001 & 03.
Steve Simpson*	7	Heworth	1987, 88, 90, 91, 92, 93 & 95.
Jonathan Bean*	7	Heworth	1990, 91, 92, 93, 94, 96, & 07.
Mark Bell*	7	Heworth	1991, 92, 93, 96, 97, 2002 & 06
John Hunter	7	Clifton Alliance	1998, 99, 2001, 04, 05, 06 & 07
James Postill	7	Clifton Alliance	1998, 99, 2001, 04, 05, 06 & 07
Alec Thompson	6	North Riding Mental Hospital	1932, 33, 34, 35, 38 & 42.
Robbie Marchant*	6	York Railway Institute	1960, 61, 63, 69, 71 & 77.
Val Toase	6	Easingwold	1968, 69, 72, 74, 79 & 82.
Ian Reed*	6	Huntington WMC	1963, 65, 74, 82, 84 & 86.
Keith Snell*	6	Stillington	1964, 72, 73, 75, 80 & 87.
Ken Johnson	6	Heworth	1974, 82, 84, 87, 88 & 90.
Paul Miles	6	Heworth	1984, 86, 90, 91, 92 & 93.

Long careers in the Myers & Burnell.

There have been some very long careers in the Myers & Burnell. Both Arthur Taylor and Ian Reed's final appearances span 25 years, just ahead of Ivor Churchill with 24 years, Keith Snell with 23 years and Dick Sykes with 22 years. Des Wyrill's career in the Myers & Burnell spanned 37 years, his final appearances being 28 years apart. Reg Baines played in only two finals, one for Clarence C.& I. and one for Rowntrees, but these were 26 years apart. Alf Aveyard and Joe Littlewood opened the innings in nine finals for the N.R.M.H./Clifton Hospital and were still opening the batting in 1958, a partnership at least 26 years old. Alf Aveyard and Ivor Churchill were still playing in the Myers & Burnell in 1962, 30 years after Alf's first appearance and an amazing 36 years after Ivor's first. Bert Brennen appeared in five finals for three different teams from 1939 to 1960 and was still playing in the Myers & Burnell for Clifton Hospital in 1972 a career of at least 33 years. Norman Pearson played in 33 consecutive competitions for Stamford Bridge between 1952 and 1985. Noel Hare played for Escrick Park and occasionally for York in the competition for 27 seasons between 1951 and 1978 and may have played prior to 1951. As mentioned earlier, Bill Reader played for Escrick Park from 1939 until 1997. His first Myers & Burnell game was in 1939 and his last, 50 years later, in 1989. He may have gone on for a few more years but for the fact that Escrick Park no longer felt they had a strong enough side to enter the competition after 1989.

Teams appearing in three or more finals.

Several teams have been finalists on ten or more occasions. The North Riding Mental Hospital and its successors, Clifton Hospital and Clifton Alliance, have appeared in eighteen finals, winning ten. Heworth have featured in sixteen finals and won five. York in various guises made fifteen final appearances and had ten wins. Acomb were in the final fourteen times and won six of them. Dringhouses appeared twelve times winning on six occasions. Woodhouse Grange appeared in the final on ten occasions winning five. The other teams winning five times are Clifton C.C. and Easingwold.

Tadcaster appeared in four consecutive finals between 1935 & 1938 and seven finals in the nine years between 1933 & 1941.

Clifton C.C. appeared in six finals in the nine years between 1942 & 1950.

Heworth appeared in four consecutive finals between 1990 & 1993 and eleven finals in the sixteen years between 1982 & 1997.

Clifton Alliance appeared in seven of the last ten finals between 1998 & 2007.

Below is a list of all teams who have appeared in three or more finals.

Team	Finals	Wins	R-Up	Team	Finals	Wins	R-Up
N.R.M Hospital	6	5	1	York R.I.	6	3	3
Clifton Hospital	5	3	2	Stamford Bridge	5	0	5
Clifton Alliance	7	2	5	York Ramblers	4	4	0
Total	18	10	8	Huntington W.M.C.	4	3	1
Heworth	16	5	11	Sheriff Hutton Bridge	4	2	2
York	15	10	5	Escrick Park	4	1	3
Acomb	14	6	8	New Earswick	4	0	4
Dringhouses	12	6	6	Rowntrees	3	2	1
Woodhouse Grange	10	5	5	Sessay	3	2	1
Easingwold	9	5	4	Thirsk	3	2	1
Tadcaster	9	4	5	Cawood	3	1	2
Clifton C.C.	8	5	3	Dunnington	3	1	2

Teams retaining the trophy.

A measure of the competitive nature of the Myers & Burnell is that only seven teams have ever successfully defended the trophy;

York Ramblers in 1928 & 1929.

North Riding Mental Hospital 1932, 1933, 1934 & 1935.

Clifton C.C. in 1946 & 1947.

York R.I. in 1960 & 1961.

Dringhouses in 1966 & 1967.

Woodhouse Grange in 1989 & 1990.

York in 2004, 2005 & 2006.

York Ramblers won the original Cup outright with their third win in 1928 which was also the last final to be played at Bootham Crescent and they then became the first team to win the replacement Cup, defending their title in the first final at Wigginton Road.

The North Riding Mental Hospital won four years in a row from 1932 to 1935, a unique achievement. Their win in 1933 was their third and they won the replacement Cup outright only five years after it was donated by John Kaye and although he was happy to provide another replacement the Hospital decided to hand it back to be played for annually under the condition it could never be won outright again. They promptly won it again in 1934 and 1935 and following their 1935 victory the Hospital authorities withdrew their side from the competition. The reason for the withdrawal was thought to be embarrassment at dominating the competition in such an overwhelming way and the Chief Medical Superintendent Dr. Russell seems to have felt it only fair to give other teams the opportunity to win the Cup. However it was reported that the organisers and the donor John Kaye tried to persuade the authorities to reconsider. In addition a number of the Hospital players were not happy with the decision and both Dr. Fraser, the Hospital's senior Doctor and George Harling the senior Nurse who had both captained the side, put pressure on Dr. Russell to reconsider. The side thankfully returned in 1937 and once again reached the final in 1938, this time losing to Tadcaster.

Dringhouses won the last final played at Wigginton Road in 1966 and the first played at Clifton Park the following year.

Woodhouse Grange narrowly missed out on becoming only the second team to win in three consecutive years. Having been successful in 1989 and 1990 they lost in the 1991 final to Heworth by just three runs.

York then achieved that feat winning in 2004, 2005 and 2006, the runners-up on each occasion being Clifton Alliance.

R.A.F. and Army sides in the Myers & Burnell.

York has a history as a military centre, with barracks at Fulford and Strensall and various military units having H.Q. located in the City. Most of these encouraged sporting activity and fielded teams in various sports. Several cricket teams emerged locally and evening cup cricket suited them, being much less of a commitment than league cricket, especially for units who faced constantly changing personnel and frequent redeployments. The earliest instance of a local military team in the York area is the game between York Garrison and Yorkshire Gentlemen at Wigginton Road in 1885. The Royal Army Medical Corps entered a side in the Myers & Burnell in 1922 and by 1925 they had been joined by a team from Northern Command, whose H.Q. was located in Fishergate, and the Royal Army Signals Corps followed them in 1927. By the mid 1930's the Royal Army Pay Corps (later to play as the Royal Engineers & Army Pay Corps), Royal Army Ordnance Corps and the 5th Battalion West Yorkshire Regiment were also regular entrants. After the outbreak of the Second World War many new R.A.F. bases sprang up around York and these too had cricket teams. The first to enter was R.A.F. Shipton in 1942 followed by a Royal Air Force XI in 1944, R.A.F. Melbourne in 1945 and R.A.F. Rufforth in 1946. Teams from bases at Linton and Acaster Malbis took part in 1951 and as late as 1955 a team simply called R.A.F. York entered. Many of these airmen stayed in the area following demob and the York Nondescripts C.C. formed in 1946 came to have a strong R.A.F. contingent.

Probably the strongest team ever to play in the Myers & Burnell, this photo shows the side before their semi-final game against Easingwold, eight of whom had played 1st class cricket. Only three players in this picture can be definitely identified; John Quarmby who played for York C.C. in the Yorkshire League is 2nd left in the middle row. Group Captain Christopher William Mitchell Ling DFC, AFC, who played 1st class cricket for the R.A.F. is seated centre in the middle row. C.R. Knight who played 1st class cricket for Jamaica is seated on the right at the front. The following members of this side who also played 1st class cricket were; Francis Woodhead who took 320 wickets for Nottinghamshire C.C.C. in 141 games, his Nottinghamshire teammate David Jones, Captain Neville Shelmerdine (Lancashire C.C.C. and the R.A.F.), Wing Commander Richard Peter Hugh Uttley (Hampshire

C.C.C. and the R.A.F.), Flying Officer Lyall (R.A.F.) and Alfred Harper (R.A.F.). The remaining two players are Alfred William Himpson (London Counties C.C.) and J.Ellis who played for Elland C.C. in the Huddersfield League. Woodhead and Uttley missed the final, their places being taken by Pilot Officer James Stuart Crawford and Ferian, about whom I have been unable to find any information.

Wing Commander Uttley was a fascinating character. After a private education at St. John's College Portsmouth he went straight into the R.A.F. As well as playing nearly 40 games as an amateur for Hampshire, he played for the Gents v the Players at the Oval and made several appearances for the R.A.F. He left the service after the War and stayed in the York area, becoming a monk at Ampleforth Abbey in later life and was known as DOM Richard Uttley OSB, OBE, TD. He died at Ampleforth in 1968.

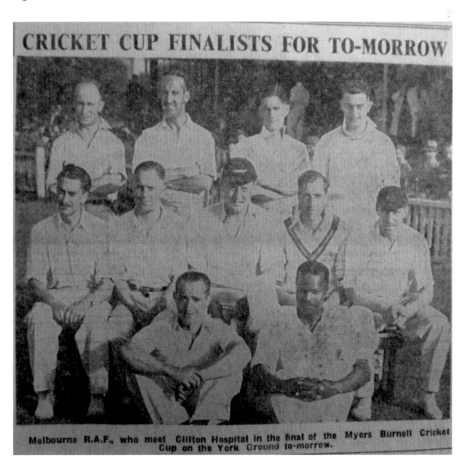

CRICKET CUP FINALISTS FOR TO-MORROW

Melbourne R.A.F., who meet Clifton Hospital in the final of the Myers Burnell Cricket Cup on the York Ground to-morrow.

The R.A.F. Melbourne side that won the cup in 1945

York Nondescripts C.C. 1946

This is one of only two known photographs of the York Nondescripts, taken in front of the pavilion at Wigginton Road in 1946. This photo, captioned "Originals", shows all the founding members. Sixteen of the players pictured have 54 Myers & Burnell final appearances and four centuries between them. The other known photo, taken later the same season, includes another five players with a further 13 finals between them.

Back row; Mr.Marquis (Scorer), David Douglas (New Earswick & York C.C.), Percy Poole (N.R.M.H. & Clifton Hospital), Dr. Philip M. Sawkill (Stamford Bridge & York C.C.), John R.F. Temple (Clifton C.C. & York an XI), George Curry (York Revellers), Flying Officer John M.J. Quarmby (R.A.F. Melbourne & York C.C), Bob Ferguson (York an XI), Jimmy Birrell (York an XI), George A. Harling (N.R.M.H. & Clifton Hospital).

Front row; Dick Lund (York City Amateurs, York Zingari & York an XI), Alf A. Aveyard (N.R.M.H. & Clifton Hospital), Les Hutson (York C.C.), B.E. Randall (York an XI), Henry Lund (York City Amateurs), Eric N. Kay (Long Marston & Acomb), Ken Lockwood (Rowntrees), Ivor Churchill (N.R.M.H. & Clifton Hospital), Harry Metcalfe (York C.C.). The two players who never featured in the Myers & Burnell were Les Hutson, who was a professional with York and therefore ineligible, and Harry Metcalfe who played 2nd and 3rd XI cricket for York and later became club secretary.

The other five Nondescripts who appear in the later photo were, Vic Bedford (Clifton C.C, York Zingari, Acomb and Rowntrees), Harry Houseman (York City Amateurs & Woodhouse Grange), Ernie Sanders (York an XI) , William A Kay (York an XI) and Bill Pearson (Clifton C.C. & York an XI).

The "Knavesmire sides".

Mention was made of Ovington C.C. becoming the first side that were based on the Knavesmire to win the Myers & Burnell Cup and this was a source of some pride to Ovington, as it was felt that some of the more established clubs tended to look down on the sides who played on the Knavesmire. These teams rented pitches from the Corporation, later the Council, on what is known as the Little Knavesmire, that stretch of land that lies between Knavesmire Road and Albermarle Road. There were several "squares" of varying quality cut across the site. In 1922 Terrys C.C. rented pitch number 16 at a cost of two guineas per season but the following season the rent had risen alarmingly to £15. These rents did not include any close cutting or rolling and only occasional mowing of the outfield. Some of these pitches were shared with others, some used exclusively by one team and most had no changing facilities, the exceptions being Ovington C.C. and the Alliance C.C. who shared an old air raid shelter on the Albermarle Road side of the site. The building, much improved nowadays, is still the pavilion of Ovington C.C, the only remaining club on the Knavesmire. The Knavesmire was a hotbed of cricket in York from late in the 19th century, a feature of cricket on the Knavesmire being the large crowds who came to watch the Evening League and particularly evening cup cricket. The geography of the Knavesmire lent itself to spectating, with the wall that ran along the pavement on the west side of Albermarle Road giving a superb grandstand view some 20 or 30 feet above the playing area. The gentle slope at the base of the wall that ran down to the boundary allowed many rows of spectators a clear view of proceedings and crowds in excess of a thousand were not unusual for big games such as cup finals and local derbies. Many players started their careers in Knavesmire teams before moving on to play at a higher standard, the prime example being Charlie Hall, a quick bowler who began with Priory Street Methodists and went on to play for York C.C. and Yorkshire C.C.C. A regular for the County 2nd XI he also played 23 games for the 1st XI between 1928 and 1934, when Yorkshire won the Championship three times and were never out of the top five, taking 45 wickets at an average of 27.24 for the county. Charlie ended his career with Woodhouse Grange and was in their side that won the Cup in 1958; he must surely have been a handful on the Knavesmire's sporting wickets in his early days. Not all sides played on the Little Knavesmire. Such was the popularity of the venue that despite the rising rents there was always a waiting list for pitches and as a result some sides played on the main part of the Knavesmire. Scarcroft played on a pitch behind the cheap ring opposite the main grandstand on what was the Polo Ground, the Baptists original pitch was in the "four shilling ring" and the Myers & Burnell works team played on an improvised pitch behind the Chase Hotel (now the Marriott on Tadcaster Road). These pitches had the disadvantage of being open to the cattle which then freely grazed on that part of the Knavesmire, so a pre-match clear up was essential for anyone using them. A list of clubs and teams that have used the Knavesmire over the years appears below, the only one remaining today being Ovington Cricket Club, although some of the clubs such as York, Alliance, Stockton & Hopgrove and Rowntrees continue to play elsewhere.

Ovington*	Gansolite
Baptists*	Gas Board
Alliance	Groves W.M.C.
York*	York Revellers*
Salem (Congregational Church Guild)	York Station Staff*
Terrys*	Rowntrees*
Scarcroft*	York Wesley Brotherhood
Priory Street Methodists	Old Priory Juniors
York Butchers	York Electricity Works*
Southlands*	South Bank W.M.C.*
Fishergate Old Boys*	Yardmasters
Stockton & Hopgrove*	New Central W.M.C.*
Myers & Burnell*	Adams Athletic
Waddington AC	Yorkshire Evening Press
Ardua	York Corporation Highways*

* Indicates teams that took part in the Myers & Burnell.

Rowntrees receive the Cup in 1954. Originally the side had played on the Knavesmire when the factory was based in the city centre at Tanners Moat but moved to Mille Crux in the early part of the 20th century when the factory re-located to the Haxby Road site.

Below is a list of teams who have competed in the Myers & Burnell since it's inception. The year indicated is the earliest known date they entered.

Burton Lane Club & Institute	1919	Clifton C.C.	1924
Poppleton	1919	Northern Command	1925
Rowntrees	1919	Stockton-on-Forest (Later Stockton and	1925
York Y.M.C.A	1919	Hopgrove)	
Civil Service	1919	North Riding Mental Hospital	1926
York Police	1919	(Later Clifton Hospital, Clifton Hospital	
Dringhouses	1919	Alliance and Clifton Alliance)	
Stamford Bridge	1919	Royal Army Signal Corps	1926
Huntington	1919	Long Marston	1926
Haxby	1919	L.N.E.R. York Goods Clerical Staff	1926
Monkgate Primitive Methodists	1919	York Catholics	1927
Bishopthorpe	1919	New Earswick	1927
York Revellers	1919	Southlands	1927
York N.E.R.	1919	Ainsty Nomads	1927
Riccall	1919	Bootham Park	1927
Heworth	1919	York Post Office	1928
St.Thomas's	1919	St.Clement's	1928
St.Michael-le-Belfrey	1919	London & N.E. Railway Locomotive	1929
Osbaldwick	1919	St.Denys'	1929
Old Priory Adult School	1919	Cooke, Troughton & Simms	1929
Acomb Wesleyans	1920	Baptist Church	1929
Escrick Park	1920	St.Luke's	1929
York Ramblers	1920	Tockwith	1930
Acomb C.C.(2ndXI) (1st XI 1921)	1920	L.N.E.R. Locomotive	1930
Gibbs & Co. York	1920	Yorkshire Insurance	1930
Layerthorpe Adult School	1920	The Retreat	1930
City Amateurs	1920	Cawood	1931
St.Martin's	1920	Hessay Ramblers	1931
Heworth Parish Church	1920	Royal Army Pay Corps	1932
South Bank W.M.C.	1920	York Commercial Travellers	1932
Crockey Hill	1920	5th Battalion West Yorkshire Regiment	1932
Clifton Church Institute	1920	Stillington	1932
New Central W.M.C.	1920	Brown Brothers & Taylor	1932
York Electricity Works	1921	Tadcaster	1933
York Banks	1921	Royal Engineers and Army Pay Corps	1934
8th Co. Royal Army Medical Corps	1922	York Railway Institute	1934
Terrys	1922	Royal Army Ordnance Corps	1935
Fishergate Old Boys	1922	Scarcroft	1935
York C.C."B". (Later York Reserves, York	1922	Yapham	1937
an XI, York Nomads and York)		Magnets Sports Club Tadcaster	1937
Heslington	1922	Ovington	1937
Strensall	1922	Deighton	1938
Henry Leetham & Sons	1922	Marston & Tockwith Junior Imperials	1938
Fulford W.M.C.	1922	(later Long Marston Imperial League)	
St.Martin's & St.Luke's	1922	York Corporation Highways	1938
York Station Staff	1922	York Zingari	1939
York Clarence Institute (Clarence C. & I.)	1922	Easingwold	1943
Sheriff Hutton	1923	Sugar Beet Factory (later Poppleton Sugar	1943
York Wanderers	1923	Beet Factory & British Sugar Sports Club)	
York Co-op (York Co-op Employees Club)	1924	National Fire Service	1943

R.A.F. Shipton	1943	Myers & Burnell	1952
Yard Masters Staff	1943	Woodhouse Grange	1954
The Home Guard	1944	R.A.F. York	1955
Royal Air Force XI	1944	Ebor Gogues	1957
R.A.F.Melbourne	1945	National Glass Works (later Glass Works)	1957
R.A.F. Rufforth	1946	Askham Bryan	1957
The Clubs Brewery Athletic Club	1946	Bushells	1958
York Corporation Employees Club	1948	Copmanthorpe	1958
Yorkshire Herald Sports Club	1948	St. John's College	1964
Ainsty Building East	1948	Selby Londesborough	1967
York City Mental Hospital	1948	Melbourne	1967
Wheldrake	1948	N.M.U. Rowntrees	1967
York and Northumbrian G.T.C.	1951	Bilton-in-Ainsty	1968
Naburn Hospital	1951	Rufforth	1968
Wighill Park	1951	Sheriff Hutton Bridge	1970
R.A.F. Acaster Malbis	1951	Huby	1981
Pocklington British Legion	1951	Sessay	1981
R.A.F. Linton	1951	Crayke	1981
Askham Bryan	1951	Bubwith	1983
Dunnington	1951	Hemingbrough	1983
Aldby Park	1951	Londesborough Park	1984
Bootham Conservatives	1951	Hovingham	1984
Poppleton Road Old Boys	1951	Alne	1985
Haxby and Wigginton	1951	Thorp Arch and Boston Spa	1988
Naburn Hospital	1951	Pocklington	1988
Fulford United	1952	Thirsk	1996
Stewarts Sports Club Pocklington	1952		

Once again this list has proved difficult to compile as complete draws
are only available for certain years.
Any additions or amendments will be gratefully received.

The 1944 winners Acomb team pictured with the Cup at Wigginton Road.

Back row; Vic Bedford, Lawrence Bean, Gordon Foster, George Maltby, Cyril Wiles (Captain), Eric Kay, Allan Bryan, John Bradley, Jack Pinder.
Kneeling; Matt Oates and Alan Dalby.

The original Cup returns.

Sometime in the late 1960's the York Ramblers were contacted by the York Education Committee to say that one of their teachers who lived in the Badger Hill area had found under his stairs "an old cup with your name on it". The then Secretary of the Ramblers, Viv Littlewood, arranged to collect the cup which turned out to be the original Myers & Burnell Cup which they had won outright and loaned to the Education committee in 1929. The Cup was kept by the Ramblers and eventually came into the hands of Norman Brown who took over as Secretary in 1981 and for the next few years it had pride of place on his front room sideboard with all his other cricket memorabilia. When the Ramblers club finally folded in 1988 it was decided amongst the remaining members to loan the Cup to York C.C. for display and safekeeping and this was done by George Myerscough, Viv Littlewood and John Hutt who in discussion with York C.C. agreed for it to be used as the runners-up trophy for the Myers & Burnell Cup. It was first awarded in 1989 and continued to be used until the competition's demise in 2007. That this Cup survives at all is a minor miracle as it could so easily have been lost after the schools ceased to play for it. More remarkably, it only just survived the Second World War. In 1941 Poppleton Road School won the trophy, and the following April the School, with the Cup inside, took a direct hit from a German bomb during the "Baedeker raid" on York. The boys themselves managed to retrieve the Cup somewhat battered from the debris and suitably repaired and re-polished it was next competed for in 1943 when Poppleton Road very nearly won it again, finishing runners-up by just three runs. Fittingly they went one better in 1944 and the Cup returned to their newly repaired school.

1944 and the boys and teachers of Poppleton Road School proudly pose with the
original Myers & Burnell Cup which they rescued from bombed remains of their
school in 1942.

Heworth were regular finalists over the years. Here the 1986 side pose before the
final against Osbaldwick at Clifton Park, on which occasion they were runners-up.
Back row: Pete Machin, Trevor Ward, Kev Wilson, Paul Miles, Paul Mosey, Dave
Wood, Mal Caddie.
Front row: Nick Carter (12th man), Graham Cooper, Ian Reed (Capt.), Dave Simpson,
Steve Precious.

Woodhouse Grange were another club who regularly featured in the Myers & Burnell final. The 1990 side seen here with the York Invitation Trophy also won the Pocklington Shield and the Myers & Burnell.

Back row: Steve Johnson, Dave Gilbertson, Peter Head, Brian Stow, Russ Bilton, Mike Newhouse.

Front row: Paul Mosey, Stuart Craven, Dick Whaley, Simon Gill (Capt.), Mike Burdett. Missing from the photo are Ian Wilson and Steve Young who replaced Stow and Whaley in the Myers & Burnell final.

Clifton C.C. v Stillington 1966 preliminary round.

Finally under the heading "miscellaneous" I must mention the only Myers & Burnell game that was won entirely single handedly and the only game I know of which was won by a woman. Ann Musgrave was for many years Secretary of Clifton C.C. and when in 1966 it proved impossible to complete their preliminary round with Stillington before the end of May deadline owing to the weather, it was agreed to decide the result by the toss of a coin. With neither captain available she and the Stillington President Arthur Midgley met in her back garden in Acomb to settle the outcome. Arthur tossed the coin and Ann called correctly to secure her side a 1st round clash with Rowntrees. Ann's husband Clive played for Clifton C.C. for many years and their son Richard played in the very last Myers & Burnell final for Clifton Alliance. Ann herself was quite a trailblazer becoming secretary of Clifton C.C. in her early 20's as well as being a member of their selection committee, not a common occurrence in the 1960's.

Toss decides match

Neither captain was available this morning when Clifton and Stillington tossed to decide which side was to play Rowntrees in the first round of the Myers Burnell Cup. So the honours were performed by Clifton's secretary Mrs. Ann Musgrave and Stillington's president Mr. A. D. Midgley. The result of the toss—Clifton won. Their preliminary round tie was twice put off by rain.

The headline says it all, from The Press May 1966.

Chapter Eight
Some notable Finals.

The competition has produced many thrilling contests and exciting finishes, none more so than in the finals. The tone was set in the very first final in 1919 played at Bootham Crescent in which Heworth triumphed by just five runs. After batting first they were all out setting St. Michael-le-Belfry 147 to win and despite 74 n.o. from Arthur Henry Naylor St. Michael's were bowled out for 142. Unfortunately there were no detailed accounts published apart from the bare essentials found on the scorecard and a brief write up, but the immediate popularity of the competition ensured much more detailed coverage in future years, with reports in the local newspapers allowing us to appreciate the intensity and excitement of some of these great games.

** Indicates the team batting first.

The 1922 Final

York Ramblers 113-9 v Southbank W.M.C.** 109 all out

Played on Saturday 19th August at Bootham Crescent, each side being allowed one completed innings.

Southbank batted first and lost four wickets for less than 30 runs, all clean bowled, with three by Harry Moult and the other by G. Tindhill. A. Pannett and Jack Prest then rescued the situation with an invaluable sixth wicket stand, Pannett making 41 and Prest 16, but once they went the lower order failed and the innings ended at 109. Moult finished with figures of 10-1-39-6, all clean bowled while H. Walker took two, Tindhill one and there was one run-out.

The Ramblers looked to have a fairly easy task but Jack Prest bowled superbly to see the back of the first four batsmen with around 35 runs on the board. G. Tindhill and the Ramblers skipper Major Harry O. Johnson then steadied things and began to slowly build a partnership, but after Pannett bowled Tindhill for 13, despite Johnson continuing to bat carefully wickets fell cheaply at the other end, only the Ramblers number ten F. Welch putting up a fight. When Welch was bowled by R. Skilbeck for 20 Johnson was joined by last man Sam Buttery still needing 11 runs for victory. After spending some time cautiously picking up singles the game was tied by a three from the captain, who then won the game in the next over with a splendid four to the leg side to end on 24 n.o. Jack Prest ended with figures of 14-0-48-5, Pannett took three wickets and Skilbeck the other.

The 1926 Final

North Riding Mental Hospital** 69 all out v Acomb 59 all out

Played on Saturday 14th August at Bootham Crescent, each side allowed one completed innings.

After their record breaking scores in the semi-finals a high scoring game was widely anticipated; Acomb had scored 294 for 7 to beat Osbaldwick in the first semi-final and a week later the Hospital scored 336-7 to beat Rowntrees. Despite a good batting wicket the bowlers of both teams "held complete mastery throughout" according to *The Yorkshire Herald* and the game "was one of the most sensational affairs in the history of the ground". This was quite a statement since it had been the headquarters of the York club for 45 years and had seen many great contests involving the best teams from around the County, including several first class sides. The Hospital batted first and were very soon in trouble. S. Strange opened the bowling for Acomb and proved almost unplayable, clean bowling four of the top five including S. Tichener and Ivor Churchill, the two centurions from the semi-final, for four and two respectively. A carefully compiled 25 by Hubert Dryland batting at number four appeared to be the only glimmer of hope for the Hospital, as the last seven batsmen managed only 31 between them. Strange bowled throughout to take 6 for 36 from 12 overs, being ably aided by A. Wray with 2 for 12 from 6.3 overs and Alan Dalby 2 for 14 from five overs to leave Acomb needing only 70 to win.

The Acomb innings also saw a sensational start, with opener Captain Francis Roupell, their centurion from the semi-final, being immediately bowled by F. Slater for a duck and the crowd sensed another top order collapse. But Alan Dalby and the skipper J. Robson then began to make the pitch look relatively easy, taking the score to 44 before Robson was lbw to Herbert Freestone. Needing only 26 more with eight wickets remaining and the bowling looking the most benign it had been all afternoon Acomb looked to be home and dry. Following Robson's departure the Hospital captain Dr. William Fraser made an inspired change and switched Slater to the other end, where according to *The Gazette* he became "absolutely unplayable" the last eight wickets falling for a mere 13 runs. Slater took a further six wickets at a cost of only five runs, Ivor Churchill taking the other two to finish with 2 for 17 from six overs, leaving the Acomb players and spectators stunned. Slater's final figures were 7 for 19 from 10.3 overs, three of which were maidens and all his victims were clean bowled. Alderman W. H. Birch presented the Cup to the Hospital captain Dr. Fraser and went on to praise both the competition which had "done so much to lift community spirits since its inception" and congratulated both teams on "their great struggle and the excellent spirit in which it had been fought out". He also reminded the crowd that both teams "had taken a high place in the cricket history of the district for over 50 years". Accepting the Cup Dr. Fraser praised "the sportsmanship of the Acomb team" and sympathised with them "on losing such a fine fight". The game remained the lowest scoring final in the competition's history, the Hospital's winning total the smallest ever and only three teams were ever dismissed for less than Acomb's total, even after 1958 when the finals were reduced to 18 eight ball overs per side. The only game coming close was in 1974 when Easingwold met Heworth in the final, a full account of that game being included later in this chapter.

The 1927 Final

Bootham Park 190-8 v Acomb** 188 all out

Played on Saturday 6th August at Bootham Crescent, each side allowed one innings restricted to a maximum duration of 2½ hours with no limit on the number of overs.

111

This was the first occasion on which a time limit had been imposed on a team's innings in a final, and both teams understandably seemed to struggle a little to adapt to the format. Acomb failed to use up their allotted time due to some over-eager lower order hitting and Bootham Park on the other hand batted rather too cautiously in the early part of their innings which would have cost them the game, had it not been for the generosity of Acomb's over rate.

Acomb batted first and made 188 all out off 54 overs in two hours and 20 minutes, skipper J. Robson making 55 and R. Hields 54. The only other contributions of note came from C. Lancaster with 11 and former Ramblers skipper Harry Johnson with 15. Henry Dalton bowled throughout to take six wickets at a cost of 62 runs and J. C. Allin took three wickets in 16 overs at a cost of 53 runs.

Despite having an opening partnership that had already registered two century stands in the competition, Bootham Park appeared to suffer a bout of "big match" nerves and they batted "far too slowly at the beginning" according to *The Herald*. O. Shaw took more than 1½ hours to score 36 and after the other opener Henry Dalton had been dismissed for 16, Shaw and the 18 year old Arthur Nelson Taylor "laboured things rather excessively for a long time" and "their running between the wickets was particularly dilatory". Once Shaw went Harry Rawson followed almost immediately and only the arrival of Allin livened things up. With 90 runs still needed and less than an hour left Taylor seemed to realise his side's plight. As batsmen came and went he picked up the scoring rate and towards the end "hit with great vigour". As the clock ran down seven runs came from what was the penultimate over and when the last over started a further seven were required. The first ball was a dot, the second saw W. Dawson run out attempting a second run from a drive by Taylor who took another single off the third ball. The new man, skipper Dr. Minski, pushed his first ball for a single and Taylor coolly drove a four through the covers to win with a ball to spare and end on 92 n.o. Taylor showed great composure for such a young man, his first 50 taking 82 minutes and the last 42 coming in 38 minutes to produce a breathtaking finish. Bootham Park were helped considerably by the fact Acomb had bowled eight more overs than their opponents in an innings lasting only 10 minutes longer.

The 1945 Final

R.A.F. Melbourne** 146 all out v Clifton Hospital 132 all out

Played on Saturday 4th August at Wigginton Road, each side allowed one innings restricted to a maximum of 50 overs without time limit.

The 1945 final was contested by the possibly the strongest two sides ever to play in the competition. The R.A.F. side contained at least seven players with first class experience, David Jones (Notts.), Neville Shelmerdine (Lancs.), C. R. Knight (Jamacia), Alfred William Himpson (London Counties), Lyall (RAF), Harper (RAF) and Captain Christopher W.M. Ling (RAF). In addition J. Ellis played in the Bradford League, John M.J. Quarmby in the Yorkshire League and amazingly two other first class players, Wing Commander Richard P.H. Uttley (Hants.) and Francis Woodhead (Notts.) who had both played in earlier rounds failed to make the side for the final. Despite their apparent overwhelming strength R.A.F. Melbourne were very nearly beaten in a final lasting over five hours and played in "blazing sunshine and watched by a crowd of over 2,000" according to *The Press*. Batting first they were bowled out for 146 inside their allotted 50 overs, their skipper Group Captain Ling securing some respectability with a "well made" 37 before being run out. He came in with the score on 21 for 2 and was seventh out with the score at 139, the only other sizeable contribution coming from opener Alfred Harper with 27. The strong R.A.F. batting line-up had struggled against the bowling of Ivor Churchill, Harry Lowe and Syd Appleyard, two wickets for Churchill, one for Lowe and two run outs, together with a superb 5 for 24 from Syd Appleyard seemed to have given their side a slight edge.

The Hospital's response was a steady start by Joe Littlewood and Alf Aveyard against some "very quick and accurate bowling" from the Jamaican C. R. Knight. However the introduction of Flying Officer John Quarmby saw the removal of both openers and despite 24 from Percy Poole the Hospital found themselves in trouble at 57 for 5. Ivor Churchill and Harry Lowe set about rescuing the situation and in the words of *The Press* sports correspondent *"Citizen"*, "hit the hitherto tight bowling so freely that the spectators sat back with the expectancy of a Hospital win". He went on to say that "they would have seen it too, but for a superb red-hot return catch by Quarmby when Churchill hit a full-pitched ball with all the strength of his arms and bat". That was the turning point of the match and despite Lowe remaining undefeated on 25 the lower order just failed to make the runs finishing 132 all out. Quarmby, who after the war turned out for York Nondescripts, ended with 6 for 26 and was well supported by 3 for 47 from Pilot Officer James Stuart Crawford. That the Hospital could give such a talented side a run for their money was a result of the recruitment policy in operation at that time. From medical staff downwards, excellence in one or more sports was a prerequisite for an interview and with several of the senior doctors and administrators being keen cricketers it was inevitable they would always have a very useful team. It has been suggested some of the Hospital cricketers over the years may have been good enough to play County Cricket, but the benefit of a home provided with the job and the guarantee of year round full-time employment proved more lucrative than professional cricket.

The 1948 Final

Acomb 154-2 v Dringhouses** 151-9

Played on Saturday 14th August at Wigginton Road, each side allowed one innings of 50 overs.

Although this game was not quite as closely fought as some of the other games listed here, but for a sporting gesture by one captain to the other it might have been much closer, and the fact that one of the participants was playing a different sport at a different venue for part of the game make it well worth recording.

Dringhouses batted first and in the face of some accurate bowling from Matt Oates and Len Vyle they lost half their wickets for 75 runs before the situation was rescued to some extent by wicketkeeper Ted Outhwaite with 26 and skipper John Lawson with 33. But the Acomb change bowlers Eddie Cooper (2 for 33) and Phil Dalby (1 for 40) chipped in to help Oates see Dringhouses end on 151 for 9 at the close of innings. The only other significant contribution came from Len Rodwell with 24 while Matt Oates finished with figures of 4 for

114

54 from 25 overs and Len Vyle 2 for 19. Mention must be made of Alf Patrick, who went in at number eight and scored eight before being bowled by Oates. An unremarkable innings one might imagine, but for the fact that for the first part of the Dringhouses innings Alf was actually playing in a York City F.C. practice match at nearby Bootham Crescent. He had scored two goals before being allowed to leave at half-time to make the short dash to Wigginton Road and join his Dringhouses team mates.

The target was what would be described as "slightly below par" by today's T.V. pundits, but the Acomb reply got off to a poor start with opener Allan Bryan lbw to Stan Hayton for only three. Alf Patrick then demonstrated his athleticism as a fielder with a pick up and throw from cover point to run out Roy Nicholson who *The Herald* described as "completing what appeared to be a leisurely single". The return was described as "lightning" by *The Gazette* and "an electrifying throw" by *The Press*. At this point the score was 21 for 2 and before any further addition to the score a third wicket fell when Acomb captain Eddie Cooper was given out stumped. This appeared to leave Acomb in a tight spot, but before Cooper was halfway off the field he turned round and returned to the crease, "which at the time puzzled the spectators" reported *The Press*. What had occurred was the Dringhouses captain John Lawson, who was fielding next to the square leg umpire, was convinced Ted Outhwaite had failed to take the ball properly, withdrew the appeal and asked the umpire to recall Cooper. This sporting gesture proved to be a pivotal point in the match as Cooper along with Vic Bedford put on 133 runs without further loss to see Acomb to victory with three overs to spare. Whether this incident played on the minds of the Dringhouses players or not was a matter of conjecture, but their usual brilliant fielding deserted them and although Bedford made a faultless 54 not out, Cooper who ended on 85 n.o. was dropped no less than eight times.

The 1951 final

Ovington** 110 all out v Stamford Bridge 105 all out

Scheduled to be played on Saturday 11th August at Wigginton Road, each side allowed one innings of 50 overs. The game was postponed due to wet weather and was rearranged to be played on the following Monday and Tuesday evenings, each side having one evening to bat, but with the overs reduced to a maximum of 40 each.

The final was according to *The Press* "eagerly anticipated" as the two un-fancied teams had reached the final by beating several sides considered to be much stronger than themselves. Ovington disposed of New Earswick, Magnets, Ramblers, Bishopthorpe and Easingwold, while Stamford had seen off York (regarded as that year's favourites), Riccall, Rowntrees (the new favourites in the absence of York) and Escrick Park.

With the pitch and outfield still damp from the weekend's rain, batting conditions were difficult, the uneven bounce from the wicket and the damp outfield making boundaries very hard to come by. Ovington took first knock and the innings got off to a disastrous start as Jack Allison clean bowled four of the top five cheaply, with only Jack Haxby showing any resistance. According to *The Press* report he "defied the Stamford Bridge attack for more than two hours to retrieve Ovington from their desperate plight". He opened the innings and was eighth out for 53, the only other significant contribution coming from wicketkeeper Gerry Pragnell "with a carefree contribution of 15 in only 10 minutes". *The Press* suggested that "a similar bolder policy by some of the other lower order batsmen may have paid dividends". The innings ended at 110 as Pragnell was dismissed off the last ball of the 39th over by Allison who bowled throughout to end with 7 for 46 from his 20 overs. Terry Barker took 2 for 26 from 10 overs three of which were maidens and the other wicket was a run out.

The following evening Stamford looked to be "labouring slowly but surely towards victory" at 65 for 2, Derek Ainley having taken both wickets. His opening partner Brian Hanson and change bowlers Ken Newton, Brian Boyes and Stan Bell were all economical but never really troubled the Stamford batsmen. Ainley was recalled to the attack and with his second ball clean bowled Wally Pearson for 30 and in his second over he bowled Tom Barton for two, Stamford however still seemed in control as Charlie Sherwood continued to pick up runs with relative ease and looked set to take his side to victory before he was brilliantly stumped by Pragnell, who was standing up to Ainley's decidedly quick bowling. With two overs left Stamford required 15 runs to win with three wickets in hand. The penultimate over yielded nine runs but skipper Dr. Phillip Sawkill was lost to an unlucky run-out, dropping his bat taking a single and after a moment's hesitation failing to make his ground for a second run. Stamford needed six off the final over but Ainley bowled Terry Barker and Fred Sherwood with the first two balls to win the game and give him figures of 9 for 40 from 16.2 overs two of which were maidens. Skipper Ted Coulson received the Cup from the Lord Mayor Alderman John Harold Kaye, the donor of the trophy.

The Stamford Bridge team who were runners-up in 1951 seen here before the semi-final. They appeared in five finals, sadly never managing to win one.
Back row; Wally Pearson, Charlie Sherwood, Dr. Philip Sawkill (Captain), Brian Wood, Eric Pateman, Frank Lindsay, Jack Allison.
Front row; Terry Barker, Harvey Beaumont, Tom Barton, Fred Sherwood. Wally Hallaways replaced Harvey Beaumont in the final.

The 1954 Final

Rowntrees** 131-8 v York an XI 125 all out

Started on Saturday 7th August at Wigginton Road, each side allowed one innings of 50 overs. The game was interrupted by rain and completed on the evening of Monday 16th August.

Rowntrees were captained by the veteran Reg Baines, who played in the Myers & Burnell for over 30 years, and had former York players Ken Lockwood and Vic Bedford in their ranks. The York team, a mix of youth and experience captained by John Richardson were thought to be favourites, but both sides had beaten some strong opposition on the way to the final.

Rowntrees batted first on a soft wicket and made a bad start. With the score on nine they lost both openers Baines and A. Wright and number three Ken Lockwood without addition to the score. Youngsters John Raine and John Fawcett then put on 46 runs before Raine was unluckily run-out, while Fawcett went on to make 43, *The Press* reporting that "he played some attractive shots and showed a sound defence". The rate of scoring which was rather slow at the beginning of the innings began to increase with breezy contributions from Ken Moor (31) and Ken Robertson (18) and the innings closed at 131 for 8. Bill Pearson with 3 for 36 from 14 overs and Terry Barker 2 for 34 from 11 overs were the pick of the York bowlers while Mick Cockerill and Geoff Wilkinson took a wicket each.

York's start was no better than their opponent's, Ted King having Alf Nicholls and Frank Cawkill lbw with successive balls to leave York 3 for 2 after five overs. Charlie Boddy and a youthful John Bond then began to rebuild the innings but Boddy was deceived by Ken Lockwood's "wrong un" with the score on 23, and 11 runs later despite some stylish strokes, Bond also fell to the spin of Lockwood who continued to torment his former club. Very soon afterwards Mick Cockerill was neatly stumped for two by Bedford, the other former York player, to give Lockwood his third wicket. With rain threatening Bill Pearson and skipper Richardson continued to pick up runs, but as the rain arrived Dennis Ramsey bowled Richardson for 13 with the last ball of the 32nd over and the umpires immediately took the players off with Pearson unbeaten on 26 and the score 71 for 6. No further play was possible so the game would be resumed and played to a finish on a rearranged date as per the rules, but due to continued poor weather and a busy fixture list on the York ground the first available date was Monday 16th August. Even this was only possible thanks to Dringhouses and New Earswick agreeing to a postponement of their Senior Charity final due to be played on the evenings of the 16th and 17th. Unfortunately for York, Terry Barker, a Railway Fireman, was unable to get time off work and the rules stipulated that in the event of an interrupted game teams could not be changed, so York resumed on the Monday evening with only ten men "in poor light with a fine drizzle falling". Pearson and 17 year old Michael Storr knew they had only two batsmen to follow them and Pearson adopted a supporting role as Storr showed a composure beyond his years. Lockwood struggled for control with a damp ball and Storr took full advantage, scoring freely. Despite losing Pearson who was run-out for 32 with the total at 96 "he continued merrily on" as the Rowntrees bowlers and fielders were hampered by the conditions. Baines juggled his bowlers in an effort to get a breakthrough and he was rewarded when Baines himself bowled Wilkinson off his pads at 115 for 8 and Moor at the other end produced a much needed maiden. Baines' next over cost just four runs, so with three overs to go 13 were needed. In the next over Storr and his new partner Andrew Lodge threw the bat at everything but scored only four runs and Storr was lucky to survive after a mistimed stroke went high in the air only for first slip to drop what should have been a simple catch for the wicketkeeper. Baines bowled the 49th over, his first four balls conceding two runs. Storr was of course keen to have the strike in the final over, and took a single of the fifth ball, leaving Lodge to negotiate the sixth. Unfortunately "Lodge was rapped on the pad plumb in front of his wicket and the game was over" leaving Storr on 39 n.o. and York an agonising six runs short. *The Press* felt "Rowntrees fully merited their success with a good all-round performance under difficult conditions, but the York side was more than a little unlucky."

The 1960 Final

York Railway Institute** 103-7 v Ebor Gogues 102-9

Played on Thursday evening 28th July at Wigginton Road, each side allowed one innings of 18 eight ball overs with no restrictions on the bowlers.

Geoff Britton the R.I. captain won the toss, as he had in every round so far, and decided to bat on a good looking wicket in excellent light. Openers Robbie Marchant and Tony Keel continued the form they had showed in the earlier rounds scoring at five an over with some ease, but with the score at 45 both openers departed to catches off the bowling of Alan Kenworthy, and with the score advanced by only a single Norman Garland fell lbw to Danny Stephens. Peter Morritt and Pete Taylor fared little better and soon the score was 66 for 6. A seventh wicket stand of 35 between skipper Britton (12) and wicketkeeper John Bradley (22*) pulled things round but the final total of 103 for 7 looked inadequate in the circumstances. Kenworthy finished with 3 for 50 from nine overs and Stephens 4 for 35 from six overs.

Alan Kenworthy opened the innings for Ebor Gogues, having scored 285 runs in the competition without being dismissed, but this form deserted him and he was bowled for one in the first over by Clive Hendry. Roy Walker was caught at the wicket off Clive Kellett with the score on 14 in the fourth over but despite this setback Joe Valente and John Falshaw "found little difficulty and had the score moving at a regular six runs an over" according to *The Press*. Valente's innings ended at 21, bowled by Hendry but his next three balls cost 11 runs, Geoff Atkinson hitting his first ball for four, the second for six almost onto Wigginton Road and taking a single of the next. Robbie Marchant restored some sanity, bowling Atkinson with the first ball of the next over, but Ebor Gogues "were now well ahead of the run rate and despite the loss of Roy Nicholson and Falshaw seemed well set for victory". Dave Blissett and skipper Bert Brennen were scoring at a run a ball and took 11 from the 17th over. Needing only four from the last over to be bowled by Hendry, with four wickets in hand the batsmen may have relaxed, for as *The Press* put it "probably hoping to make the winning hit, Blissett swung at the first ball and was bowled"...... "Ray Sutton made nothing of the first ball he received and was bowled by the next one. Danny Stephens did not score from the next two, while Brennen at the other end was anxious to get the strike. A pushed single by Stephens gave Brennen the chance he wanted, but he missed with a shot which might have produced a boundary and became Hendry's sixth victim. The last ball of the match went straight through to the keeper John Bradley and Dave Firminger and Stephens galloped a bye to be beaten by one run". Hendry had taken three wickets for one run in the last over to finish with 6 for 42 from nine overs but remarkably he nearly didn't play in the final. Having missed two early rounds through injury he declined to upset the team in the semi-final and allowed his replacement Wilf Jackson to play. Jackson would have played in the final had he himself not been injured in the replayed semi-final allowing Hendry back in.

The 1964 Final

Stillington** 92-8 v Civil Service 83 all out

Played on Thursday evening 23rd July at Wigginton Road, each side allowed one innings of 18 eight ball overs with no restrictions on the bowlers.

Batting first Stillington were restricted to 92 for 8, Civil Service's pace man Duncan Steel doing the damage, his 7 wickets costing only 23 runs off nine overs. Only three batsmen got into double figures; John Wyrill run out for 23, a young Dennis North with 11 and Ray Midgley with 27, leaving the pre-match favourites Civil Service in a strong position.

However the pace of Stillington's opening bowlers Malcolm Denton and Colin Minton proved too much for the Service top order. After they "hurled down a fiery over apiece the world seemed to have collapsed around Civil Service's heads" according to Keith Meadows reporting in *The Press*. They had lost four wickets for five runs in two overs, and when this quickly became 13 for 5, victory seemed a long way off. However Bill Shaw had other ideas and he and Maurice Cram began to claw things back, with steady singles at first before Shaw cut loose with a four and "a mighty six". Denton then swung things back in his side's favour with three more wickets, only for Shaw to launch two more sixes into the crowd leaving 24 needed off the last three overs. Shaw's fine innings came to an end in the penultimate over at 46 with a smart stumping by John Fowler off the bowling of John Wyrill and the last wicket fell off the last ball of the game with Civil Service 10 runs short of victory. Denton finished with the excellent figures of 6 for 26 from nine overs.

121

The 1974 Final

Easingwold** 86 all out v Heworth 48 all out

Played on Thursday evening 24th July at Clifton Park, each side allowed one innings of 18 eight ball overs with no restrictions on the bowlers.

On a difficult wicket which favoured the bowlers Easingwold took first knock and lost openers Val Toase and Stuart Burton with the score on 15, the Heworth bowlers Jim Collis and Colin Armstrong proving a handful for the batsmen. However skipper Dennis Hutchinson and Jeff Robinson made it look a different wicket, taking the total to 67 before Collis bowled Robinson for 25 and Hutchinson was run out a short time later for 31, after which the bowlers once more gained the upper hand. Easingwold slipped from 67 for 2 to 78 for 9, with the only other significant contribution being a breezy 15 from Stuart Reynolds who was last out at 86 with three balls of the innings left. Collis took 3 for 50 from his nine overs and Armstrong 5 for 32 from 8.5 overs.

Set a seemingly modest total, Heworth had no answer to the pace of Colin Minton and Ken Skilbeck. Minton had Colin Henderson lbw to the first ball of the innings, Ken Johnson was dropped behind from the second, survived the third but was bowled by the fourth. Guy Raines survived two loud appeals for lbw from Skilbeck before he was bowled by him with the score on 12 and Skilbeck followed this up with the wickets of Robert Turner, Jerry Dunnington and Ian Reed in the next couple of overs to leave Heworth in deep trouble at 28 for 6. Minton then swiftly despatched Alec Fyrth, John Fowler, Pete Johnson and Colin Armstrong to see Heworth all out for 48 in the 15th over. Minton finished with 6 for 27 from 7.3 overs and Skilbeck 4 for 20 from seven overs.

The 1984 Final

Heworth 160-9 v Acomb** 156-4

Played on Thursday evening 19th July at Clifton Park, each side allowed one innings of 18 eight ball overs with a maximum of five overs per bowler.

An eagerly anticipated final between two of the top clubs of the era, Acomb were the holders and Heworth had already this year won the Pocklington Shield and the Sawkill Cup. Both teams were captained by outstanding local players of entirely different temperaments. Dick Sykes for Acomb, one of the best bats seen in local cricket, could also bowl and keep wicket as well as being an excellent tactician who was invariably calm and quietly spoken. His opposite number Ian Reed, a brilliant bowler who could also bat, was fiercely competitive and often outspoken. He wore his heart on his sleeve and led from the front so it promised to be an interesting final.

Acomb batted first on a good wicket, Bob Graves (49) and Chris Simpson (35) giving them a great start and this was followed up with 44 from the hard hitting Dave Tute at number three. Only Ian Reed of the Heworth bowlers showed any control, his five overs costing just 23 runs for one wicket, while all the other bowlers, Steve Precious, Steve Young and Neil Armstrong went for more than nine runs an over as Acomb closed on a very respectable 156 for 4.

The Heworth reply was impressive. Steve Taylor and Mick Hammerton had put on a hundred for the first wicket by the 12th over, but then four consecutive run-outs for the addition of only 18 runs "set the game alight" reported Peter Vine in *The Press*. Dick Sykes then bowled the dangerous Ian Wilson for 25 and had Steve Precious lbw for one while Steve Young was well caught at the wicket by Billy Carter off Tony Hinder for two, leaving Heworth 139 for 7 in the penultimate over. Paul Miles then came out to join Kev Wilson, and his skipper's instructions to get the 18 runs required in "odd ones" were completely ignored as he proceeded to smash his first three deliveries from Dick Sykes for fours and swung the game back in Heworth's favour. A quick single followed and consecutive two's from Kev Wilson tied the scores but Wilson was then bowled by Sykes leaving Miles on strike for the

123

last over with Neil Armstrong coming out to join him at the other end. Hinder bowling the last over had Miles dramatically caught by keeper Carter off the first ball but then skipper Reed came in and played a dead bat to his first ball before cutting the next for four between gully and cover point to end a superb contest.

Proud moment: Bill Carter, captain of the Acomb team, proudly displays the Myers and Burnell trophy they won by beating Stamford Bridge in last night's final. From the left: Dave Tute, Richard Sykes, Malcolm Pepper, Chris Simpson, Andy Leaning, Dave Robinson, Mike Robinson, Bob Graves, Andy Thrall, Tony Haines and Bill Carter.

The Acomb team that won the 1983 Myers & Burnell 35 years after their previous success. Nine of the players went on to play in the final the following year only to be narrowly defeated by Heworth in a thrilling game.

The 1993 Final

Heworth** 129-5 v Easingwold 128-7

Played on Thursday evening 22nd July at Clifton Park, each side allowed one innings of 18 eight ball overs with a maximum of five overs per bowler.

Heworth batted first on a night that promised rain. Tight bowling from Martin and Alan Robinson restricted the scoring to the extent that Heworth were only 15 without loss in the fifth over, which soon became 15 for 1 as Martin Robinson clean bowled Des Wyrill for seven. The arrival of wicketkeeper Chris Mead saw the scoring rate pick up and he and Jonathan Bean took the score beyond 50 before

Bean went for 27, caught behind by Kevin Hollinrake off the bowling of his brother Keith. Hollinrake took another catch soon afterwards to send Steve Simpson back for nine, the bowler this time being Paul Redshaw. The rain started after eleven overs with the score on 70 for 3 and seemed to affect the batsmen more than the fielding side, but Mead continued to accumulate runs and John Corcoran chipped in with 12 before he became Martin Robinson's second victim. Jason Gatus was then unluckily run out after scoring a single, the damp surface not helping running between the wickets. Paul Miles was next in and batted well with Mead to see the score to a competitive 129 for 5, Miles being eight n.o. and Mead 52 n.o. The pick of the bowlers were Keith Hollinrake with 1 for 26 from five overs and Martin Robinson with 2 for 32 from his five overs.

Martin Robinson and Andrew Dawson then gave their side a great start with a half-century opening stand in less than ten overs before Martin Sigsworth uprooted Dawson's off stump when he had made 33. His partner Robinson soon followed for 25, caught by skipper Trevor Walton off the bowling of Steve Simpson. Keith Hollinrake only made five before becoming Walton's only wicket. Alan Robinson the Easingwold skipper then played a lone hand as his team mates rather lost their way against some tight bowling, particularly by Walton whose four overs cost only four runs. Despite this Easingwold still seemed to be in the game, Ian Dobson staying for a while for 12, but Ronnie Alexander could only add five, both being dismissed by Simpson and the departure of Robinson for 32 appeared to signal the end. However Paul Moore and Paul Redshaw took things to the wire and with four needed off the last ball to tie, Redshaw was run out going for a fourth run. What was to be the last ever single innings final had proved to be one of the most exciting and certainly one of the closest. Steve Simpson with 3 for 33 from five overs was the most successful bowler in terms of wickets but Trevor Walton's 1 for 4 from four overs had undoubtedly won the match for his side. It had been an impressive all-round performance by Heworth throughout the competition, Steve Simpson and Martin Sigsworth having taken 24 wickets between them, backed up superbly by Trevor Walton who always bowled economically. Paul Miles had 13 dismissals behind the stumps as well as scoring runs at crucial moments and the out fielding was excellent. The batsmen rarely had to chase big totals but when runs were needed Chris Mead, Jonathan Bean and Des Wyrill all played their parts.

The 1994 Final

Sessay 142-6 & 145-9 v Woodhouse Grange** 155-3 & 131-9

Played on Sunday 21st August at Clifton Park, each side allowed two innings of 16 eight ball overs, with a maximum of four overs per bowler.

This promised to be a good final with two top local sides pitted against each other. Woodhouse were in a period of dominance locally and nationally and were rightly regarded as experts in knock-out cricket, while Sessay were also a force in local cricket and had had a great year in local cup cricket, winning the York Invitation on the same ground a week earlier.

Woodhouse batted first and reached 155 for 3 thanks to an unbroken fourth wicket stand of 102 between Paul Mosey and Mike Burdett who made batting look easy on a good wicket.

In reply Sessay reached 142 for 6. After opener John Flintoff had limped off with a calf injury and three more early wickets had fallen Dwane Atkinson (36), Richard Till (32), Darren Atkinson (21*) and Dan Copeland (19) rescued the innings.

In their second innings Woodhouse skipper Simon Gill (37) and Stuart Craven (33) put on 56 for the first wicket before 16 year old Matthew Till was introduced into the attack by Sessay skipper Richard Wentworth. The move paid immediate dividends, as he removed both openers for only 11 runs with four overs of superbly controlled leg-spin and backed up by brother Richard, who also took two wickets, they saw Woodhouse fall away to 131 for 9. Of the nine Woodhouse wickets that fell to bowlers in the match the Till family took eight, with Keith taking two to add to the six taken by his cousins Matthew and Richard.

Set 145 to win Sessay appeared to stall initially and despite 34 from Neil Lawson at number four "the match seemed to be slipping from Sessay's grasp" reported Chris Houseman in *The Press*. Things went from bad to worse for Sessay "as three run-outs decimated their middle order", two of these being by ex-Yorkshire player Colin Johnson who was ineligible to play, but was allowed on as substitute fielder. Dan Copeland and Richard Till pulled things round but 46 were still

126

needed off the last three overs. "Copeland's dismissal (for 19) saw the injured Flintoff hobble to the crease to increase the tempo", which he did, including two enormous sixes to the mid-wicket boundary, but 18 were still required off the last over. Flintoff scored two from the first ball but was bowled by Peter Head with the second. Skipper Wentworth then came in and he and Richard Duffield scrambled 14 off the next five deliveries to leave two needed off the last ball. A good delivery from Head speared into the legs of Duffield went off his pads to keeper Mike Burdett. The batsmen set off for a single and Burdett's shy at the wicket which would have won the game for Woodhouse narrowly missed, the resulting overthrow allowing the Sessay pair back for the winning run.

This was the first ever two innings per side final, an innovation which was introduced to try to revive interest in the competition which at the time was on the wane, although personally I believe that the problem was not the format but simply a steady decline in the popularity of cup cricket and evening cricket as a whole. Many of the smaller clubs were finding it harder to raise teams to take on what was inevitably becoming a smaller nucleus of "big" clubs dominating local cricket. This has continued to be the case and has seen the end of most of the once popular cup competitions and the effect is still evident in the current "pyramid system" in local cricket, which concentrates an ever decreasing pool of talent amongst a few strong clubs at the top. The real answer lies in finding a way of converting more of the vast number of junior cricketers into senior cricketers. We seem to have a greater junior membership across local clubs than ever, but far fewer of these players go on to play senior cricket than ever before. Little or no cricket on "free to air" television is also a major factor in the decline of the game. The greed and short-sightedness of the ECB and the Counties has caused long term damage to grass-roots cricket and without a strong grass-roots base cricket will struggle in the years to come.

The demise of evening cricket and particularly cup cricket is a cause of sadness for many cricketers of previous generations, mine included, providing as it did excitement, sometimes bitter rivalry and often tremendous camaraderie in equal measure. We made many friends (and occasional enemies!) and it is missed by all those who took part and by the many spectators who spent so many summer evenings enjoying these contests.

Chapter Nine

Winners, runners-up and final scorecards 1919 to 2007.

This chapter contains tables with a list of winners and runners-up for each year of the competition from 1919 to 2007, followed by a detailed scorecard for each final.

The scorecards are hopefully fairly simple to follow;

Column one. Gives the date each final was scheduled to be played and details of subsequent dates of any postponed or interrupted games. Also in this column, against the first final in 1919, appear brief details of the format for the final, semi-finals and early rounds. After 1919 details of the format are only given against years in which the format changed.

Column two. Gives the year.

Column three. Gives the winning side, the team, in batting order, and indicates both captain and wicketkeeper where known. The bowling figures immediately following the team refer to the opposition and generally show the most successful bowlers. In addition wicketkeepers with three or more victims and the occurrence of three or more run-outs are listed where known. Column five gives the same information for the runners-up.

Column four. Gives the players individual scores, the team total and the number of overs in the innings. Column six gives the same information for the runners-up.

** indicates that team batted first.

Full names of players are given where known, although some only have initials and a very small number only have surnames. The accuracy of names cannot be guaranteed as a number of discrepancies occur between and within written reports and even club score-books. Similarly with team lists it has proved very difficult in some cases to be certain of the exact make up of teams. I have gone to considerable lengths to try to make these lists as accurate as possible, but I will be happy to hear from anyone who can correct any mistakes.

	Myers & Burnell Cup 1919-1993				
year	WINNERS	SCORE	CAPTAIN	RUNNERS-UP	SCORE
1919	Heworth**	146 all out	J.W.Wheatley	St.Michael-le-Belfry	142 all out
1920	York Ramblers**	146 all out	Maj.Harry O. Johnson	Escrick Park	69 all out
1921	Dringhouses	92-1	Harold Arnold	Escrick Park**	89 all out
1922	York Ramblers	113-9	Maj.Harry O. Johnson	Southbank WMC**	109 all out
1923	Escrick Park**	160 all out	Claude W. Thompson	Dringhouses	74 all out
1924	Rowntrees**	159 all out	Major George Herbert	Dringhouses	106 all out
1925	York City Amateurs	100-1	Henry Lund	Haxby**	94 all out
1926	North Riding Mental Hospital**	69 all out	Dr.William A.Fraser	Acomb	57 all out
1927	Bootham Park	190-8	Dr.Minski	Acomb**	188 all out
1928	York Ramblers**	244-7	Eddie Legard	Clarence C.& I.	211 all out
1929	York Ramblers	185-8	Harry Moult	Clifton CC**	171 all out
1930	Acomb**	168-9	Maj.Harry O. Johnson	Long Marston	123 all out
1931	York Reserves**	124 all out	R.A.Castle	York Station Staff	75 all out
1932	North Riding Mental Hospital**	160 all out	George A.Harling	Escrick Park	127 all out
1933	North Riding Mental Hospital**	236 all out	Dr.William A.Fraser	Tadcaster	178 all out
1934	North Riding Mental Hospital**	235-7	George A.Harling	New Earswick	188 all out
1935	North Riding Mental Hospital	127-3	George A.Harling	Tadcaster**	125 all out
1936	Tadcaster**	164 all out	Noel W.Herbert	York Railway Institute	42 all out
1937	Clifton C.C.	70-5	Bill Taylor	Tadcaster**	64 all out
1938	Tadcaster**	175 all out	Johnny Munford	North Riding Mental Hospital	107 all out
1939	York Zingari	115-7	Vic Bedford	Acomb**	113 all out
1940	Tadcaster**	140 all out	Ernie Stubbs	New Earswick	81 all out
1941	York Railway Institute**	164 all out	Bob Stather	Tadcaster	68 all out
1942	Clifton CC	147-7	Jack R.Pulleyn	Clifton Hospital**	146 all out
1943	Clifton Hospital**	182 all out	George A.Harling	York an XI	146 all out
1944	Acomb**	154-9	Cyril Wiles	Clifton C.C.	82 all out
1945	RAF Melbourne**	146 all out	Group Captain Ling	Clifton Hospital	132 all out
1946	Clifton C.C.**	121 all out	Jack R.Pulleyn	York Railway Institute	83 all out
1947	Clifton C.C.	232-9	Jack R.Pulleyn	Acomb**	231-9
1948	Acomb	154-2	Eddie Cooper	Dringhouses**	151-9
1949	Clifton CC "A"**	144-9	Herbert Harrison	Dringhouses	102 all out
1950	Clifton Hospital**	198-7	Ivor Churchill	Clifton C.C.	99 all out
1951	Ovington**	110 all out	Ted Coulson	Stamford Bridge	105 all out
1952	Dringhouses**	182 all out	Stan Fawcett	York an XI	126-9
1953	Clifton Hospital	199-7	Joe McConnon	New Earswick**	198 all out
1954	Rowntrees**	131-8	Reg Baines	York an XI	125 all out
1955	Dringhouses**	136-8	Stan Fawcett	York an XI	129 all out
1956	York an XI	133-5	John R. Richardson	Stamford Bridge**	132 all out
1957	Magnets Sports Club**	155 all out	Dennis Firn	Ebor Gogues	129 all out
1958	Woodhouse Grange**	250-8	Tommy H.Hobson	Rowntrees	168 all out
1959	Tadcaster	90-2	Cyril Mason	New Earswick**	89 all out
1960	York Railway Institute**	103-7	Geoff N.Britton	Ebor Gogues	102-9
1961	York Railway Institute	72-6	John Bradley	Heworth**	71 all out
1962	Cawood	110-6	Eric Gibson	Dringhouses**	106 all out
1963	Huntington W.M.C.	85-6	Derek Magson	York Railway Institute**	83 all out
1964	Stillington**	92-8	Cecil Wood	Civil Service	83 all out
1965	Huntington W.M.C.	98-5	Derek Magson	York an XI**	95 all out
1966	Dringhouses	105-3	Geoff Limbert	Woodhouse Grange**	102-7
1967	Dringhouses**	121-8	Geoff Limbert	Heworth	69 all out
1968	Easingwold	104-5	Dennis Hutchinson	Dringhouses**	103-6
1969	York an XI (Nomads)	139-3	Tony F.J.Temple	Easingwold**	135-4
1970	Dringhouses	103-6	Keith Cowl	Dunnington**	102 all out

131

Year	Winner	Score	Captain	Runners-up	Score
1971	York an XI**	142-6	Tony F.J.Temple	Stamford Bridge	119-4
1972	Easingwold**	143-5	Dennis Hutchinson	Sheriff Hutton Bridge	79-9
1973	Huntington W.M.C.**	90 all out	Wally Baynes	Sheriff Hutton Bridge	86-7
1974	Easingwold**	86 all out	Dennis Hutchinson	Heworth	48 all out
1975	Sheriff Hutton Bridge**	150-6	Mick R. Oldfield	Cawood	47 all out
1976	Dunnington**	156-6	Pat Wood	Huntington W.M.C.	118 all out
1977	York an XI	108-2	Alec Backhouse	Tadcaster**	104 all out
1978	Sheriff Hutton Bridge**	162-3	Mick R.Oldfield	Cawood	141-7
1979	Easingwold	102-3	Peter Gilleard	Stamford Bridge**	99-8
1980	York an XI	118-3	Alec Backhouse	Woodhouse Grange**	117-8
1981	Sessay	130-1	John Flintoff	Acomb**	128-7
1982	Easingwold**	172-7	Stuart Reynolds	Heworth	158-7
1983	Acomb**	148-2	Billy Carter	Stamford Bridge	122-8
1984	Heworth	160-9	Ian Reed	Acomb**	156-4
1985	Crayke**	136-4	Andy Gilleard	Sessay	123-9
1986	Osbaldwick**	135-6	Dave Rippon	Heworth	124 all out
1987	York an XI**	125-6	Paul Jackson	Heworth	100-8
1988	Thorp Arch and Boston Spa**	131-5	Stephen Booth	Heworth	110-8
1989	Woodhouse Grange	105-1	Dick Whaley	Acomb**	104-8
1990	Woodhouse Grange	96-6	Simon Gill	Heworth**	95 all out
1991	Heworth**	116-4	David Simpson	Woodhouse Grange	113-7
1992	Pocklington**	122-5	Kevin Smith	Heworth	98 all out
1993	Heworth**	129-5	Trevor Walton	Easingwold	128-7

** Batted first

Years in Green played at Bootham Crescent	Teams in blue played for the original cup
Years in Black played at Wigginton Road	Teams in black played for the replacement cup
Years in Red played at Clifton Park	Teams in red won the original cup as runners-up

Scores in Black 50 over/time format

Scores in Blue 18x8 ball over format

Myers & Burnell Cup 1994-2007

year	WINNERS	SCORE	CAPTAIN	RUNNERS-UP	SCORE
1994	Sessay	142-6 & 145-9	Richard Wentworth	Woodhouse Grange**	155-3 & 131-8
1995	Acomb	113-5 & 139-4	Dick Sykes	Dunnington**	127-5 & 122-5
1996	Woodhouse Grange**	121-6 & 116-4	Mark Burton	Heworth	113-4 & 115-9
1997	Heworth	116-5 & 93-7	Martin E.Sigsworth	Easingwold**	85-8 & 122-7
1998	Thirsk	177-3 & 65-4	Dave Greenlay	Clifton Alliance**	121-6 & 119-9
1999	Clifton Alliance**	202-3 & 149-5	Duncan Naylor	Thirsk	131-5 & 127-8
2000	Thirsk**	125-4 & 152-6	Dave Greenlay	Easingwold	99 all out & 148-6
2001	Clifton Alliance**	142-8 & 139-7	Duncan Naylor	Acomb	116-7 & 143-7
2002	Osbaldwick*	144-1 & rsp	Steve J. Young	Heworth**	116-6 & 150-8
2003	Acomb**	157-2 & 138-3	Dave Sykes	Woodhouse Grange	134-4 & 150-4
2004	York**	169-4 & 142-6	Nick Kay	Clifton Alliance	124 all out & 167-7
2005	York**	182-9 & 186-9	Nick Kay	Clifton Alliance	163-8 & 130-6
2006	York	203-3 & 50-2	Nick Kay	Clifton Alliance**	150 all out & 99 all out
2007	Woodhouse Grange	Not known	Steve Burdett	Clifton Alliance	Not known

* Rain stopped play run rate used	Teams in black won the replacement cup	
** Batted first	Teams in red won the original cup as runners-up	

Played at Clifton Park on a Sunday afternoon games consisting of two innings each side (16x8 ball overs)

Date and format	Year	The finals 1919-1993 Winner	Score	Runner-up	Score
Sat 23rd Aug	1919	**Heworth ****		**St. Michael le Belfry**	
Final one complete		Claude E.Anson	25	Captain A.E.Dent	7
innings each		Charlie Trendall	35	H.W.Masterman	5
		J.W.Wheatley (Capt.) (Wkt.)	34	E.J.Webb	19
Semi's 2 nights		Major S.M.Dowsett	1	Arthur Henry Naylor	74*
1 comp inns each		Arthur Nettleton	0	Jack E.Sweeting	15
		H.Herbert	9	A.Clayton	2
		A.G.Simpson	14	G.H.Douglas	10
Early rounds 1hr		William Ware	0	George Herbert Naylor	0
30 mins per side		H.Craig	4	W.Mennell	0
on one evening		George Ware	7	J.Badger	6
		Arthur Henry Smith	1*	J.Chatterton	1
		extras	16	extras	3
		A.E.Dent 5 wkts	146 all out	H.Herbert 4 wkts	142 all out
		Jack E.Sweeting 3 wkts		William Ware 3 wkts	
Sat 14th Aug	1920	**York Ramblers****		**Escrick Park**	
		Jimmy Duck	16	Joe Reader	17
		F.W.Adamson	15	Herbert Sanders	14
		J.Robson	10	Francis Edward Digweed	5
		Harry Moult	0	Edwin Reader	0
		T.Anthony	44	Dr.Morrison	0
		Gerald Simpson	0	Claude W.Thompson (C&W)	20*
		P.Backhouse	3	George H.Stancliffe	0
		Maj.Harry O. Johnson (Capt.)	27	George Streetly	3
		H.Walker	0	Arthur Skilbeck	0
		J.Peek	3*	Ray Ellar	5
		Sam Buttrey	6	Luke Cecil Dennison	0
		extras	22	extras	5
		Luke Cecil Dennison 12-5-15-4	146 all out	Jimmy Duck 11-0-21-6	69 all out
		Ray Ellar 15-3-26-4			
Sat 13th Aug	1921	**Dringhouses**		**Escrick Park****	
		S.Mayo	41*	R.Pratt	8
		A.Shaw	1	Claude W.Thompson (C&W)	13
		C.Lancaster	43*	Joe Reader	1
		Billy Wilkinson	dnb	Dr.Morrison	15
		Harold Arnold (Capt.)	dnb	Tommy Hobson	0
		Fred Lancaster	dnb	Edwin Reader	31
		E.Wagstaff	dnb	Herbert Hodgson	6
		Joe Stoker	dnb	Ernie Sanders	5
		R.Bird	dnb	Ray Ellar	0
		G.Roper	dnb	George Streetly	0
		Fred Davison	dnb	Luke Cecil Dennison	2*
		extras	7	extras	8
		Edwin Reader 1 wkt.	92-1	Fred Davison 4 Wkts.	89 all out
				Billy Wilkinson 3 wkts	
Sat 12th Aug post	1922	**York Ramblers**		**Southbank WMC****	
to Sat 19th Aug		F.W.Adamson	12	W.Thompson	7
		N.Herbert	8	W.Skilbeck	8
		T.Anthony	12	W.Eshelby	9
		G.W.Dawson	2	A.Prest	1
		G.Tindill	13	A.Pannett	41
		Maj.Harry O. Johnson (Capt.)	24*	H.Hoyle	8
		Arthur R.Birch	0	Jack Prest	16
		Harry Moult	5	R.Skilbeck	3
		H.Walker	1	J.Johnson	1
		F.Welch	20	Constantine Authbert	0
		Sam Buttery	3*	A.Rowarth	1
		extras	13	extras	14
		Jack Prest 14-0-48-5	113-9	Harry Moult 10-1-39-6	109 all out
		A.Pannett 3 wkts		all clean bowled	

133

Sat 18th Aug part	1923	**Escrick Park****		Dringhouses	
finished replay on		Joe Reader	12	W. "Billy" Wilkinson	27
Sat 1st Sept post		Rev.Roger Franklen Cardale	41	A.Shaw	3
to Sat 8th Sept		Edwin Reader	32	Herbert Fawcett	4
		Luke Cecil Dennison	0	L.Flanagan	11*
		H.Rudd	3	Harry Lawson	0
		Claude W.Thompson (Capt.)(Wkt.)	5	Joe Stoker	4
		George Streetly	6	Harold Arnold (Capt.)	4
		A.L.Butterworth	10	R.Bird	16
		Ray Ellar	3	W.Wood	0
		G.Storr	6	E.Shaw	0
		R.Rochester	2*	W.Bradley (Wkt.)	0
		extras	40	extras	5
		E.Shaw 14-6-19-6	160 all out	Rev.R.F.Cardale 9.2-1-33-7	74 all out
			off 49.4 overs		off 18.2 overs
Sat 16th Aug post	1924	**Rowntrees****		Dringhouses	
to Sat 23rd Aug		Major George Herbert (Capt.)	56	W.Rafton	1
		James Irving Waterhouse	17	H.Waterworth	5
		George H. Huggons (Wkt.)	0	A.Shaw	12
		Thomas Edward Hornshaw	9	Billy Wilkinson	21
		Robert William Kirby	44	L.Flanagan	13
		James Hepworth	0	S.Downs	23
		Arthur Baxter	0	Fred Davison	11
		B.Webster	9	Harold Arnold (Capt.)	2
		Arthur Brassey	12	Herbert Fawcett	0*
		Arthur Harbottle	0	R.Bird	0
		John Henry Clayton	4*	F.Dunderdale	1
		extras	8	extras	17
		Fred Davison 4 Wkts	159 all out	Arthur Brassey 5 Wkts	106 all out
		A.Shaw 3 wkts		Arthur Harbottle 3 wkts	
Sat 15th Aug	1925	**York City Amateurs**		Haxby**	
		Charlie Trendall	60	Fred W.Carr (Capt.)	18
		Arthur Nelson Taylor	25	A.D.Young	2
		F.W.Wood	15	C.S.Baxter	8
		Henry Lund (Capt.& Wkt.)	dnb	E.Wrigglesworth	12
		H.C.Greenwood	dnb	W."Harold" Annequin	1
		Dick Lund	dnb	Fred Bryan	8
		F.Hare	dnb	C.Wrigglesworth	9
		W.F.Cox	dnb	Harry Jefferson	6
		R.Freer	dnb	Arthur Edwin Beresford	12
		Harry Houseman	dnb	Federick Henry Cordukes	9*
		Joe Triffitt	dnb	A.B.Pearcey	7
		extras	0	extras	2
		A.B.Pearcey 5-1-28-1	100-1	Joe Triffitt 15-3-57-7	94 all out
			off 28 overs	Dick Lund 14.2-2-35-3	off 29.2 overs
Sat 14th Aug	1926	**North Riding Mental Hospital****		Acomb	
		S.Tichener (Wkt.)	4	Capt.Francis L.L.F.Roupell	0
		F.Slater	0	Alan Dalby	26
		Ivor Churchill	2	J.Robson (Capt.)	24
		Hubert H.Dryland	25	Maj.Harry O.Johnson	2
		George B.Sprigg	0	C.Lancaster	0
		Herbert Freestone	7	B.Appleby	0
		George Alfred Harling	6	G.Exelby	0
		Dr.William A.Fraser (Capt.)	9	H.Leadley	3*
		William Hill	5	T.A.Holmes	0
		Charles McQuade	2	S.Strange	0
		William Craven	2*	A.Wray	0
		extras	7	extras	2
			69 all out		57 all out
		S.Strange 12-1-36-6	off 23.3 overs	F.Slater 10.3-3-19-7	off 22.3 overs

134

Sat 6th Aug	1927	**Bootham Park**		**Acomb****	
2 hrs 30 mins each		Henry Dalton	16	J.Robson (Capt.)	55
no limit on overs		O.Shaw	36	Alan Dalby	5
		Arthur Nelson Taylor (Wkt.)	92*	C.Lancaster	11
		Harry Rawson	0	R.Hields	54
Semi's 2 nights		J.C.Allin	7	H.Leadley	4
1 comp inns each		A.Armitage	4	Maj.Harry O.Johnson	16
		H.Richardson	9	B.Appleby	1
		G.Buckingham	0	W.Skilbeck	8
		W.W.Dawson	10	S.Strange	15
Early rounds 1hr		Dr.Minski (Capt.)	1*	A.Wray	1
30 mins each on		Unknown	dnb	A.Leadley	1*
one evening		extras	15	extras	17
		Maj.Harry O.Johnson 7-1-33-3	190-8	Henry Dalton 27-7-62-6	188 all out
			off 61.5 overs	J.C.Allin 18-2-33-3	off 54 overs
		The 62nd over was the last within the time limit			in 2hrs 20 min
Sat 11th Aug	1928	**York Ramblers****		**Clarence C.& I.**	
		Eddie Legard (Capt.)	54	E.Stathers	0
		Arthur R.Birch	4	A.Burdett	10
		Joe Triffitt	77	F.Boyes	10
		G.Cooper	18	H.Higgins	8
		Harry Moult	5	Reg Baines	90
		J.R.A.Freer	40*	H.Baines	17
		F.Welch	9	H.Scaife	9
		Cecil William Hamilton	9	R.Richmond	16
		A.Horner	11	Harry Brazier (Capt.)	20*
		S.W.Robinson	dnb	J.L'Anson	14
		S.G.Spencer	dnb	R.Hutchinson	0
		extras	17	extras	17
		H.Scaife 20-1-81-3	244-7	Harry Moult 17.4-2-64-4	211 all out
			off 57 overs	Cecil W.Hamilton 21-3-78-4	off 46.4 overs
			time expired		in 2 hrs 15 min
Sat 17th Aug	1929	**York Ramblers**		**Clifton CC****	
		F.W.Adamson	8	Sammy Toyne	0
		Arthur R.Birch	1	H.G.Henderson	8
		Joe Triffitt	34	Vic Bedford (Wkt.)	10
		Harry Moult (Capt.)	36	J.T.Davis	3
		Eddie Legard	14	J.Tremlin	27
		J.R.A.Freer	18	W."Bill"Taylor	2
		E.Peacock	30	R.Angrave	5
		A.Horner	35*	D.Gell	29
		F.Welch	3	S.Harrison	24
		S.G.Spencer	0*	C.Myton (Capt.)	19
		Mortimer	dnb	J.L'Anson	17*
		extras	6	extras	27
		H.G.Henderson 14-1-68-3	185-8	Harry Moult 22-4-33-5	171 all out
			off 38 overs	A.Horner 18-3-54-3	off 51.5 overs
Sat 16th Aug	1930	**Acomb****		**Long Marston**	
2 hrs 30 mins each		Maj.Harry O.Johnson (Capt.)	20	George Dickinson	12
no limit on overs		H.Leadley	19	Lawrence Griffith-Jones	1
		C.G.Shepherd	71*	Eric N.Kay (Capt.)	27
		R.Hields	2	C.W.Griffith-Jones	2
Semi's 2 nights		J.W.Hields	6	N.Clayton	1
1 comp inns each		G.Pratt	13	L.Jackson	8
		Peter Carlton	8	Harry Dickinson	6
		J.Thompson	2	Harold Kay	8
Early rounds 1hr		C.Blackburn	0	Edward Dickinson	36
30 mins each max		S.Strange	9	Tom Dickinson	1
28 overs		H.Alcock	6*	John S."Jock"Hall (Wkt.)	10*
		extras	12	extras	11
		Harry Dickinson 8-1-17-3	168-9	C.G.Shepherd 11.2-1-26-4	123 all out
		time expired	off 58 overs	C.Blackburn 11-3-28-4	off 46.2 overs

135

Sat 8th Aug post	1931	**York Reserves****		**York Station Staff**	
Mon 17th & Tue		R.Needham	29	G.Swinn	9
18th, post on 17th		R.A.Roberts	4	J.Taylor	6
played on 18th and		Herbert Harrison	12	J.Robson (Wkt.)	38*
19th		H.Wheatley	0	M.Wake	0
		Roy S.Nicholson	10	J.Watters	4
		Harold F.Hornshaw	9	W.Robson	1
		R.S.Barber	2	Jim C.D'Arcy	4
		E.L.Green	20	George G.Cross (Capt.)	2
		J.H.Clayton	14	T.Meek	2
		R.A.Castle (Capt.)	2	G.Tomes	1
		Tommy W.White	5	W.Wilson (sub for A.Jackson	1
		extras	17	who played on 18th) extras	7
		Jim C.D'Arcy 6 for 45	124 all out	Tommy W.White 14-4-24-5	75 all out
				Roy S.Nicholson 4 for 20	
Sat 6th Aug	1932	**North Riding Mental Hospital****		**Escrick Park**	
		Joe Littlewood	23	Arthur "Pom" Elmhirst (Wkt.)	36
		Alf A. Aveyard	6	H.Hodgson	3
		Alec Thompson	25	Vic Hale	0
		George William Appleby	57	David Wormald	10
		Ivor Churchill	2	Eric C.O. Thompson (Capt.)	43
		Fred Oliver	13	Jack Elmhirst	4
		Percy Poole	11	George Streetley	0
		Matt Storey	3	Herbert Scaife	1
		Tommy Robinson (Wkt.)	14	Luke Cecil Dennison	4
		George Alfred Harling (Capt.)	3	Bill Yeoman	8
		Ernie Marshall	0*	Ray Ellar	1*
		extras	3	extras	17
		Ray Ellar 14-1-49-5	160 all out	Ernie Marshall 12-0-42-5	127 all out
		Jack Elmhirst 16.5-3-61-5	off 39.5 overs	Ivor Churchill 3 for 30	off 34.2 overs
Sat 12th Aug	1933	**North Riding Mental Hospital****		**Tadcaster**	
50 overs each no		Joe Littlewood	2	Ken Steele (Capt.)	4
time limit		Alf A. Aveyard	124*	G.Morrell	3
		Alec Thompson	21	Fred W.Shearsmith	2
		George William Appleby	7	George Shearsmith	10
Semi's 40 overs		Tommy Robinson (Wkt.)	29	George Marsh	52
each over 2 nights		Ivor Churchill	31	Johnny Munford	53
first time		Percy Poole	2	H.Tomkinson	2
		Fred Oliver	1	G.Tomkinson	1
		Matt Storey	7	J.Clifford	28
		Ernie Marshall	4	H.Metcalfe	12
		Dr.William A.Fraser (Capt.)	0	Alf E.Whitelock	0
		extras	8	extras	11
		Alf Whitelock 6 for 60	236 all out	Ernest Marshall 3 for 61	178 all out
		J.Clifford 3 wkts	in the 49th over	Ivor Churchill 3 for 30	in the 45th over
Sat 11th Aug rsp	1934	**North Riding Mental Hospital****		**New Earswick**	
NE at 29-0 in reply		Joe Littlewood	14	R.S.Guffick (Capt.)	48
finished Mon 20th		Alf A. Aveyard	54	Herbert Freer	20
Aug		Alec Thompson	0	Cyril Charlton	1
		Ivor Churchill	27	Eric Bryan	7
		George William Appleby	68*	John R.A.Freer	6
		Tommy Robinson (Wkt.)	43	Bill Hardaker	34
		Percy Poole	8	Ian Douglas	1
		Fred Oliver	15	Les Beck	28
		Matt Storey	1*	John Greaves	3
		George Alfred Harling (Capt.)	dnb	G.Douglas	0
		Ernie Marshall	dnb	John Randles	25*
		extras	5	extras	15
		Guffick 1-30, Douglas 1-33,	235-7	Ivor Churchill 3 for 30	188 all out
		Bryan 1-35, Hardaker 1-36,	off 50 overs	Alec Thompson 4 wkts	in the 48th over
		H.Freer 1-38, Charlton 1-58.			

Sat 10th Aug 1935

North Riding Mental Hospital		Tadcaster**	
Alf A. Aveyard	31	Ken Steele	15
Joe Littlewood	48	Norman Swinden	3
Tommy Robinson (Wkt.)	5	B.Lumby	49
Alec Thompson	11	Noel W.Herbert (Capt.)	24
George William Appleby	22*	H.Metcalfe	8
Percy Poole	dnb	George Shearsmith	0
Ivor Churchill	dnb	Fred W.Shearsmith	6
George Alfred Harling (Capt.)	dnb	D.Pickering	8
Ernie Marshall	dnb	T.Whitehead	2
Fred Oliver	dnb	Alf E.Whitelock	1*
Matt Storey	dnb	J.Clifford	0
extras	10	extras	9
J.Clifford 2 wkts	127-3	George W. Appleby 5 for 18	125 all out
	in the 39th over		in the 35th over

Sat 8th Aug 1936

Tadcaster**		York Railway Institute	
Ken Steele	2	Billy Moore	1
Norman Swinden	1	George Baker	5
H.Metcalfe	27	Bob Stather	0
Fred W.Shearsmith	16	Frank Baker	4
George Shearsmith	12	Tommy White	1
Johnny Munford	14	Jim C.D'Arcy	14
Noel W.Herbert (Capt.)	39	Bill Bell	0
D.Pickering	10	L.Milner	4
Ernie Stubbs	6	Tommy W.White	0
C.Dixon	1	Harry Brazier (Capt.)	0
Alf E.Whitelock	24*	Jack Birch	8
extras	12	extras	5
Tommy W.White 19-3-70-5	164 all out	Ernie Stubbs 8.1-7-1-8	42 all out
Jim C.D'Arcy 16.1-3-45-4	off 49.1 overs	(including hat-trick)	off 16.1 overs

Sat 7th Aug 1937

Clifton CC		Tadcaster**	
F.Oxtoby	5	Norman Swinden	5
T.D.Kilvington	0	Ken Steele	17
Vic Bedford (Wkt.)	41	H.Metcalfe	7
G.R.Toes	12*	Noel W.Herbert (Capt.)	3
R.D.Winn	0	Fred W.Shearsmith	0
Bill Taylor (Capt.)	3	George Shearsmith	16*
Bill Yeoman	dnb	E.Stubbs	3
E.Hide	dnb	J.J."Johnny" Munford	0
H.W.Hodgson	dnb	J.Clifford	2
Jim S.Blackburn	dnb	Alf E.Whitelock	2
F.Greetham	dnb	G.E.Fawcett	9
extras	9	extras	0
Ernie Stubbs 7.4-2-24-4	70-5	G.R.Toes 16-4-32-6	64 all out
	off 19.4 overs	Jim S.Blackburn 15.2-2-32-4	off 31.2 overs

Sat 6th Aug 1938

Tadcaster**		North Riding Mental Hospital	
Ken Steele	73	Joe Littlewood	18
D.Pickering	8	Alf A.Aveyard	9
Fred W.Shearsmith	0	Arthur Nelson Taylor (Wkt.)	23
Norman Swinden	6	Les Pearson	0
Noel W.Herbert	29	Ray Needham	5
Johnny Munford (Capt.)	36	George William Appleby	15
Alf E.Whitelock	1	Fred Oliver	1
Ernie Stubbs	0	Alec Thompson	21*
George Shearsmith	5*	Ivor Churchill	12
W.Steele	5	George Alfred Harling (Capt.)	0
G.E.Fawcett	1	Bob Carter Snr.	1
extras	11	extras	2
Bob Carter Snr. 10-0-65-5	175 all out	Ernie Stubbs 14.3-1-24-4	107 all out
Alec Thompson 19-3-38-3	off 49 overs		off 36.3 overs
Arthur N.Taylor 2ct & 1stumped			

Sat 12th Aug	1939	**York Zingari**		**Acomb****	
		Vic Bedford (Capt.) (Wkt.)	52	J.Thompson	13
		R.Tyson	0	Matt Oates	13
		Bert Brenen	3	F.Pannett	2
		Claude Skilbeck	22	J.Hetherton	12
		T.W.Keel	24	T.Kitchen	2
		L.Pickard	5	Jack Pinder	26
		Dick Lund	1	A.Illingworth	11
		L.Beck	3*	S.Strange	16
		Frank Richardson	0*	W.Greenwood	0
		Bill Yeoman	dnb	N.Fearne	7
		Cole	dnb	W.Ainley	6*
		extras	5	extras	5
		J.Thompson 16-2-42-5	115-7	Frank Richardson 19.4-2-49-5	113 all out
			off 36 overs		off 40.4 overs
Sat 10th Aug	1940	**Tadcaster****		**New Earswick**	
		Ken Steele	15	David Douglas (Wkt.)	2
		D.Pickering	1	Eric Bryan (Capt.)	13
		H.Metcalfe	1	Stan Robinson	22
		Fred W.Shearsmith	7	Billy Walls	6
		Noel W.Herbert	3	Herbert Freer	5
		Alf E.Whitelock	10	Ken Shaw	3
		George Shearsmith	7	Cyril Coultate	12
		Ernie Stubbs (Capt.)	19	John Greaves	12
		Norman Swinden	4	John Randles	0
		W.Steele	44	G.Horseman	0
		A.Thomlinson	26*	John Smith	2*
		extras	3	extras	4
		G.Horseman 11.2-1-37-4	140 all out	Ernie Stubbs 11.3-2-27-6	81 all out
		Herbert Freer 9-1-36-3	off 38.2 overs	N.W.Herbert 6-0-34-3	off 23.3 overs
Sat 9th Aug	1941	**York Railway Institute****		**Tadcaster**	
		N.Ogden	2	W.Steele	11
		D.Shaw	42	George Shearsmith	5
		G.Ingleby	36	Fred W.Shearsmith	5
		Frank Baker	1	Noel W.Herbert	3
		Bob Stather (Capt.)	45	G.Chignell	12
		R.Brown	0	Ernie Stubbs (Capt.)	6
		Jim Blackburn	1	John Marriott	1
		Jack Birch	0	A.Thomlinson	11
		Peter Morritt	22	D.Pickering	0
		G.R.Smith	3	Ernest Mason	0
		W.H."Harry" Brazier	1	J.Pope	2*
		extras	11	extras	12
		John Marriott 10.2-2-59-7	164 all out	R.Brown 10-1-20-5	68 all out
			off 32.2 overs	G.Ingleby 10-0-36-4	off 20 overs
Sat 8th Aug	1942	**Clifton CC**		**Clifton Hospital****	
		W.Steele	49	Joe Littlewood	22
		H.W.Hodgson	19	Alf A. Aveyard (Capt.)	22
		Richard M.T.Kneebone	13	J.Hebden	9
		A.Broadhurst	30	Alec Thompson	12
		R.Leadley	11	Percy Poole	26
		R.Horwell	0	Ray Needham	18
		Jim P.Pulleyn	3	Ivor Churchill	22
		F.Crosby	5*	Tommy Robinson (Wkt.)	0
		Jack R.Pulleyn (Capt.)	8*	George William Appleby	1
		Huggins	dnb	Fred Oliver	5*
		Ted King	dnb	Syd Appleyard	2
		extras	9	extras	7
		Alf Aveyard 2 for 28	147-7	R.Horwell 6 for 51	146 all out
		J.Hebden 2 for 42		Ted King 3 for 47	

138

Sat 14th Aug	1943	**Clifton Hospital****		**York an XI**	
		Joe Littlewood	17	Ernie Sanders	4
		Alf A.Aveyard	46	Bob Ferguson (Wkt.)	7
		Lewin	13	Alf Nicholls	59
		J.Hebden	23	R.Freer	9
		Ray Needham	15	Peter B.Pickering	25
		Percy Poole	7	Jimmy Birrell	0
		Tommy Robinson (Wkt.)	29	William A.Kay (Capt.)	13
		Ivor Churchill	6	P.C.Laverack	3
		Kenyon	14	Frank Richardson	3
		Syd Appleyard	1	B.E.Randall	4
		George Alfred Harling (Capt.)	2*	Dick Lund	4*
		extras	9	extras	15
		Jimmy Birrell 4 for 40	182 all out	Alf Aveyard 4 for 22	146 all out
		P.C.Laverack 3 for 39		Ivor Churchill 3 for 46	
Sat 26th Aug	1944	**Acomb****		**Clifton CC**	
		Alan Dalby	9	H.W.Hodgson	14
		Allan Bryan	14	D.Fairclough	14
		Jack Pinder	16	R.W.Wilkinson	0
		Eric N. Kay	43	M.Henry	1
		Vic Bedford (Wkt.)	15	Richard M.T.Kneebone	9
		Matt Oates	3	Jack R.Pulleyn (Capt.)	2
		Gordon Foster	30*	Jim Blackburn	13
		George Maltby	4	C.Needham	8
		Lawrence Bean	2	Ted King	10*
		Cyril Wiles (Capt.)	2	P.A.Benson	2
		John Bradley	0*	B.Mitchell	3
		extras	16	extras	6
		Jack R.Pulleyn 8-3-17-5	154-9	Matt Oates 15-1-39-5	82 all out
			off 50 overs	Alan Dalby 15.5-3-37-4	off 30.5 overs
Sat 4th Aug	1945	**RAF Melbourne****		**Clifton Hospital**	
		Alfred Harper	27	Joe Littlewood	14
		Sgt.David Jones	8	Alf Aveyard	19
		Capt.Neville Shelmerdine	5	George William Appleby	3
		C.R.Knight	17	Percy Poole	24
		Group Captain Christopher Ling (C)	37	Tommy Robinson	5
		Ferian	17	Ivor Churchill	27
		Pilot Officer James S. Crawford	0	Les Pearson	1
		J.Ellis	10	Arthur Nelson Taylor (Wkt.)	2
		Flying Officer Lyall	3	Harry Lowe	25*
		Alfred William Himpson	2*	Syd Appleyard	2
		Flying Officer John M.J.Quarmby	0	George Alfred Harling (Capt.)	1
		extras	20	extras	9
		Syd Appleyard 5 for 24	146 all out	John Quarmby 6 for 26	132 all out
				Crawford 3 for 47	
Sat 3rd Aug	1946	**Clifton CC****		**York Railway Institute**	
50 overs each no		Harold F.Hornshaw	1	Billy Moore	18
time limit		Bill Pearson	4	George Mortimer	1
		Herbert Harrison (Vice Capt.)	23	Richard Powell	12
		Arthur Broadhurst	69*	J.Thompson	0
Semi's 40 overs		Bill Roberts	1	N.Ogden	0
each over 2 nights		Jim P.Pulleyn	0	Bob Stather (Capt.)	26
		Len Bennett	5	Jack Birch	13
		Jim Blackburn	5	R.Bell	6
		Jack R. Pulleyn (Capt.)	7	Bill Bell	2*
early rounds max		George A. Edwards (Wkt.)	1	F."Biddy" Lazenby	0
28 overs no time		Harry Craven	0	Cyril Audaer	2
limit		extras	5	extras	3
		Cyril Audaer 5 for 26	121 all out	Harry Craven 4 for 26	83 all out
		J.Thompson 4 for 41			

Sat 9th Aug	1947	Clifton CC		Acomb**	
		Bill Roberts	3	Eddie Cooper (Capt.)	28
		Bob Leadley	25	Len Vyle	21
		Harold Hornshaw	73	Alan Dalby	20
		Herbert Harrison (vice Capt.)	14	Eric N.Kay	74
		Arthur Broadhurst	45	Roy S.Nicholson	51
		Jim P.Pulleyn	24	Gordon Foster	14
		Bob Crosby	1	Vic Bedford (Wkt.)	4
		Jim Blackburn	5	Jack Pinder	0
		Jack R.Pulleyn (Capt.)	22*	Matt Oates	5
		George A. Edwards (Wkt.)	1	Phil Dalby	0
		Harry Craven	4*	Tom Victor Ludolf	0*
		extras	15	extras	14
		Phil Dalby 18-1-83-4	232-9	Harry Craven 18-2-62-4	231-9
		Matt Oates 11-0-51-3	in the 44th over		off 50 overs
Sat 14th Aug	1948	Acomb		Dringhouses**	
		Eddie Cooper (Capt.)	85*	John Patrick	24
		Allan Bryan	3	Bruce Connell	1
		Roy S.Nicholson (Vice Capt.)	7	Ted Outhwaite (Wkt.)	26
		Vic Bedford (Wkt.)	54*	Frank Tuesley	8
		Phil Dalby	dnb	John Lawson (Capt.)	33
		Matt Oates	dnb	Stan Fawcett	4
		Len Vyle	dnb	Len Rodwell	24
		Alan Dalby	dnb	Alf Patrick	8
		Gordon Foster	dnb	Billy "Nucker" Brown	10*
		Peter Carlton	dnb	Tom "Tucker" Arnold	7
		Tommy Bamford	dnb	Stan Hayton	1*
		extras	5	extras	5
		Stan Hayton 1 for 61	154-2	Matt Oates 25 overs 4 for 54	151-9
			in the 47th over		off 50 overs
Sat 6th Aug	1949	Clifton CC "A"**		Dringhouses	
		Bert Brenen	16	Bruce Connell	2
		H.W.Harvey	6	Frank Tuersley	2
		Harold F.Hornshaw	11	Peter N.L.Terry	23
		Arthur Broadhurst	5	Alf Patrick	6
		K.S.Milne	28	Ted Outhwaite (Wkt.)	33
		Bill Roberts	2	John Lawson	0
		Jim Blackburn	15	Stan Fawcett	16
		Harry Craven	15*	Billy "Nucker" Brown	0
		George A.Edwards (Wkt.)	10 (0 on sheet)	Len Rodwell	7
		G.B.Lawson	24*	Tom "Tucker" Arnold (Capt.)	5
		Herbert Harrison (Capt.)	dnb	Stan Hayton	2*
		extras	12 (7 on sheet)	extras	6
		Billy Brown 21-3-52-4	144-9	Herbert Harrison 14.2-3-40-6	102 all out
		scorecard incorrect	off 50 overs		off 39.2 overs
Sat 12th Aug post	1950	Clifton Hospital**		Clifton CC	
several times		Alf A.Aveyard	43	H.W.Harvey	13
Sat 17th Sept rsp		Joe Littlewood	4	Bill Roberts	2
finished Sun 18th		Percy Poole	51	Harold F.Hornshaw	9
		Ronnie Freer	74*	Herbert Harrison (Capt.)	4
		Joe McConnon	0	M.Smith	21
		Arthur Nelson Taylor	9	Arthur Broadhurst	1
		Ivor Churchill (Capt.)	3	Brian Prest	6
		Tommy Robinson (Wkt.)	3	Jim S.Blackburn	20
		Stan Page	2*	Harry Craven	8
		Syd Appleyard	dnb	John R.F.Temple	11
		Len Freer	dnb	G.B.Lawson	2*
		extras	9	extras	2
		Brian Prest 2 for 33	198-7	Alf Aveyard 4 for 18	99 all out
		Herbert Harrison 2 for 48	off 50 overs	Syd Appleyard 4 for 46	off 37.3 overs

Sat 11th Aug post	1951	**Ovington****		**Stamford Bridge**		
Mon 13th & Tue		Ken Newton	14	Brian G.Wood	11	
14th Aug evenings		Jack Haxby	53	Frank Lindsay	3	
		G.Wright	0	Wally Pearson	30	
		Derek Ainley	10	Charlie E.Sherwood	34	
		Peter Mowbray	4	Tom Barton	2	
		Ted Coulson (Capt.)	0	Eric Pateman	4	
		Geoff Limbert	5	Jack Allison	2	
		Stan Bell	3	Wally Hallaways	5*	
		Brian Hanson	0	Philip M.Sawkill (Capt.)(Wkt.)	6	
		Gerry Pragnell (Wkt.)	15	Terry Barker	2	
		Brian Boyes	0*	Fred Sherwood	0	
		extras	6	extras	6	
		Jack Allison 20-4-46-7	110 all out	Derek Ainley 16.2-2-40-9	105 all out	
			off 39 overs		off 39.2	
Sat 9th Aug post	1952	**Dringhouses****		**York an XI**		
Wed 13th & Thurs		John Shaw	70	George Watson	3	
14th Aug evenings		John Lawson	9	Alf Nicholls	33	
reduced to 40 overs		Phil Dalby	30	John R.Bond	2	
per side		Derek Pattinson	2	Eddie Hibberson (Capt.)	1	
		Peter N.L.Terry	11	Reg Docking	37	
		Alf Patrick	26	Jack Pinder	15	
		Pete Knapton	12	Geoff Wilkinson	2	
		Stan Hayton	0	John Pitt	4	
		Stan Fawcett (Capt.)	7	Alan Barker	9	
		John Patrick (Wkt.)	0	Tony Wright (Wkt.)	4	
		Malcolm Blakey	0	H.Chignell	0	
		extras	15	extras	16	
		Geoff Wilkinson 10.5-0-35-5	182 all out	Stan Hayton 20-4-49-5	126-9	
		John Pitt 11-0-55-3	off 40 overs	Malcolm Blakey 20-1-61-3	off 40 overs	
Sat 8th Aug	1953	**Clifton Hospital**		**New Earswick****		
		Percy Poole	5	Lewis Barker	45	
		Alf A.Aveyard	69	Norman Coates	0	
		Len Freer	35	Herbert Freer	44	
		Les Pearson	9	W.E."Eric" Bryan	22	
		Joe Littlewood	0	Arthur Duckworth	0	
		Tommy Robinson (Wkt.)	6	Harold Anderson (Capt.)	13	
		Joe McConnon (Capt.)	26	Billy Walls (Wkt.)	2	
		Fred Oliver	13*	Bernard Goodhall	14	
		Stan C.Page	24*	Maurice Richards	19	
		Bob Carter Snr.	dnb	Wilf Anderson	16	
		Jimmy Hughes	dnb	Dick Wilks	15*	
		extras	12	extras	8	
		Herbert Freer 3 for 39	199-7	Joe Littlewood 4 for 64	198 all out	
			Off ? Overs	Bob Carter Snr. 3 for 61	off 45 overs	
Sat 7th Aug	1954	**Rowntrees****		**York an XI**		
part finished rsp		Reg Baines (Capt.)	3	Alf Nicholls	2	
finished on Monday		A.Wright	5	John R.Bond	13	
evening 16th Aug		Ken Lockwood	0	Frank Cawkill	0	
		John Raine	13	Charlie Boddy	8	
		John Fawcett	43	Bill Pearson	32	
		Vic Bedford (Wkt.)	4	John R.Richardson (Capt.)	13	
		Ken Moor	31	Mick Cockerill	2	
		Ken Robertson	18	Michael Storr	39*	
		Dennis Ramsey	6*	Geoff Wilkinson	5	
		Peter "Pip" Long	1*	Andrew Lodge (Wkt.)	3	
		Ted King	dnb	Terry Barker	0 (absent)	
		extras	7	extras	8	
		Bill Pearson 14-6-26-3	131-8	Ken Lockwood 19-6-43-3	125 all out	
			off 50 overs		off 49 overs	

Sat 6th Aug	1955	**Dringhouses****		**York an XI**	
		Pete Knapton	12	George Watson	46
		A."Bunny" Parker	52	John R. Bond	1
		Derek Pattison	6	Bert Brennen	2
		John Lawson	32	Alf Nicholls	4
		Alf Patrick	0	Eddie Hibberson	3
		Stan Hayton	0	John R. Richardson (Capt.)	22
		Stan Fawcett (Capt.)	16*	Mick Cockerill	11
		John Patrick (Wkt.)	0	Alwyne Yorke	5
		Frank Tuersley	8	Andrew Lodge (Wkt.)	9
		Laurie Thompson	1*	Geoff Wilkinson	15
		Freddie Smith	dnb	Alan Barker	0*
		extras	9	extras	11
		Alan Barker 17-3-41-4	136-8	Stan Hayton 18.2-4-32-4	129 all out
		Mick Cockerill 12-2-25-3	off 50 overs	Derek Pattison 14-1-55-4	off 44.2 overs
Sat 11th Aug	1956	**York an XI**		**Stamford Bridge****	
post to14th&15th		Michael Storr	10	Wally Pearson (Capt.)	23
then 16th & 17th		George Watson	35	Brian G.Wood	8
then 21st & 22nd		Norman Morse	39*	Norman Pearson	9
finished 4th sept		Mick Cockerill	0	Roy Lawson	46
reduced to 40 overs		Geoff Britton	6	Harvey Beaumont	6
per side		John R. Richardson (Capt.)	32	Don Walton	12
		John Falshaw	4*	Wally Hallways	0
		Bert Brennen (Wkt.)	dnb	Terry Barker	9
		Eddie Hibberson	dnb	Tom Barton	0
		Alan Barker	dnb	Claude Walton (Wkt.)	5
		Geoff Wilkinson	dnb	Des Burgess	2*
		extras	7	extras	12
		Des Burgess 2 for 36	133-5	Mike Cockerill 3 for 38	132 all out
		Terry Barker 2 for 50	in the 37th over	Geoff Wilkinson 3 for 39	in the 40th over
Sat 10th Aug	1957	**Magnets Sports Club****		**Ebor Gogues**	
post several times		Eric Cross	28	John Wagstaffe	24
played mon & tue		Ray Hardy	7	John Falshaw	10
26th & 27th Aug		Lance Conroy	13	M.West	0
35 overs each by		Clive Birdsall	5	Roy S.Nicholson	25
agreement		George Wilstrop	7	Bert Brennen (Capt.) (Wkt.)	24
		Dennis Firn (Capt.)	13	Ian Hallas	25
		Eric Stones (Wkt.)	7	George McClennan	2
		Basil Jewitt	35*	V.Purves	7
		Cyril Conroy	5	N.Dumachie	2
		W.Roseigh	8	R.Charnock	3*
		Stan Hall	9	A.Dickinson	0
		extras	18	extras	7
		Ian Hallas 5 for 60 from 17 overs	155 all out	Cyril Conroy 11-1-38-6	129 all out
		John Falshaw 3 wkts	in the 34th over		in the 35th over
Sat 9th Aug rsp	1958	**Woodhouse Grange****		**Rowntrees**	
WHG 250-8		George Shepherdson	26	Reg Baines	4
Rowntrees 46-2		Clive B. Kay	79	John Bond	63
finished mon 11th		Steve Megginson	1	John Pitt	1
		Alisdair Swann	44	George Watson	51
		Ted Outhwaite (Wkt.)	59	M.Watson	7
		Charlie Hall	6	Ken Lockwood	9
		Derek Nicholson	27	Harry Harvey	13
		Jack R.Knowles	3	Ted King	1
		Tommy H.Hobson (Capt.)	1*	Vic Bedford (Wkt.)	10
		Eddie Richardson	2*	Ken Moor (Capt.)	0
		Trevor N. Kay	dnb	Dennis Ramsey	1*
		extras	2	extras	8
		John Pitt 25-2-110-5	250-8	Steve Megginson 6-1-21-4	168 all out
		Ken Moor 9-0-52-3	off 50 overs	Geo. Shepherdson 8.5-1-29-3	off 42.5 overs

142

Thurs 30th July 1959

Tadcaster		New Earswick**	
Maurice Wade	7	Lewis Barker	29
Don Whitley	53	Pete Sedgwick	8
Eric Wallis	13	A.Dale	2
W.Morley	13	John Skilbeck	2
Barry Firn	dnb	Bernard Goodhall	1
Doug MacKay (Wkt.)	dnb	Norman Coates Snr.	13
Dennis Thirkill	dnb	Wilf Anderson	2
Norman Swinden	dnb	Pete Jerrum	5
Cyril Mason (Capt.)	dnb	Dick Wilks	4
Sam Lawrence	dnb	Norman Coates Jnr.	15*
Dave Swift	dnb	P.Wray	4
extras	4	extras	4
Dick Wilks 7-0-38-2	90-2	W.Morley 9-0-30-5	89 all out
	off 13.6 overs	Sam Lawrence 7-0-33-5	off 18 overs

18 eight ball overs each on one night no restrictions on bowlers

All rounds 18 x 8 each on one night no restrictions on bowlers

Thurs 28th July 1960

York Railway Institute**		Ebor Gogues	
Robbie Marchant	27	Alan Kenworthy	1
Tony Keel	18	Roy Walker	9
Norman Garland	1	Joe Valente	21
Peter Morritt	2	John Falshaw	14
Pete Taylor	9	Geoff Atkinson	11
Dick Powell	8	Roy S. Nicholson	4
Geoff N.Britton (Capt.)	12	Dave Blissett	26
John Bradley (Wkt.)	22*	Bert Brenen (Capt.)	13
Ken Marshall	2*	Ray Sutton	0
Clive Hendry	dnb	Danny Stephens	1*
Clive Kellett	dnb	Dave Firminger	0*
extras	2	extras	3
Danny Stephens 6-0-35-4	103-7	Clive Hendry 9-0-42-6	102-9
Alan Kenworthy 9-0-50-3	off 18 overs	Robbie Marchant 5-0-25-3	off 18 overs

Wed 26th July 1961

York Railway Institute		Heworth**	
Robbie Marchant	28	Joe Shaw	28
Tony Keel	1	Alf Nichols	1
Dick Powell	17	Alan Martindale	7
Norman Garland	14	Jerry Dunnington	6
Geoff N. Britton	5	David F.Miller	1
Peter Morritt	2	Dennis G.Martindale	0
Ken Marshall	2*	Tony Moore	1
Terry Adams (Wkt.)	1*	Ken Roscoe (Wkt.)	13*
John Bradley (Capt.)	dnb	Tommy Baram (Capt.)	5
Wilf Jackson	dnb	Dave Wilson	4
Clive Hendry	dnb	Terry Precious	1
extras	2	extras	4
Tony Moore 9-0-34-3	72-6	Clive Hendry 9-0-39-5	71 all out
	off the last ball of the 18th over	Wilf Jackson 9-1-26-4	off 18 overs

Friday 27th July 1962

Cawood		Dringhouses**	
Peter Wright	26	Derek Pattison	14
Eric Gibson (Capt.)	28	Norman Young	29
Brian Hall	21*	Alan Franks	8
Pete Braithwaite	6	Don Paver	31
Eddie Howcroft	18	Alf Patrick	3
Dave Kellett	3	Dave Burrows	3
Pat Brough	3	Brian Wilson (Wkt.)	5
Stan Warner (Wkt.)	2*	Roly Pattison	0
Garry Stead	dnb	Ray Varney	1
Ken Thompson	dnb	Stan Fawcett (Capt.)	0
Michael Elcock	dnb	Alan Burrows	0*
extras	3	extras	12
Alan Burrows 6-0-28-3	110-6	Pete Braithwaite 9-0-39-6	106 all out
Roly Pattison 9-0-60-3			off 18 overs

143

Thurs 25th July	1963	**Huntington WMC**		**York Railway Institute****		
		Sid Hepton	7	Tony Keel	9
		Peter Sedgwick	2	Robbie Marchant	32
		Stan Bell	14	Geoff N. Britton (Capt.)	4
		Lenny Watson	25*	Peter Morritt	0
		Derek Magson (Capt.)	9	Ken Marshall	2
		Frank Gibson (Wkt.)	0	Peter Taylor	6
		Mick Storr	9	Don Pringle	5
		Brian Baines	5*	Clive Hendry	4
		Ian Reed	dnb	Howard Lewis	2
		Ben Mitchell	dnb	Keith Crosby	6*
		Robert Sedgwick	dnb	Terry Adams (Wkt.)	3
		extras	14	extras	10
		Tony Keel 4 for 39	85-6	Ian Reed 7 for 31	83 all out
			off 17.5 overs	Frank Gibson 3ct & 1st	
Thurs 23rd July	1964	**Stillington****		**Civil Service**		
		Norman Morse	3	J.R."Dick" Shaw (Capt.)	0
		John Wyrill	23	David Stevenson	2
		Dennis North	11	Eric Stephenson	2
		Ray Midgley	27	Duncan Steel	1
		Alan Grainger	6	George Patterson	2
		Dave Spavin	1	Bill Shaw	46
		Keith Snell	4	Maurice Cram	10
		Malcolm Denton	8	John Gibb	6
		John Fowler (Wkt.)	0	Ian Davis	0
		Cecil Wood (Capt.)	3*	Pete Robinson	10
		Colin Minton	dnb	Alan Barker	0*
		extras	6	extras	4
		Duncan Steel 9-0-23-7	92-8	Malcolm Denton 9-0-26-6	83 all out
			off 18 overs		off 18 overs
Thurs 22nd July	1965	**Huntington WMC**		**York an XI****		
		John Skilbeck	8	Ray Murgatroyd	9
		Sid Hepton	50	Guy Raines (Capt.)	34
		Lenny Watson	14	Eric Chaplin	8
		Ian Reed	3	Noel Hare	15
		Mick Storr	16*	Dave Malbon	8
		Peter Glassby	3	Barry Temple	0
		Derek Magson (Capt.)	0*	Clive Robinson	5
		Fred Storr	dnb	Alan Garlick (Wkt.)	6*
		Jim Collis	dnb	Jonh R.F.Temple	0
		Frank Gibson (Wkt.)	dnb	John Teale	0
		Peter Foster	dnb	Robbie Skilbeck	0
		extras	4	extras	10
		Robbie Skilbeck 4.2-1-22-2	98-5	Jim Collis 5.3-1-24-5	95 all out
		Noel Hare 5-0-42-2	off 13.2 overs	Fred Storr 6-0-29-4	off 17.3 overs
Thurs 21st July	1966	**Dringhouses**		**Woodhouse Grange****		
		Derek Pattison	52	Peter Lynn	4
		Ray Varney	38	Tony Simpson	20
		George Myerscough	2	John Bygate	2
		Tony Stilgoe	9*	Alisdair Swann (Wkt.)	15
		Brian Myerscough	dnb	Nigel Fowler (Capt.)	13
		Pete Smales	dnb	Robert Atkin	18
		Brian Wilson (Wkt.)	dnb	Dennis Hornby	11*
		Dave Burrows	dnb	Jeff Pratt	4
		Roly Pattison	dnb	Fred Mason	3*
		Geoff Limbert (Capt.)	dnb	Terry Fountain	dnb
		Alan Burrows	dnb	Paul Lewis	dnb
		extras	4	extras	12
		Paul Lewis 2 for 31	105-3	Roly Pattison 4 for 54	102-7
			off 15 overs	Tony Stilgoe 1 for 36	off 18 overs

Thurs 20th July	1967	**Dringhouses****		Heworth	
		Derek Pattison	20	Alec Fyrth (Capt.)	7
		Andy Bulmer	18	Don Pringle	13
		Keith Cowl	4	Jerry Dunnington	11
		Tony Stilgoe	33	Geoff Powell	0
		Tony Moore	7	Chris Henderson	3
		Brian Wilson (Wkt.)	28	David F.Miller	8
		Dave Burrows	0	Barry Middleton	9
		Brian Myerscough	1	Dave Hall (Wkt.)	6
		George Myerscough	0*	Des Garness	7
		Geoff Limbert (Capt.)	dnb	Colin Armstrong	0
		Alan Burrows	dnb	Robert Toes	1*
		extras	10	extras	4
		Robert Toes 9-0-55-4	121-8	Tony Moore 7.4-0-23-6	69 all out
			off 18 overs	Tony Stilgoe 8-0-42-4	off 15.4 overs
Thurs 1st Aug	1968	**Easingwold**		**Dringhouses****	
		Val Toase	7	Derek Pattison	8
		William Bell	4	Ray Varney	7
		Dennis Hutchinson (Capt.)	39	Keith Cowl	8
		Stuart Burton	29	Andy Bulmer	1
		Jeff Robinson (Wkt.)	14	George Myerscough	25
		Pete Gilleard	5*	Dave Burrows	17
		Colin Minton	1*	Brian Wilson (Wkt.)	12*
		Geoff Skilbeck	dnb	Geoff Limbert (Capt.)	15*
		Ken Skilbeck	dnb	Peter Smales	dnb
		Colin Raper	dnb	Roly Pattison	dnb
		Peter King	dnb	Alan Burrows	dnb
		extras	5	extras	10
		Roly Pattison 9-1-46-2	104-5	Colin Minton 9-1-46-3	103-6
		and 3 run outs	off 17.4 Overs	Ken Skilbeck 9-0-47-3	off 18 overs
Thurs 24th July	1969	**York an XI (Nomads)**		**Easingwold****	
		Barry Temple (Wkt.)	32	Val Toase	0
		Robin Marchant	53*	David Curry	46
		David Hall	28	Dennis Hutchinson (Capt.)	21
		John Taylor	4	Stuart Burton	55*
		John Richardson	11*	Jeff Robinson (Wkt.)	5
		John Stillborn	dnb	Colin Raper	5*
		John Dickinson	dnb	Geoff Skilbeck	dnb
		Tony F.J. Temple (Capt.)	dnb	Bill Bell	dnb
		Dave Blissett	dnb	Pete Gilleard	dnb
		Ray Murgatroyd	dnb	Ken Skilbeck	dnb
		John Teale	dnb	Colin Minton	dnb
		extras	11	extras	3
		Geoff Skilbeck 4-0-25-1	139-3	John Stillborn 3-0-30-2	135-4
		Ken Skilbeck 5-0-27-1	off 16.5 overs		off 18 overs
Thurs 23rd July	1970	**Dringhouses**		**Dunnington****	
		Andy Bulmer	6	Pat Wood	0
		Alwyne Yorke	3	John Taylor	15
		George Myerscough	13	Dennis Milburn	24
		Keith Cowl (Capt.)	28	Sid Fisher	13
		Tony Stilgoe	8	Robin Smith	13
		Alan Fountain	27*	Bryan Nelson	24
		Dave Burrows	6	Dave Leeman (Capt. & Wkt.)	4
		Brian Wilson (Wkt.)	6*	Dave Bell	4
		Roly Pattison	dnb	Terry Weston	0
		Peter Smales	dnb	Brian Stacey	1
		Alan Burrows	dnb	Jim Robertson	0*
		extras	6	extras	4
		Brian Stacey 6.2-0-27-3	103-6	Tony Stilgoe 8.1-0-41-4	102 all out
			off 17.4 overs	Roly Pattison 7-1-39-3	off 17.1 overs

Thurs 22nd July	1971	**York an XI****		**Stamford Bridge**		
		Barry Temple (Wkt.)	10	Norman Pearson (Capt.)	23	
		Robbie Marchant	56*	John Beckett	6	
		Dave Hall	43	Roy Lawson	5	
		John Taylor	1	Dave Dixon	44	
		Nigel Henshall	4	Alan Jackson	23*	
		Jonathan Clarke	6	Jeff Vanham	2*	
		Tony F.J. Temple (Capt.)	4	Claude Walton (Wkt.)	dnb	
		Ray Murgatroyd	12*	Nigel West	dnb	
		Phil Crookes	dnb	Peter West	dnb	
		John Place	dnb	Jeff Bellamy	dnb	
		Paul Baines	dnb	Alan Walker	dnb	
		extras	6	extras	16	
		Pete West 9-0-65-3	142-6	Tony Temple 9-0-49-1	119-4	
			off 18 overs	John Taylor 9-0-53-1	off 18 overs	
Thurs 20th July	1972	**Easingwold****		**Sheriff Hutton Bridge**		
		Val Toase	70	Brian Shirley (Wkt.)	22	
		Stuart Burton	23	Bill Revis	3	
		Dennis Hutchinson (Capt.)	25	Keith Snell	0	
		Jeff Robinson (Wkt.)	0	Des Wyrill	1	
		Fred Cowling	6	Mick Oldfield	9	
		Colin Raper	5	Ken Magson	23	
		Ken Hudson	dnb	Wally Craven	2	
		Dominic Dziurzynski	dnb	Mick Harrison	3	
		Ken Skilbeck	dnb	Don Pringle (Capt.)	1	
		Geoff Skilbeck	dnb	Brian Poole	7*	
		Graham Inchboard	dnb	WilliamCowling	2*	
		extras	14	extras	6	
		Des Wyrill 9-0-50-2	143-5	Geoff Skilbeck 9-1-30-3	79-9	
		Mick Oldfield 7-0-62-2	off 18 overs	Ken Skilbeck 9-0-43-3	off 18 overs	
				plus 3 run outs		
Thurs 19th Aug	1973	**Huntington WMC****		**Sheriff Hutton Bridge**		
		Wally Baynes (Capt.)	0	Des Wyrill	8	
		Lenny Watson (Wkt.)	10	Bill Revis	8	
		Trevor Markham	42	Brian Shirley (Wkt.)	0	
		Ray Pudsey	1	Keith Snell	42	
		Brian Pudsey	6	Ken Magson	16	
		Barry Clancey	6	Wally Craven	3	
		Stan Whiting	7	Mick Oldfield	4	
		David Freeman	3	Brian Pool	1	
		Pete Timler	4	Don Pringle (Capt.)	1	
		Alan Baynes	1*	Sid Lusher	dnb	
		Derek Marshall	7	Albert Pattison	dnb	
		extras	3	extras	3	
		Mick Oldfield 5-0-22-3	90 all out	Pete Timler 9-0-38-4	86-7	
		Des Wyrill 8-0-44-3	off 17 overs		off 18 overs	
Thurs 24th July	1974	**Easingwold****		**Heworth**		
		Val Toase	6	Robert Turner	0	
		Stuart Burton	2	Chris Henderson	8	
		Dennis Hutchinson (Capt.)	31	Ken Johnson	0	
		Jeff Robinson (Wkt.)	25	Guy Raines	6	
		Geoff Skilbeck	0	Jerry Dunnington	10	
		Stuart Reynolds	15	Ian Reed	9	
		Graham Inchboard	2	John Fowler (Wkt.)	0	
		Colin Minton	0	Alec Fyrth (Capt.)	3	
		Bill Cowling	0	Pete M.Johnson	2	
		Ken Skilbeck	1	Colin Armstrong	8	
		Peter King	0*	Jim Collis	1	
		extras	4	extras	1	
		Colin Armstrong 8.5-1-32-5	86 all out	Colin Minton 7.3-1-27-6	48 all out	
		Jim Collis 9-1-50-3	off 17.5 overs	Ken Skilbeck 7-0-20-4	off 14.3 overs	

Thurs 24th July	1975	**Sheriff Hutton Bridge****			**Cawood**	
18 eight ball overs		Des Wyrill	67*		Dave Gibson	6
each on one night		Bill Revis	34		Eric Gibson	0
max 5 overs per		Ken Magson	18		Brian Hall	0
		Brian Shirley (Wkt.)	14		Dave Kellett (Capt.)	1
All rounds 18 x 8		Brian Nelson	3		Kev Lund	0
each on one night		Nigel Henshall	9		Ray Liddle	26*
max 5 overs per		Keith Snell	1		Peter Gibson	6
		Geoff Wyrill	dnb		Garry Stead	5
		Mick R.Oldfield (Capt.)	dnb		Ken Sayner	1
		Mick Jones	dnb		Michael Taylor (Wkt.)	1
		Roy Piercy	dnb		Nick Furniss	0
		extras	4		extras	1
		Dave Gibson 5-0-34-2	150-6		Roy Piercy 5-0-8-3	47 all out
			off 18 overs		Brian Shirley 3 St and 1 Ct	off 12.6 overs
Thurs 22nd July	1976	**Dunnington****			**Huntington WMC**	
		Pat Wood (Capt.)	19		Wally Baynes (Capt.)	11
		Terry Weston	53		Trevor Markham	39
		Doug Bartle	1		Lenny Watson	17
		Dennis Milburn	2		Brian Pudsey	10
		Dave Leeman (Wkt.)	7		Barry Clancey	13
		Steve Holden	44*		Derek Marshall	0
		Brian Stacey	4		Peter Timler	1
		Steve Whittaker	14*		Steve Sharpley	4
		Jim Robertson	dnb		Dave Clapham	0
		Ian Wilkinson	dnb		Pete Foster	7
		Robin Smith	dnb		Alan Baynes	2
		extras	12		extras	14
		Peter Timler 5-0-32-2	156-6		Robin Smith 3.6-0-18-6	118 all out
		Trevor Markham 5-0-35-2	off 18 overs		Pat Wood 5-0-28-3	off 16.6 overs
Thurs 21st July	1977	**York an XI**			**Tadcaster****	
		Alec Backhouse (Capt.)	1		Howard Conroy	52
		Robbie Marchant	42*		Ian Mackenzie	0
		Mal Pringle	3		Terry Downey	11
		Clive Robinson	51*		David Cornthwaite (Capt.)	1
		John Taylor	dnb		Derek Gilpin	14
		Alan Kenworthy	dnb		Dave Marsh	1
		Barry Temple	dnb		Barry Shann	1
		Ken Skilbeck	dnb		Ray Dowdall	14
		David Airey	dnb		Tony Stead	5
		Graham Orange (Wkt.)	dnb		Barry Emmott	0
		David Wreglesworth	dnb		Doug MacKay (Wkt.)	0*
		extras	11		extras	5
		Tony Stead 5-0-18-1	108-2		Dave Wreglesworth 2.6-0-8-4	104 all out
		David Marsh 5-0-28-1	off 16.4 overs		and 3 run outs	off 15.6 overs
Thurs 20th July	1978	**Sheriff Hutton Bridge****			**Cawood**	
		Des Wyrill	98*		Eddie Howcroft (Wkt.)	35
		Bill Revis	45		Dave Gibson	20
		Brian Shirley (Wkt.)	7		Brian Hall	23
		Alan Jackson	1		Dave Kellett	12
		Geoff Wyrill	1*		Eric Gibson (Capt.)	2
		John Hetherton	dnb		Peter Gibson	1
		Dennis Shipley	dnb		Ray Liddle	10*
		Colin Mole	dnb		Dave Thompson	5
		Mick R.Oldfield (Capt.)	dnb		Nigel Bartram	4
		Rob Littler	dnb		Nick Furniss	dnb
		Paul Graham	dnb		John Gibson	dnb
		extras	10		extras	19
		Nick Furniss 4-0-22-1	162-3		Dennis Shipley 5-0-32-4	141-7
		Eric Gibson 4-0-45-1	off 18 overs			off 18 overs

147

Date	Year	Team / Player	Score	Team / Player	Score
Thurs 19th July	1979	**Easingwold**		**Stamford Bridge****	
		Peter Gilleard (Capt.)	4	John Beckett	2
		Stuart Reynolds	53	Norman Pearson (Capt.)	0
		Geoff Skilbeck	12	John Dodds (Wkt.)	11
		Alan "Jack" Robinson	26*	Roy Lawson	47*
		Colin Minton	0*	John Flint	0
		Peter Sharpe	dnb	Graham Tipping	2
		Val Toase	dnb	Tony Wilcockson	1
		Fred Cowling (Wkt.)	dnb	Rod Burdett	1
		Martin Robinson	dnb	Pete West	16
		Ken Skilbeck	dnb	Nigel West	11*
		Ian Dobson	dnb	Unknown	dnb
		extras	7	extras	8
		Pete West 4.2-0-13-1	102-3	Colin Minton 5-0-24-3	99-8
		Nigel West 5-0-21-1	off 17.2 overs	Fred Cowling (Wkt.) 4 catches	off 18 overs
		Rod Burdett 4-0-25-1			
Thurs 24th July	1980	**York an XI**		**Woodhouse Grange****	
		Alec Backhouse (Capt.)	46	Mark Burton	?
		David Airey	36	Mike Stones	?
		Barry Temple (Wkt.)	?	John Driver	?
		Kevin Huddart	?	Russ Bilton	?
		Graham Cooper	?	Steve Johnson	?
		Bill Boddycombe	dnb	Kev Davidson	48
		Mal Pringle	dnb	Tom Mitchell (Wkt.)	?
		Keith Snell	dnb	Mike Stothard	11
		Dave Cornthwaite	dnb	Alisdair Swann (Capt.)	?*
		Phil Crookes	dnb	Peter Nolton	?*
		Dave Wreglesworth	dnb	Fred Mason	dnb
		extras		extras	
		Mike Stothard 1 wkt	118-3	Dave Cornthwaite 4-0-29-3	117-8
			Off ? Overs	Dave Wreglesworth 5-0-11-2	off 18 overs
Mon 27th July	1981	**Sessay**		**Acomb****	
		John Flintoff (Capt.)	81*	Dick Sykes	10
		Dave Harrison	21	Dave Tute	16
		Bruce Jackson	19*	Billy Carter (Capt.& Wkt.)	0
		Fred Till	dnb	John Webster	42
		David Langstaff (Wkt.)	dnb	Mal Pepper	12
		Mervyn Duffield	dnb	Joe Baxter	11
		Tom Richardson	dnb	Tony Haines	7
		Ian Till	dnb	Bob Graves	17
		James Till	dnb	George Patterson	1
		Richard Cawkill	dnb	Brian Burton	dnb
		Roy Jackson	dnb	Tony Hinder	dnb
		extras	9	extras	12
		Tony Haines 5-0-41-1	130-1	John Flintoff 5-0-26-4	128-7
			off 16 overs		off 18 overs
Thurs 22nd July	1982	**Easingwold****		**Heworth**	
		Keith M.Hollinrake (Wkt.)	2	Mick Hammerton	3
		Peter Gilleard	34	Dick Whaley	22
		Stuart Reynolds (Capt.)	33	Dave Wood	43
		Pete Sharp	9	Steve Young	47
		Martin Robinson	53	Ken Johnson	0
		Geoff Skilbeck	19	Steve Precious	8
		Alan "Jack" Robinson	0*	Ian Reed (Capt.)	0
		Ian Dobson	1	John Fowler (Wkt.)	19*
		Ken Skilbeck	dnb	Pete M. Johnson	0*
		Val Toase	dnb	Colin Markham	dnb
		Stuart Burton	dnb	Mick Cross	dnb
		extras	21	extras	16
		Steve Young 4-0-39-2	172-7	Alan Robinson 3-0-33-2	158-7
		and 3 run outs	off 18 overs		off 18 overs

148

Thurs 21st July	1983	**Acomb****			**Stamford Bridge**	
		Dave Tute	6		Norman Pearson (Capt.)	54
		Dick Sykes	70*		John Beckett	11
		Chris Simpson	44		John Flint	9
		Mike Robinson	21*		Alan Jackson	2
		Dave Robinson	dnb		John Dodd (Wkt.)	3
		Mal Pepper	dnb		Graham Tipping	0
		Andy Leaning	dnb		Roy Lawson	10
		Billy Carter (Wkt.) (Capt.)	dnb		Nigel West	0
		Tony Haines	dnb		Jeff Pratt	7*
		Bob Graves	dnb		Colin Brown	6*
		Andy Thrall	dnb		Tim Swales	dnb
		extras	7		extras	20
		Graham Tipping 4-0-30-1	148-2		Tony Haines 5-0-17-4	122-8
		John Flint 4-0-31-1	off 18 overs			off 18 overs
Thurs 19th July	1984	**Heworth**			**Acomb****	
		Steve Taylor	42		Bob Graves	49
		Mick Hammerton	52		Chris Simpson	35
		Dave Wood	1		Dave Tute	44
		Ian Wilson	25		Dick Sykes (Capt.)	4
		Ken Johnson	2		Mike Robinson	12*
		Steve Precious	1		Mal Pepper	dnb
		Steve Young	2		Billy Carter (Wkt.)	dnb
		Kev Wilson	2		Dave Robinson	dnb
		Paul Miles (Wkt.)	13		Tony Hinder	dnb
		Neil Armstrong	0*		Rich Clayton	dnb
		Ian Reed (Capt.)	4*		Andy Thrall	dnb
		extras	16		extras	12
		Dick Sykes 4-0-44-3	160-9		Ian Reed 5-0-23-1	156-4
		and 4 run outs	off 17.3 overs		Neil Armstrong 5-1-43-1	off 18 overs
					Steve Young 5-0-49-1	
Thurs 18th July	1985	**Crayke****	Crayke Wkt.		**Sessay**	Sessay Wkt.
		Andy Gilleard (Capt.)	87		John Flintoff	0
		Dennis Hutchinson	25		Bruce Jackson	5
		Norman Pipes	12		David Kay	7
		Ian Warriner	3*		David Barker	35
		Andrew Dawson	0		Jim Till	35
		Jon Wright	1*		Richard Cawkill	13
		Roger Hutchinson	dnb		Fred Till	2
		Mike Dawson (Wkt.)	dnb		Philip Hodgson	11*
		Paul Barton	dnb		Howard Clayton	1
		Simon Gilleard	dnb		David Langstaff (Capt.) (Wkt.)	0
		Michael Pipes	dnb		Martin Palliser	1*
		extras	8		extras	13
		John Flintoff 4-0-17-2	136-4		Michael Pipes 5-0-20-3	123-9
		Fred Till 2-0-32-2	off 18 overs			off 18 overs
Thurs 17th July	1986	**Osbaldwick****			**Heworth**	
		Chris Hammerton	59		Paul Mosey	14
		Mick Hammerton	3		Dave Simpson	0
		Neil Johnson	15		Trevor Ward	1
		Jon Simpson	32		Steve Precious	40
		Danny Rippon	0		Dave Wood	0
		Mark Ridsdale	10		Kev Wilson	8
		Marcus Hollis	4*		Mal Caddie	1
		Dave Rippon (Capt.) (Wkt.)	3*		Paul Miles (Wkt.)	21
		Dave Cooper	dnb		Ian Reed (Capt.)	16
		Dave Kettlestring	dnb		Pete Machin	1*
		Steve Machen	dnb		Graham Cooper	8
		extras	9		extras	14
		Pete Machin 5-0-31-2	135-6		Jon Simpson 5-0-31-4	124 all out
		and 3 run outs	off 18 overs		Marcus Hollis 3-0-27-3	off 17.6 overs
					and 3 run outs	

149

Thurs 16th July	1987	**York an XI****		Heworth	
		Paul Jackson (Capt.)	12	Mal Caddie	30
		Glenn Breusch	24	Dave Simpson	14
		Dave Tompkins	46	Tony Simpson	4
		Richard Nutall	5	Ken Johnson (Capt.)	6
		Andrew Wright	4	Nigel Briggs	4
		Nigel Bartram	8*	Kev Wilson	12
		Dick Brewster	10	Steve Simpson	14
		Julian Hughes (Wkt.)	5*	John Fowler (Wkt.)	3*
		Mark Shillito	dnb	Neil Armstrong	11
		Keith Snell	dnb	Trevor Walton	dnb
		Ian Edwards	dnb	Jerry Dunnington	dnb
		extras	11	extras	2
		Trevor Walton 5-0-36-3	125-6	Ian Edwards 5-0-18-2	100-8
			off 18 overs	Mark Shillito 4-0-30-2	off 18 overs
				and 3 run outs	
Tues 19th July	1988	**Thorp Arch & Boston Spa****		Heworth	
		Steve Lawrence	61*	Nigel Briggs	1
		Will Robinson	55	Dave Simpson	6
		Jedd Lees	0	Mal Caddie	6
		Stephen Booth (Capt.)	1	Tony Simpson	31
		Tommy Kilby	5	John Fowler (Wkt.)	3
		Mick McKay	0	Ken Johnson (Capt.)	2
		Robin Lataster	dnb	Steve Simpson	30
		David Storr	dnb	David Freeman	7
		Mike Scholey	dnb	Pete Machin	15*
		Nigel Durham (Wkt.)		Graham Morritt	dnb
		Steve Pick		Trevor Walton	dnb
		extras	9	extras	9
		Pete Machin 5-0-26-2	131-5	Steve Lawrence 5-0-37-3	110-8
		Trevor Walton 4-0-38-2	off 18 overs	Nigel Durham 2ct & 1stumped	off 18 overs
Thurs 13th July	1989	**Woodhouse Grange**		**Acomb****	
		Paul Mosey	67*	Robert Turner	7
		Stuart Craven	15	Dick Sykes (Capt.) (Wkt.)	1
		Simon Gill	9*	Joey Burton	8
		Colin Johnson	dnb	Rich Clayton	26
		Ian Wilson	dnb	Nick Crowther	5
		Steve Young	dnb	Rob Murray	29
		Dick Whaley (Capt.)	dnb	John Webster	3
		Mike Newhouse	dnb	Gary Woodworth	5
		Rich Burdett (Wkt.)	dnb	Bob Graves	3*
		Steve Johnson	dnb	Tony Haines	2*
		Graham Cooper	dnb	Brian Stow	
		extras	14	extras	15
		Brian Stow 5-3-4-1	105-1	Mike Newhouse 4-0-26-2	104-8
			off 16 overs	and 3 run outs	off 18 overs
Tues 24th July	1990	**Woodhouse Grange**		**Heworth****	
		Paul Mosey	2	Mick Hammerton	19
		Stuart Craven	7	Dave Simpson (Capt.)	13
		Simon Gill (Capt.)	14	Steve Simpson	6
		Ian Wilson	6	Ken Johnson	13
		Steve Young	1	Jonathan Bean	2
		Steve Johnson	42*	Andy Ward	16
		Russ Bilton	5	Tony Moore	8
		Mike Burdett	6*	Paul Miles (Wkt.)	5
		Dave Gilbertson (Wkt.)	dnb	Jason Gatus	8*
		Mike Newhouse	dnb	Pete Machin	2
		Graham Cooper	dnb	Trevor Walton	0
		extras	13	extras	3
		Pete Machin 5-0-11-2	96-6	Mike Newhouse 4-0-22-5	95 all out
		Steve Simpson 5-1-13-2	off the last ball		off 18 overs
		Paul Miles (Wkt.) 3 catches			

Thurs 18th July	1991	**Heworth****		**Woodhouse Grange**	
		Dave Gibson	0	Paul Mosey	9
		Dave Simpson (Capt.)	27	Stuart Craven	22
		Rick Moglia	38	Mike Burdett (Wkt.)	11
		Steve Simpson	43*	Simon Gill (Capt.)	11
		Jonathan Bean	1	Ian Wilson	2
		Jason Gatus	4*	Steve Young	0
		Paul Miles (Wkt.)	dnb	Steve Johnson	22*
		Pete Machin	dnb	Pete Head	14
		Martin Sigsworth	dnb	Mike Newhouse	9*
		Trevor Walton	dnb	Russ Bilton	dnb
		Mark Bell	dnb	Brian Stow	dnb
		extras	3	extras	13
		Steve Johnson 5-0-21-1	116-4	Steve Simpson 4-0-29-3	113-7
		Brian Stow 4-0-27-1	off 17.3 overs	Martin Sigsworth 4-032-3	off 18 overs
Thurs 16th July	1992	**Pocklington****		**Heworth**	
		Paul Jackson	55	Jonathan Bean	12
		Andy Inns	17	Dave Simpson (Capt.)	29
		Matthew Atkinson (Wkt.)	12	Steve Simpson	9
		Kevin Hinch	5	Jason Gatus	1
		Kevin Smith (Capt.)	1	Dave Gibson	12
		Martyn Nesom	16*	Rick Moglia	5
		Dick Wright	12*	Paul Miles (Wkt.)	11
		Barry Pearson	dnb	Graham Hogben	4
		Phil Stephenson	dnb	Mark Bell	3
		Steve Lyus	dnb	Graham Morritt	4*
		Richard Foster	dnb	Trevor Walton	0
		extras	4	extras	8
			122-5		98 all out
		Trevor Walton 4-0-36-2	off 18 overs	Kevin Hinch 3.6-0-19-3	off 16.6 overs
				Kevin Smith 3-0-24-2	
				and 3 run outs	
Thurs 22nd July	1993	**Heworth****		**Easingwold**	
		Des Wyrill	7	Martin Robinson	25
		Jonathan Bean	27	Andrew Dawson	33
		Chris Mead	52*	Keith M.Hollinrake	5
		Steve Simpson	9	Geoff Skilbeck	5
		John Corcoran	12	Alan "Jack" Robinson (Capt.)	32
		Jason Gatus	1	Ian Dobson	12
		Paul Miles (Wkt.)	8*	Paul Redshaw	3
		Martin Sigsworth	dnb	Paul Moore	4*
		Mark Bell	dnb	Ronnie Alexander	dnb
		Trevor Walton (Capt.)	dnb	Kevin P. Hollinrake (Wkt.)	dnb
		Graham Hogben	dnb	Paul Skilbeck	dnb
		extras	13	extras	9
		Martin Robinson 5-0-32-2	129-5	Steve Simpson 5-0-33-3	128-7
			off 18 overs		of 18 overs

151

The column "BO" lists the batting order in the 2nd innings where it varies from the 1st.

	Year	Winner	1st inn	2nd inn	BO	Runner-up	1st inn	2nd inn	BO
		The two innings finals 1994-2007							
Date and format	Year	Winner	1st inn	2nd inn	BO	Runner-up	1st inn	2nd inn	BO
Sun 21st August	1994	**Sessay**				**Woodhouse Grange****			
2 innings each		Dwane Atkinson (Wkt.)	36	4	2	Stuart Craven	23	33	
16x8 ball overs		John Flintoff	13	18	10	Simon Gill (Capt)	6	37	
4 overs max		Neil Lawson	1	34	3	Paul Mosey	62*	2	
per bowler		Richard Till	32	25	6	Tim Clark	5	0	
		Dan Copeland	19	19	5	Mike Burdett (Wkt.)	48*	0	
		Philip Hodgson	2	3	7	Steve Young	dnb	9	
All rounds 16x8		Darren W. Atkinson	21*	6	4	Roger Johnston	dnb	34*	
ball overs each		Keith Till	4*	0	8	Steve Burdett	dnb	0	
on one night		Richard Wentworth (Capt.)	dnb	13*	11	Russ Bilton	dnb	1	
max 5 per bowler		Richard Duffield	dnb	13*	9	Peter Head	dnb	3*	
		Matthew Till	dnb	1	1	Brian Stow	dnb	dnb	
		extras	14	9		extras	11	12	
		1st Inn Brian Stow 4-0-28-2	142-6	145-9		1st Inn Matt Till 4-0-27-2	155-3	131-8	
		2nd Inn S.Burdett 4-0-28-2	16 ov	16 ov		2nd Inn Matt Till 4-0-11-2	16 ov	16 ov	
		Pete Head 4-0-45-2 and 3 run				Richard Till 4-0-32-2			
		outs				Keith Till 4-0-33-2			
Sun 6th August	1995	**Acomb**				**Dunnington****			
		Chris Simpson		27		Harwood Williams		82*	
		Dick Sykes (Capt.)				Dave Simpson			
		Joey Burton				Junior Mitchum	65		
		Rob Littlewood	34	18		Darren Avey			
		Nick Crowther		64*		Jonathan Simpson			
		James Byford				Steve Simpson			
		Andy Hough				Steve Precious (Capt.)			
		Rob Murray				Mal Pepper			
		Billy Carter (Wkt.)				Neil Smallwood (Wkt.)			
		Glynn Botterill				Dave Greening			
		Dave Sykes				Mark Graves			
		extras				extras			
		1st Inn S. Precious 2 for 14	113-5	139-4		1st inn Dave Sykes 2 for 38	127-5	122-5	
		2nd Inn S.Precious 2 for 13	16 ov	? ov		2nd Inn G.Botterill 4-0-10-3	16 ov	16 ov	
Sun 18th Aug	1996	**Woodhouse Grange****				**Heworth**			
		Colin Johnson				Rick Moglia		30	
		Stuart Craven	30	60		Paul Mosey	35		
		Jonathan Bean				Guy Wilkinson	46		
		Mike Burdett (Wkt.)	39	39		Dave Bowling			
		Steve Burdet				Chris Mead		21	
		Mark Burton (Capt.)				Jason Gatus			
		Russ Bilton				Ian Lynch			
		Paul Mouncey				Mark Lynch (Wkt.)			
		Richard Burdett				Mark Bell			
		Peter Head				Martin E. Sigsworth (Capt.)			
		Steve Young				Trevor Walton			
		extras				extras			
			121-6	116-4			113-4	115-9	
			16 ov	16 ov			16 ov	16 ov	
		2nd Inn Mark Bell 2 wkts				2nd Inn P.Mouncey 6 for 26			

152

Sun 10th Aug	1997	**Heworth**				**Easingwold****			
		Kieran Powar	43	11		Martyn Piercy	9	12	
		Paul Mosey	14	24		Keith M.Hollinrake (Capt.)	31	1	
		Tom Archer	7	0		Paul Skilbeck	0	0	
		Dave Bowling	13	17		Tommy N.Darnell	3	1	
		Chris Mead	10	8		Darren Wass	4	13	
		Ian Lynch	6*	2		Paul Spence	7	25	
		Graham Hogben	1*	2		Dan Copeland	8	10	
		Mark Lynch (Wkt.)	dnb	18*		Alan "Jack" Robinson	12	49*	
		Mark Bell	dnb	1*		Paul T. Redshaw	3*	0*	
		Martin E. Sigsworth (Capt.)	dnb	dnb		Jason Sargent	3*	dnb	
		Trevor Walton	dnb	dnb		Kevin P. Hollinrake (Wkt.)	dnb	dnb	
		extras	22	10		extras	5	11	
		1st inn DanCopeland 2-0-9-2	116-5	93-7		1st inn Trev Walton 4-0-23-4	85-8	122-7	
		Paul Redshaw 4-0-24-2	16 ov	15.5 ov		2nd inn Mark Bell 4-0-14-2	16 ov	16 ov	
		2nd inn Paul Spence 4-0-23-2				Kieran Powar 4-0-19-2			
						MartinSigsworth 4-0-41-2			

Sun 2nd Aug	1998	**Thirsk**				**Clifton Alliance****			
		Andrew D. Hawke	39	0	1	Dave Taylor	0	18	
		Neil Stephenson	35	12	2	Joel Southam	16	4	
		Dave Greenlay (Capt.)	53	25	3	Darren Barton	7	6	
		Peter Kent	24*	2	4	Duncan Naylor (Capt.)	48	9	
		Des Wyrill	17*	9*	5	John Hunter	6	15	
		Simon Barton	dnb	dnb	7	Simon Dwyer	28	15	
		James Trueman	dnb	dnb	8	Peter Hunter	6*	15	
		Phil Curtis	dnb	dnb	9	Jon Bladen	dnb	5	
		Barry D.Petty	dnb	7*	6	Mick Knowles	dnb	7*	
		John Harper (Wkt.)	dnb	dnb	10	Simon Corley (Wkt.)	dnb	8	
		Josh Greenlay	dnb	dnb	11	Mick Pickering	dnb	8*	
		extras	9	10		extras	10	9	
		1st inn John Hunter 4-0-36-2	177-3	65-4		1st inn Barry Petty 4-0-17-2	121-6	119-9	
		2nd inn J.Hunter 3.6-0-18-2	16 ov	14.6 ov		2nd inn Barry Petty 4-0-9-3	16 ov	16 ov	
						Dave Greenlay 4-0-25-3			

Sun 1st Aug	1999	**Clifton Alliance****				**Thirsk**			
		Dave Taylor (Wkt.)	13	1	1	Chris Paul	1	51	4
		Ben Higgins	114*	57	2	Andrew D. Hawke	9	7	1
		John Hunter	28	dnb		Neil Stephenson	47	12	3
		Duncan Naylor (Capt.)	7	18	4	John Harper	58	4	5
		Darren Barton	11*	27*	5	Chris Hooper	0	4	6
		Dave Russell	dnb	5	6	Des Wyrill	5	19	2
		James Postill	dnb	6*	7	James Almond	0	0	7
		Simon Dwyer	dnb	22	3	Michael Megson (Wkt.)	dnb	4*	9
		Mick Knowles	dnb	dnb	8	Dave Greenlay (Capt.)	dnb	6	8
		Jon Bladen	dnb	dnb	9	Martin Harper	dnb	dnb	10
		Mick Pickering	dnb	dnb	10	Johnathan Kendall	dnb	dnb	11
		extras	29	13	11	extras	11	20	
		1st inn D.Greenlay 4-0-61-2	202-3	149-5		1st inn J.Postill 4-1-18-1	131-5	127-8	
		2nd inn D.Greenlay 4-0-35-2	16 ov	16 ov		J.Hunter, M.Knowles and	16 ov	16 ov	
						M.Pickering 1 wkt each			
						2nd inn Jon Bladen 4-0-21-3			

153

Sun 6th Aug 2000

Thirsk**				Easingwold			
Lincoln R. McCrae	10	16	2	Martyn Piercy	1	45	6
Andrew D.Hawke	18	66	1	Matthew Schenke	0	9	2
Dave Greenlay (Capt.)	7	20	3	Jonathan Marwood	0	30	3
Neil Stephenson	17	9	5	Martin J. Robinson	53	9	1
Des Wyrill	57*	15*	4	Tommy N. Darnell	7	3	5
Phil Marwood	9*	3	7	Paul Skilbeck	18	7	4
John Harper (Wkt.)	dnb	8	6	Dan Copeland	0	34	7
Jodie Robson	dnb	4*	8	Alan Robinson	0	1	8
Barry D.Petty	dnb	dnb	9	Paul T.Redshaw	4	dnb	9
Matthew Cressey	dnb	dnb	10	Adrian Leckenby	0	dnb	10
Dean Bramney	dnb	dnb	11	Jason Sargent	0	dnb	11
extras	7	11		extras	16	10	
1st inn J.Sargent 4-0-19-3	125-4	152-6		1st inn L.McCrae 3.7-0-26-3	99 ao	148-6	
2nd Inn M.Schenke 3-0-39-3	16 ov	16 ov		Barry D.Petty 4-0-10-2	15.7 ov	16 ov	
Jason Sargent 4-0-39-2				2nd Inn L.McCrae 4-0-47-2			

Sun 5th Aug 2001

Clifton Alliance**				Acomb		
Darren Reeves (Wkt.1st inn)	40	61	1	Chris Simpson	36	16
James Postill	0	0	6	Duminda D.R.Perera	13	17
Simon Dwyer	43	36	3	Andy Tute	14	2
Dave Taylor	2	0	2	Paul Hemmingway	3	8
John Hunter	18	2	5	Dick Sykes	13	30
Darren Barton	23	7	4	James Byford	1	30
Richard Hunter	0	2*	9	Dave Sykes (Capt.)	10	7
Simon Corley	4*	dnb	10	Matt Dickinson	12*	18*
Duncan Naylor (Capt.)	0	10	7	Andy Ingle	2*	1*
Dave Russell (Wkt. 2nd inn)	1*	9*	8	Andy Ward (Wkt.)	dnb	dnb
Mick Knowles	dnb	dnb	11	Steve Buckton	dnb	dnb
extras	11	12		extras	12	14
1st inn Andy Tute 4-0-26-5	142-8	139-7		1st inn John Hunter 4-0-26-3	116-7	143-7
2nd inn Dick Sykes 3-0-30-2	16 ov	16 ov		Darren Reeves 1ct & 2st	16 ov	16 ov
				2nd inn James Postill 4-1-12-2		
				Darren Reeves 2-0-25-2 +3ct		

Sun 4th Aug rsp 2002

Osbaldwick (won on run rate)			Heworth**			
Steve Jackson	74*	dnb	Richard Bowling	3	1*	9
Rich Carew	27	dnb	Dave Simpson	25	58	4
Ian Wilson (Wkt.)	33*	dnb	Michael Brooke	18	48	5
Steve J.Young (Capt.)	dnb	dnb	Shahid Khan	1	3	2
Dave Cooper	dnb	dnb	Chris Mead (Wkt.)	7	2	7
Gawaine Hogg	dnb	dnb	Tom Quinn	17*	0	8
Damien Aston	dnb	dnb	Guy Wilkinson	7	6	1
Simon Powdrill	dnb	dnb	Paul Mosey (Capt.)	15*	11	3
Simon Levison	dnb	dnb	Kashif Mahmood	dnb	3	6
Matt Thompson	dnb	dnb	Mark Bell	dnb	dnb	
Dave Thompson	dnb	dnb	Andy Bonarius	dnb	dnb	
extras	10		extras	23	18	
1st inn G.Wilkinson 4-0-27-1	144-1	rsp	1st inn G.Hogg 4-0-31-3	116-6	150-8	
	16 ov		2nd inn G.Hogg 3-0-24-3	16 ov	14 ov	
					rsp	

Sun 3rd Aug 2003 — Acomb** vs Woodhouse Grange

Acomb**				Woodhouse Grange			
Sanjay Rodrigo	68*	32		Kamran Sajid	14	32	1
Andy Tute	60	51		Nick Hadfield	55*	11	2
Dick Sykes (Wkt.)	13	2		Howard Johnson	10	16	3
Paul Hemingway	1*	31*		Steve Burdett (Capt.)	38	58*	4
Matt Dickenson	dnb	19*		Tom Quinn	6	18*	6
Scott Nichols	dnb	dnb		Rich Steele (Wkt.)	0*	5	5
Andy Sykes	dnb	dnb		Jonathan Bean	dnb	dnb	
James Byford	dnb	dnb		Dudley Cooper	dnb	dnb	
Richard Allman	dnb	dnb		Graham Smith	dnb	dnb	
Dave Sykes (Capt.)	dnb	dnb		Paul Grewer	dnb	dnb	
Tim Merrick	dnb	dnb		Ashley Quinn	dnb	dnb	
extras	15	3		extras	11	10	
1st inns S.Burdett 2-0-27-1	157-2	138-3		1st Inns J.Byford 4-0-35-2	134-4	150-4	
2nd Inns K.Sajid 4-032-2	16 ov	16 ov		2nd Inns D.Sykes 4-0-18-1	16 ov	16 ov	

Sun 8th Aug 2004 — York** vs Clifton Alliance

York**				Clifton Alliance			
Stephen Piercy	62	8	1	Dave Taylor (Wkt.)	9	9	1
Simon Mason	6	35	2	Lorenzo Ingram	9	2	2
Nick Kay (Capt.)	3	54	3	James Postill	8	68	3
Andrew Kay	74	5	4	John Hunter	12	11	4
James Pringle	4*	8	7	John Myers	28	25	5
Duncan Snell	1*	21	5	John Gilham	30	17*	6
Dan Broadbent	dnb	4 ret h	6	Jon Bladen	5	1	8
Will Warne	dnb	dnb	9	Richard Hunter	5	2*	9
Nigel Durham (Wkt.)	dnb	dnb	10	John Thornton	7	22	7
Riley O'Neill	dnb	dnb	11	Johnny Stevens (Capt.)	1*	dnb	10
Rob Flack	dnb	1*	8	Alex Renton	1	dnb	11
extras	19	6		extras	9	10	
1st inn John Hunter 4-0-16-1	169-4	142-6		1st inn Riley O'Neill 4-0-36-4	124 ao	167-7	
2nd inn L.Ingram 4-0-22-3	16 ov	16 ov		2nd inn Riley O'Neill 4-0-28-1	15.5 ov	16 ov	
				and 4 run outs			

Sun 7th Aug 2005 — York** vs Clifton Alliance

York**				Clifton Alliance			
Nick Thornicroft	21	14	1	Daniel Harris (Capt.)	83	21	1
Michael Sheedy	26	0	2	Dave Taylor	5	8	2
Dan Broadbent	22	2	8	Richard F.T.Musgrave	41	6	3
Nick Kay (Capt.)	44	67	6	Chris Malthouse (Wkt.)	4	32	4
Duncan Snell	27	18	5	John Hunter	7	9	5
Andrew Kay	16	12	7	James Postill	13	17	6
Jason English	6*	26	4	John Gilham	5*	dnb	
Tom Bartram	0	9	9	John Thornton	0	dnb	
Brendan Ledgway	0	2*	10	Johnny Stevens	0	18*	7
Mike Mortimer	7	25	3	Paul Walton	0*	9*	8
Nigel Durham (Wkt.)	0*	7*	11	Alex Renton	dnb	dnb	
extras	13	11		extras	5	10	
1st inn R.Musgrave 3-0-28-3	182-9	186-9		1st inn D.Snell 4-0-29-2	163-8	130-6	
Chris Malthouse 4 stumped	16 ov	16 ov		2nd inn Broadbent 4-0-33-3	16 ov	16 ov	
2nd inn J.Hunter 4-0-31-4				Nigel Durham 1ct & 2 st			
Chris Malthouse 1 stumped							

Sun 6th Aug	2006	**York**				**Clifton Alliance****			
		Stephen Piercy	28	dnb		John Myers	52	5	2
		Dan Broadbent	2	dnb		John Gilham	16	4	1
		Duncan Snell	72*	dnb		John Hunter	7	21	3
		Nick Kay (Capt.)	42	dnb		James Postill (Capt.)	15	4	4
		Jason English	43*	dnb		Paul Boraston	21	2	5
		Tom Bartram	dnb	12*	4	Darren Barton	12	32	6
		Dan Wilson	dnb	5	1	Paul Walton	5	8	7
		Ben Hough	dnb	4	3	John Thornton	3	2	9
		Mark Bell	dnb	dnb		Nathan Briggs	3	10	8
		Alex Collins	dnb	25*	2	Alex Renton	1*	7	10
		Nigel Durham (Wkt.)	dnb	dnb		Johnny Stevens (Wkt.)	1	0*	11
		extras	16	4		extras	14	4	
		1st inn Alex Renton 4-0-44-2	203-3	50-2		1st inn Nick Kay 4-0-27-3	150 ao	99 ao	
			16 ov	5.2 ov		and 3 run outs	16 ov	15.4 ov	
		2nd inn Alex Renton 2-0-11-2				2nd inn Mark Bell 3.4-0-29-4			
						Nigel Durham 2st 1 ct			
	2007	**Woodhouse Grange**				**Clifton Alliance**			
		Nick Hadfield				James Packman			
		Jonathan Bean				Richard Musgrave			
		Andrew Bilton				Chris Malthouse			
		Steve Burdett (Capt.)				John Hunter (Capt.)			
		Mike Burdett (Wkt.)				Darren Barton			
		Paul Grewer				James Postill			
		Simon Dwyer				Danny White			
		Joel Hughes				John Gilham			
		Tom Quinn				Simon Corley (Wkt.)			
		Dave Suddaby				Alex Renton			
		Andrew Anderson				Barry Sayer			
		extras				extras			
		Woodhouse won, both score-books are lost and no press report can be found.							
		** batted first							

Chapter Ten

The other local competitions.

This final chapter details winners and in some cases runners-up, where known of other local knock-out cricket competitions. Also included are some brief details of the origin and format if known. Most of these competitions were run by local clubs and as with the Myers & Burnell no systematic records appear to have been kept. The information has been gathered from the trophies themselves where available, the recollections of club members and snippets picked up from the archives at the British Library at Boston Spa while researching the Myers & Burnell. As a result there is much less detail in this chapter, but I felt it was important to record as many competitions as possible before they become forgotten.

The two local competitions that are well documented are the Senior and Junior Charity Cups. The Charity Cups Committee kept detailed records of both competitions from their beginnings in 1930 until their demise in 2014 and later lodged the entire archive in York Library. The archive contains a wealth of information, with comprehensive results for most years and some fascinating correspondence relating to the administration of the competitions and the distribution of the proceeds. It is available to view on request and well worth a look at for anyone with an interest in local cricket.

As with the chapters relating to the Myers & Burnell many details are missing and some may be inaccurate so any further information would be gratefully received.

There are some competitions for which I have found insufficient information to provide a worthwhile summary amongst which are; The Pocklington Shield, the Major Walker and Sundella Cups at Malton, the C.I.U. Cup, the Derek Magson and Hallas Cups at Huntington and the Frank Piercy at Sheriff Hutton Bridge. If you have any information that would allow me to complete my lists, or you or your club have details of a competition I have overlooked, I would be delighted to hear from you.

A brief history of the Charity Cups

Inspired by the success of the Myers & Burnell Cup a group of local businessmen and cricket enthusiasts decided in 1929 to set up a knock-out cricket competition with the aim of raising money for the York County Hospital. The inaugural meeting was held in the County Hospital boardroom and according to the minutes a "valuable silver trophy has been donated by a well known local tradesman and sportsman". This was Henry Foster, a local butcher and President of the Butchers Guild, and also captain of the York Butchers C.C., who was elected President of the of the new competition. A committee was formed and rules were drawn up restricting entry to teams within a 10 mile radius of York Post Office. Why this landmark was chosen is not clear, but perhaps it was felt that York Minster had already been appropriated by the Myers & Burnell, or that the Post Office had a more egalitarian feel which would reflect the make up of the competing clubs. It is a fact that until after the Second World War many more of the smaller clubs and what might be described as "working class" and works teams participated in the Charity Cups rather than in the Myers & Burnell, and several of the more established clubs did not enter the Charity Cups in the early years.

A meeting in early 1930 stated that the name should be "The York County Hospital Cricket Cup Competition" and that the wooden base of the Cup should have fixed to it an inscribed plate reading "York County Hospital Cricket Cup". A resolution was passed that games should take place on the competing clubs' grounds, except for the final and semi-finals which would be played on neutral grounds to be organised by the committee. Early rounds were to be "time games" with one and a quarter hours batting per side on the same evening, and two hours each in the semi finals and final, these to be played over two evenings. By 1932 semi-finals were reduced to one and a half hours each, over two evenings "if needed", with the final still being two hours per side on two nights. By 1933 all games were to be "overs games", with early rounds being 25 six ball overs each played on one night, increasing to 35 overs each on consecutive nights in the semi-finals and to 45 overs each in the final, again on consecutive nights. Entry was initially set at two shillings and sixpence per team and a collection was to be made at each game using collection boxes provided by the committee, the proceeds after expenses to go to the County Hospital. An advertisement was placed in the local press seeking entries and it was stated that the Cup would be "on display in Mr H. Staveley's shop window in Micklegate". Games were to be arranged "so as not to clash with Evening League fixtures or the Myers & Burnell Cup". The first winners in 1930 were surrounded by controversy. Called York Collegiate, the team consisted of several players with connections to the York club amongst them Dr Philip Sawkill and Harry Rayson who captained the side and the team was essentially a collection of talented players from various clubs. Fairly soon a "strong rumour", as the committee described it in their minutes, spread amongst the local cricketing community that the York club, who organised the Myers & Burnell, were backing the Collegiate team in an effort to discredit the competition and prevent it becoming a rival to the Myers & Burnell. Any potential loss of income at this time was taken seriously by the York club who had narrowly avoided financial ruin some years earlier. With the passage of time the truth of this accusation is impossible to prove, but the committee received many written complaints from local clubs which were taken very seriously and were recorded in the minutes of the 1930 A.G.M. and as a result York Collegiate never took part in the competition again. Despite this the competition was deemed a success and so many entries were received for the 1931 season that it was decided to split them into two sections with the clubs deemed "Senior" being in one and those deemed "Junior" being assigned to another. In April 1931 a second Cup was donated by Henry Foster and a motion was passed to have each Cup engraved "York Hospital Cup". However this engraving never happened as can be seen on the Cups today, one being engraved "Senior Charity Cricket Cup" and the other "Junior Charity Cricket Cup". When this happened is not known but by October 1934 the committee's minutes show that they had changed their name to the "York Charity Cups Competition" and the proceeds were to be distributed to several good causes including the County Hospital. The new Cup for the Junior section was identical to the original which was described as "a valuable silver trophy", although a close examination of both Cups reveals that neither have hallmarks or makers marks of any description. At some point between 1935 and 1958 all games became two innings on one evening consisting of sixteen six ball overs per side. A proposal to switch to eight ball overs was defeated at the 1958 A.G.M. but by 1970 games were sixteen eight ball overs per side and in 1985 this was changed to eighteen eight ball overs, this format remaining in place until the demise of the competition in 2014. Another proposal that was defeated at the 1958 A.G.M. was to increase the radius for competing clubs to 15 miles from the Post Office, but by 1970 the radius had extended to 25 miles.

So in 1931 two competitions were run, the Senior section being won by York Station Staff who played on the Knavesmire and had been runners-up to York Collegiate in the previous year. The Junior section was won by Scarcroft, who played on the "Polo ground", a piece of the Knavesmire behind the popular ring opposite the main Grandstand. The Senior Charity developed into one of York's most prestigious competitions possibly second only to the Myers & Burnell. Several clubs that no longer exist such as Sand Hutton, Clarence C.& I., York Revellers and York Zingari all appeared in the 1930's and the early years of the War saw the rise of York Railway Institute and military teams such as the Royal Army Ordnance Corps and the Royal Observer Corps. The competition was then suspended for three years from 1944, after which Ainsty Building Estates made two consecutive finals as runners-up in 1947 and winners in 1948. A strong side that contained players such as Claude Skilbeck, Tommy Hobson and three of the Kay family, William, Noel and Clive, they made a brief but successful appearance in local Cricket winning the York and District Senior League in their debut season of 1947. They never finished outside the top five and had lost only 12 of their 67 league games in the four seasons played before they folded after the 1950 season. They were replaced by York Civil Service, who also took over their ground on Boroughbridge Road. From the early 1950's the finals were generally dominated by the major local sides from the Senior League who also featured in the Myers & Burnell. A "double" of the Senior Charity and Myers & Burnell was a cherished achievement only accomplished on eight occasions after the War, one each by Acomb, Clifton Alliance, Heworth, Osbaldwick and Sheriff Hutton Bridge and three by York.

The Junior Charity featured many smaller clubs and works or trade teams such as York Butchers, Corporation Highways, Poppleton Sugar Factory and Church sides such as Albany Street Methodists, along with Old Boys teams from the likes of Haxby Road School and the Minster Choir School. There were also many local villages that have long since lost their cricket teams, including Murton, Naburn, Haxby, Poppleton, Shipton-by-Beningbrough, Sutton-on-Forest and East Cottingwith to name but a few. The 1954 winners were Ogle's Sports, a team put together by George Ogle, a garage owner on the Hull Road near Barmby Moor, containing several players from nearby clubs such as Woodhouse Grange, Pocklington and Yapham and captained by Alasdair Swann. From the 1960's onward the competition was mainly made up of Senior League second teams and lower division first teams along with Saturday League sides. However, Thornton and East Cottingwith from the East Riding Independent Evening League featured in six finals between 1976 and 1982.

The 1961 Junior final was delayed due to Dringhouses claiming to be unable to raise a side but the committee refused to believe this and awarded the Cup to Terrys, the confectionary factory side. Terrys refused to accept the Cup under those circumstances and requested a postponement, but the committee were adamant and declared them the winners. After much pressure from Terrys the committee relented and the final was duly played two weeks late, Dringhouses emerging the winners. Terrys could be said to have held the trophy for a fortnight, the shortest period on record. Justice was done to Terrys for their sporting gesture when they won the trophy in 1964 and 1967. The 2012 competition ended disappointingly after the semi-final between Heworth and the Retreat ended with claims of ineligible players. The resulting correspondence became "very acrimonious" in the words of the committee, to the point that they looked to play the final between the other two semi-finalists. This proved impossible due to the clubs involved being reluctant to play, so the Cup was not awarded.

Both competitions ended after the 2014 season. Despite the decline in the popularity of evening cricket, both competitions continued to attract sufficient teams to remain viable, but nevertheless they folded after the 2014 season. The committee were unable to recruit a new secretary or attract enough new members to run the competitions efficiently. The amount of behind the scenes work that went into organising these competitions, dealing with the never ending objections and complaints from competing clubs, securing sponsorship and distributing the profits to the various good causes was tremendous and can only really be appreciated when one reads through the minutes and vast amount of correspondence contained in the archives at York Library. Both local cricketers and charities alike owe a debt of gratitude to the likes of Claude Skilbeck, George Simpson, Nigel Collinson, Tim Murphy, Don Layfield, Chris Houseman, Alan Robinson and many others who helped run the Charity Cups over the years.

year	WINNERS	SCORE	CAPTAIN	RUNNERS-UP	SCORE
	Senior Charity Cup				
1930	York Collegiate	178	Harry G.Rayson	York Station Staff	108
1931	York Station Staff	74-2	George G.Cross	Poppleton	65 all out
1932	Sand Hutton	182-5	H.Milne	Clarence C.& I.	109 all out
1933	York Reserves	164-9	R.A.Castle	Rowntrees	148 all out
1934	York Reserves		R.A.Castle	Clarence C.& I.	
1935	Clifton C.C.	94-5	Bill Taylor	Rowntrees	91 all out
1936	York Revellers		S.J.Moor	Escrick	
1937	Clifton C.C.		Bill Taylor	Acomb	
1938	Sand Hutton	109-2	H.Milne	Clarence C.& I.	75 all out
1939	York Zingari *	127-4	Vic Bedford	Stamford Bridge	126 all out
1940	York Railway Institute	67-8	Bob Stather	Stamford Bridge	37 all out
1941	Royal Army Ordnance Corps	131-5	G.Hodgkinson	Royal Observer Corps	128 all out
1942	Ovington	108-5	Billy Goodall	York Railway Institute	103 all out
1943	Clifton C.C.		Jack R.Pulleyn	York Railway Institute	
1944	No Competition war		No Competition war	No Competition war	
1945	No Competition war		No Competition war	No Competition war	
1946	No Competition war		No Competition war	No Competition war	
1947	York Railway Institute	211 all out	Billy Moore	Ainsty Buiding Estates	168 all out
1948	Ainsty Building Estates		William A.Kay	York Railway Institute	
1949	York Railway Institute	117-4	George Mortimer	Rowntrees	116 all out
1950	Clifton C.C.	132-5	Herbert Harrison	York Railway Institute	131 all out
1951	Clifton C.C.		Herbert Harrison	Rowntrees	
1952	Woodhouse Grange	161-6	Tommy H.Hobson	Rowntrees	137 all out
1953	Dringhouses		Stan Fawcett	Rowntrees	
1954	Dringhouses	76-5	Stan Fawcett	New Earswick	74 all out
1955	Woodhouse Grange	132-9	Tommy H.Hobson	Haxby	125 all out
1956	Dringhouses		Stan Fawcett	Stamford Bridge	
1957	Dringhouses		Stan Fawcett	York Ramblers	
1958	Stamford Bridge	89 all out	Wally Pearson	Huntington W.M.C.	53 all out
1959	York Railway Institute		Geoff N.Britton	Woodhouse Grange	
1960	Woodhouse Grange		Tommy H.Hobson	York Ramblers	
1961	Heworth		Tommy Baram	Haxby	
1962	Woodhouse Grange		Alisdair Swann	York an XI	
1963	York an XI	153-7	Tony F.J.Temple	New Earswick	146 all out
1964	Huntington W.M.C.		Derek Magson	Sheriff Hutton Bridge	
1965	Sheriff Hutton Bridge		Jimmy Rhodes Jnr.	Dringhouses	
1966	Sheriff Hutton Bridge	130-6	Jimmy Rhodes Jnr.	Heworth	129 all out
1967	Rowntrees		Lol Morse	Woodhouse Grange	
1968	Sheriff Hutton Bridge	153-8	Chris Tate	Woodhouse Grange	
1969	Sheriff Hutton Bridge		Chris Tate	Heworth	
1970	York Civil Service	36-2	John Freer	Dringhouses	35 all out
1971	Heworth	98-2	Alec Fyrth	York Railway Institute	97-9
1972	York an XI	81-3	John Taylor	Tadcaster Town	80-6
1973	Easingwold	113-4	Dennis Hutchinson	Huntington W.M.C.	44 all out
1974	York an XI	97-6	John Taylor	Acomb	96 all out
1975	Sheriff Hutton Bridge	95-8	Mick R.Oldfield	Dringhouses	94 all out
1976	Huntington W.M.C.	72-2	Wally Baynes	Sheriff Hutton Bridge	70-8
1977	Huntington W.M.C.	122-5	Wally Baynes	Heworth	93-8
1978	Dunnington	114-5	Dave Leeman	Sheriff Hutton Bridge	113-8
1979	Acomb		Denzil Webster	Stamford Bridge	
1980	York an XI	114-7	Andrew Tate	Acomb	111-9
1981	Stamford Bridge	69-1	Norman Pearson	Easingwold	68 all out

Year	Winner	Score	Captain	Runner-up	Score
1982	Stamford Bridge	121 all out	Norman Pearson	Easingwold	105 all out
1983	Huntington	81-1	Wally Baynes	Stamford Bridge	80 all out
1984	Osbaldwick	104 all out	Dave Rippon	Stamford Bridge	92 all out
1985	Heworth	156-0	Ian A.Reed	Osbaldwick	142-7
1986	Osbaldwick	125-6	Dave Rippon	Acomb	120-7
1987	Bubwith	109-9	Andy Ward	Dunnington	102 all out
1988	Osbaldwick**	43-4 rsp	Dave Rippon	Heworth	76-8
1989	Heworth	124-1	Ken B.Johnson	Osbaldwick	120-8
1990	Acomb***	120-5 tie	Robert W.Turner	Osbaldwick	120-7
1991	Osbaldwick	151-6	Dave Wood & Dave Rippon	Sheriff Hutton Bridge	67-7
1992	Heworth		Dave Simpson	Sheriff Hutton Bridge	
1993	Heworth		Trevor Walton	Osbaldwick	
1994	Heworth	184-2	Trevor Walton	Bilton-in-Ainsty	174-7
1995	Acomb	171-2	Rich Clayton	Clifton Hospital Alliance	169-6
1996	Heworth		Martin E.Sigsworth	Dunnington	
1997	Osbaldwick	151-7	Pete Machin & Dave Kettlestring	Dunnington	112-7
1998	Clifton Alliance	154-6	Duncan Naylor	Heworth	146-5
1999	Heworth	152-4	Dave Simpson	Osbaldwick	143-4
2000	Clifton Alliance	180-3	Duncan Naylor	Heworth	109-7
2001	Clifton Alliance	184-3	Duncan Naylor	Heworth	97-8
2002	Acomb CC		Dave Sykes	Pocklington	
2003	Clifton Alliance	124-7	Duncan Naylor	York	123-6
2004	York	157-7	Nick Kay	Osbaldwick	81 all out
2005	Woodhouse Grange	125-1	Steve Burdett	Clifton Alliance	124-6
2006	York	133-9	Nick Kay	Clifton Alliance	121-8
2007	York		Nick Kay	Woodhouse Grange	
2008	Woodhouse Grange****	128-8	Steve Burdett	York	128-9
2009	Clifton Alliance	155-6	Richard F.T.Musgrave	York	104 all out
2010	Woodhouse Grange		Steve Burdett	Sessay	
2011	York		Nick Kay	Sessay	
2012	York	135-4	Dan Woods	Clifton Alliance	133-6
2013	Woodhouse Grange		Nick Hadfield	York	
2014	Woodhouse Grange		Steve Burdett	Easingwold	
	* The Cup has Clifton CC engraved for 1939, but the committee minutes state York Zingari were the winners and congratulate them on winning at their first attempt and also winning the Myers & Burnell.				
	** rain stopped play, run rate used for the first time.				
	*** tie, run rate used.				
	**** tie, won on fewer wickets lost.				

163

	Junior Charity Cup				
year	WINNERS	SORE	CAPTAIN	RUNNERS-UP	SCORE
1931	Scarcroft	91 all out	A.Graham	Southlands	68 all out
1932	Scarcroft	93 all out	A.Graham	Ovington	67 all out
1933	Rowntrees 2nd XI	88-6	H.Connell	Murton	86 all out
1934	Haxby Road Old Boys	137 all out	W.Thompson	Albany Street Methodists	100 all out
1935	Murton	110 all out	E.Walker	Naburn	72 all out
1936	Corporation Highways		W.Hields	Askham United	
1937	Stockton-on-Forest		S.Swan	Riccall	
1938	Riccall	86-9	J.S.Halkon	Rowntrees 2nd XI	85 all out
1939	Hopgrove		Les Pears	Naburn	
1940	Hopgrove		Fred Allen	Poppleton Sugar Factory	
1941	No competition War			No competition War	
1942	No competition War			No competition War	
1943	No competition War			No competition War	
1944	No competition War			No competition War	
1945	No competition War			No competition War	
1946	No competition War			No competition War	
1947	York Journeyman Butchers	69 all out	J.W.Hudson	Haxby	65 all out
1948	York Railway Institute		Bob Stather	Stillingfleet	
1949	St.Olave's	101all out	A.S.Lane	Osbaldwick	50 all out
1950	Ovington 2nd XI		A.Thompson	York Butchers	
1951	Sheriff Hutton Bridge		Jim Rhodes Snr	Poppleton	
1952	Wheldrake		George Beilby	RAF Linton	
1953	Fulford United		W.Hayes	Wheldrake	
1954	Ogles Sports Club	176-5	Ernie Bagley	Shipton	33-9 (10 men only)
1955	Minster Choir School OB	132-8	J.Turner	Long Marston	79 all out
1956	Sheriff Hutton Bridge	127-8	Gerry Grinham	Long Marston	105 all out
1957	Sheriff Hutton Bridge	136-7	Gerry Grinham	Minster Choir School OB	134-7
1958	Sutton-on-Forest	71-6	Jack Woodliffe	Dunnington	69 all out
1959	Askham Bryan		Phil Hopwood	Dringhouses 2nd XI	
1960	Dunnington		Jim Burniston	Haxby	
1961	Dringhouses 2nd XI		John Lawson	Terrys *	
1962	Kelfield		Francis Golton	Sheriff Hutton Bridge	
1963	Dringhouses 2nd XI	107-3	John Lawson	Heslington	106 all out
1964	Terrys		R.Sturdy	Heworth 2nd XI	
1965	Fulforgate W.M.C.	107 all out	C.Johnson/KGrant	Heworth 2nd XI	99 all out
1966	Clifton Hospital	99-9	Joe McConnon	Civil Service 2nd XI	79 all out
1967	Terrys		S.Whiting	N.M.U. (Rowntrees)	
1968	Dringhouses 2nd XI	151 all out	Stan Fawcett	Acomb 2nd XI	140 all out
1969	Woodhouse Grange 2nd XI	194-7	D.Milner	Poppleton	160 all out
1970	Dunnington 2nd XI		Jim Burniston	Osbaldwick	
1971	Sheriff Hutton Bridge 2nd XI	96-5	Albert Pattison	Heworth 2nd XI	95-9
1972	Wheldrake	77 all out	John Jackson	Sheriff Hutton Bridge 2nd XI	73 all out
1973	Heworth 2nd XI	94-5	Colin Armstrong	Dunnington 2nd XI	93-8
1974	Heworth 2nd XI	81 all out	Eric Wrighton	Dunnington 2nd XI	79-8
1975	Easingwold 2nd XI		Bill Dunnill	Long Marston	
1976	East Cottingwith		Nigel Room	Easingwold 2nd XI	
1977	Heworth 2nd XI		Guy Raines	Thornton	
1978	Heworth 2nd XI		Ray Pudsey	East Cottingwith	
1979	Heworth 2nd XI		Mark J.L.Smith	Stillingfleet	
1980	Thornton	98-7	Stuart Craven	Long Marston	91 all out
1981	Tadcaster Town 2nd XI		Barry A.Shann	Dunnington 2nd XI	
1982	Thornton	85-1	Stuart Craven	Osbaldwick	84-9

Year	Team	Score	Name	Opponent	Score
1983	Heworth 2nd XI	119-5	David Freeman	Sheriff Hutton	63-8
1984	Heworth 2nd XI		David Freeman	Escrick Park	
1985	Heworth 2nd XI	87-7	David Freeman	Escrick Park	86 all out
1986	Clifton Hospital Alliance	57-5	Ian Burden	Burythorpe	55-9
1987	Burythorpe	140-4	Geoff Milner	Crayke	110-8
1988	Sheriff Hutton Bridge 2nd XI		Colin Mole	Not Known	
1989	Tadcaster Town		Malcolm W.Marsh	Not Known	
1990	Stamford Bridge 2nd XI		Rod Burdett	General Accident	
1991	York Railway Institute		Alfie Hill	Not Known	
1992	Heworth 2nd XI		Andy Ward	Not Known	
1993	Huntington		Neil Atkinson	Not Known	
1994	Osbaldwick 2nd XI	111-8	Dave Rippon	Stockton & Hopgrove	74 all out
1995	Osbaldwick 2nd XI	156-8	Dave Rippon	Dunnington 2nd XI	108-9
1996	Cawood		Matthew Kellett	Acomb 2nd XI	
1997	Acomb 2nd XI		John Webster	Yapham	
1998	Huntington		Not known	Long Marston	
1999	Aldby Park		A.Craven	Rowntrees	
2000	Heslington		Paul Clark	Heworth 2nd XI	
2001	Heslington		John Myers	Cawood	
2002	Tadcaster Magnet		Martin Lambert	Wilberfoss	
2003	Acomb 2nd XI		James Byford	Stillington	
2004	Heworth 2nd XI		Joel Johnson	New Earswick	
2005	Clifton Alliance 2nd XI	162-3	Duncan Naylor	Long Marston	116-9
2006	Stamford Bridge 2nd XI		Martin Veysey	Osbaldwick 2nd XI	
2007	Clifton Alliance 2nd XI	97-3	John Myers	Westow	96-6
2008	Woodhouse Grange 2nd XI		Marcus Smith	Burn	
2009	Tadcaster Magnet		Paul Clark	Dringhouses 2nd XI	
2010	York 2nd XI		Simon Hall	Hemingborough	
2011	Stockton & Hopgrove		Rich Kerrison	York 2nd XI	
2012	NOT AWARDED**				
2013	Tadcaster Magnets		Paul Smith	Acomb 2nd XI	
2014	Woodhouse Grange 2nd XI		Paul Grewer	Stockton & Hopgrove	
	* awarded cup				
	** dispute				

165

The Acomb Invitation

The Acomb Invitation Trophy was first played for in 1958 and became one of the major evening competitions in the York area. The Trophy itself, originally called the "York and District Challenge Cup Competition", was donated in 1890 by Mr Riley-Smith, from the brewing dynasty in Tadcaster, and played for annually. Little is known of this competition except for the fact that the final was played on the York Cricket Club ground at Bootham Crescent. It was won in 1890 and 1891 by Acomb who defeated Heworth Revellers in the 1891 final and they went on to win it outright as a result of a third victory sometime later in the 1890's. The Cup was promptly placed in the safety of the club's bank where it stayed until it was withdrawn to use as the Invitation Trophy. It is a fine looking silver cup with engraved scroll work and scenes of a game of cricket on both sides. Initially the final was a 40 overs per side game played on Sunday afternoons changing from 1965 onward to being played on a Wednesday evening as a 20 six ball over game and later changed again to 16 eight ball overs with a limit of four overs per bowler. Originally all games were played at Acomb, but from 1981 onward early rounds were played on the competing clubs' grounds, with the semi-finals and final played at Acomb. A handicap system was also introduced in later years to encourage lower league teams to enter.

Acomb Invitation					
year	WINNERS	RUNNERS-UP		WINNERS	RUNNERS-UP
1958	York Railway Institute	Civil Service	1983	Heworth	Easingwold
1959	Woodhouse Grange	Not known	1984	No competition	No competition
1960	Woodhouse Grange	Not known	1985	Tadcaster	Not known
1961	York Railway Institute	Not known	1986	Woodhouse Grange	Not known
1962	York Railway Institute	Not known	1987	Tadcaster	Not known
1963	No competition	No competition	1988	Heworth	Not known
1964	No competition	No competition	1989	Woodhouse Grange	Stamford Bridge
1965	Civil Service	Not known	1990	Pocklington	Not known
1966	York Railway Institute	Heworth	1991	Heworth	Osbaldwick
1967	Dringhouses	Heworth	1992	York	Not known
1968	Civil Service	Easingwold	1993	York	Heworth
1969	Sheriff Hutton Bridge	Tadcaster	1994	York	Easingwold
1970	Sheriff Hutton Bridge	Easingwold	1995	Bilton-in-Ainsty	Heworth
1971	Easingwold	Sheriff Hutton Bridge	1996	Clifton Alliance	Heworth
1972	Dringhouses	Easingwold	1997	Clifton Alliance	Easingwold
1973	Sheriff Hutton Bridge	Easingwold	1998	Clifton Alliance	Osbaldwick
1974	Huntington W.M.C.	Woodhouse Grange	1999	Clifton Alliance	Osbaldwick
1975	Sheriff Hutton Bridge	Dringhouses	2000	York	Easingwold
1976	Sheriff Hutton Bridge	Easingwold	2001	York	Not known
1977	Easingwold	Sheriff Hutton Bridge	2002	Easingwold	York
1978	Sheriff Hutton Bridge	Tadcaster	2003	Clifton Alliance	Heworth
1979	Heworth	Woodhouse Grange	2004	Clifton Alliance	Acomb
1980	Easingwold	Heworth	2005	Heworth	Not known
1981	Thorp Arch & Boston Spa	Sheriff Hutton Bridge	2006	Clifton Alliance	York
1982	Sheriff Hutton Bridge	Heworth			

The Sawkill Cup

The Sawkill Cup (an elegant silver cup complete with lid) was run by Stamford Bridge from 1952 until 2014. The Cup was presented to Doctor Philip Sawkill in 1951 and he graciously donated it to be used as a trophy for a knock-out competition to be organised by the Stamford Bridge club. The Cup is engraved on the front "The Sawkill Cricket Cup" and below can be found the following inscription "Subscribed for by the associates of Dr P.M. Sawkill as an appreciation of 25 years captaincy of the Stamford Bridge Club 1927-1951". Until 1963 the early rounds were 24 six ball over games played on the clubs' grounds with the semi-finals and final being spread over two nights, these being played at Stamford. From 1964 onward all games became 20 six ball overs per side (changing to 18 eight ball overs in 1970) with the final played at Stamford on a Friday evening.

The Sawkill Cup					
year	WINNERS	RUNNERS-UP		WINNERS	RUNNERS-UP
1952	Ovington	Not known	1984	Heworth	Pocklington
1953	Woodhouse Grange	Not known	1985	Acomb	Not known
1954	Ovington	Woodhouse Grange	1986	Heworth	Acomb
1955	York Civil Service	Not known	1987	Acomb	Not known
1956	Yapham	Ovington	1988	Woodhouse Grange	Not known
1957	Huntington W.M.C.	Not known	1989	Pocklington	Woodhouse Grange
1958	Escrick Park	Huntington W.M.C.	1990	Heworth	Not known
1959	York Ramblers	Not known	1991	Woodhouse Grange	Londesborough Park
1960	Dringhouses	York Ramblers	1992	Heworth	Dunnington
1961	Dringhouses	Not known	1993	Heworth	Woodhouse Grange
1962	Pocklington Nomads	Not known	1994	Easingwold	Heworth
1963	Dringhouses	York Ramblers	1995	Woodhouse Grange	Osbaldwick
1964	Dringhouses	Not known	1996	Woodhouse Grange	Not known
1965	Huntington W.M.C.	Yapham	1997	Easingwold	Clifton Alliance
1966	Woodhouse Grange	Not known	1998	Heworth	Clifton Alliance
1967	Woodhouse Grange	Not known	1999	Easingwold	Osbaldwick
1968	Old Malton	Stockton & Hopgrove	2000	Woodhouse Grange	Dringhouses
1969	Sheriff Hutton Bridge	Dunnington	2001	Acomb	Not known
1970	Sheriff Hutton Bridge	Not known	2002	Dunnington	Not known
1971	Heworth	Londesborough Park	2003	Dunnington	Not known
1972	Heworth	Not known	2004	Woodhouse Grange	Not known
1973	Londesborough Park	Heworth	2005	Heworth	Not known
1974	Dunnington	Not known	2006	Heworth	Not known
1975	Escrick Park	Not known	2007	Acomb*	Heworth
1976	Pocklington	Not known	2008	Dunnington	Not known
1977	Acomb	Not known	2009	Clifton Alliance	Not known
1978	Dunnington	Heworth	2010	Dunnington	Not known
1979	Woodhouse Grange	Not known	2011	Woodhouse Grange	Not known
1980	Woodhouse Grange	Not known	2012	Woodhouse Grange	Not known
1981	Heworth	Not known	2013	Woodhouse Grange	Not known
1982	Forge Valley	Not known	2014	Woodhouse Grange	Not known
1983	Heworth	Not known			
	* game tied Acomb won on bowl out				

The Isaac Poad / York invitation Cup

This cup was actually called the Arthur Brown Trophy, but it was generally known by most local cricketers as the Isaac Poad having been donated by Isaac Poad & Sons, a well known and long established local seed and potato merchant. The Cup was named after their Chairman Arthur Brown, a keen sportsman who was a Director of York City F.C. and President of Cliftonville A.F.C. It was first contested in 1976 and it later became known as the York Invitation using the same trophy with sponsorship from Harowell Shaftoe solicitors. The last final took place in 1996. The trophy is a handsome silver cup with a batsman on the lid. It was competed for by six local teams invited by the York club, with the home club entering their Ridings XI and East Yorkshire Cup XI. The format was 18 eight ball overs per side with a maximum of five overs per bowler played on one evening and all games were played at Clifton Park.

	The Isaac Poad / York Invitation				
year	WINNERS	RUNNERS-UP	year	WINNERS	RUNNERS-UP
1976	Huntington W.M.C.	Stamford Bridge	1987	Woodhouse Grange	Not known
1977	Sheriff Hutton Bridge	Huntington W.M.C.	1988	Acomb	Sheriff Hutton Bridge
1978	York Ridings XI	Sheriff Hutton Bridge	1989	Woodhouse Grange	Not known
1979	York Ridings XI	Not known	1990	Woodhouse Grange	Not known
1980	Dringhouses	York Ridings XI	1991	Woodhouse Grange	Osbaldwick
1981	Easingwold	York Ridings XI	1992	Heworth	York an XI
1982	Sessay	Not known	1993	Woodhouse Grange	Sheriff Hutton Bridge
1983	Stamford Bridge	Osbaldwick	1994	Sessay	Not known
1984	Easingwold	Stamford Bridge	1995	Clifton Hospital Alliance	Stamford Bridge
1985	Woodhouse Grange	Not known	1996	Acomb	Not known
1986	Acomb	Sheriff Hutton Bridge			

The Harry Southwood Memorial Trophy

Known generally as the Southwood Cup, the competition was run by Heworth C.C. from 1970 until 2001. The Cup was named in memory of Harry Southwood, a local plumber, who was a long serving member of the club and was involved in their revival after the Second World War. The original Cup is inscribed "The Harry Southwood Memorial Trophy" and was competed for from 1970 until 1999. Another Cup donated by the Nag's Head public house and inscribed "Heworth Cricket Club Harry Southwood Nag's Head Cup" was played for in 2000 and 2001.

	The Harry Southwood Memorial Trophy		
year	WINNERS		WINNERS
1970	Rowntrees 2nd XI	1986	Dunnington
1971	Shepherd Engineering Services	1987	Dringhouses
1972	Sorrells	1988	Dringhouses
1973	British Rail Chief Finance Officers	1989	Stamford Bridge
1974	Rowntrees 2nd XI	1990	Dringhouses
1975	Dringhouses	1991	Acomb
1976	Dunnington	1992	Stamford Bridge
1977	Rowntress 2nd XI	1993	Dunnington
1978	The Mitres	1994	Stamford Bridge
1979	Huntington W.M.C. 2nd XI	1995	Dunnington 2nd XI
1980	Rowntrees	1996	Osbaldwick 2nd XI
1981	Osbaldwick	1997	Acomb
1982	Osbaldwick	1998	Dunnington 2nd XI
1983	Stamford Bridge	1999	Not known
1984	Huntington CC	2000	Clifton Alliance 2nd XI
1985	Osbaldwick	2001	Acomb

The Midgley Cup

The Cup is solid silver and was presented by the Stillington C.C. President Arthur Midgley and was first played for in 1951. The competition was always well supported with up to twenty five teams entering each year. All the rounds were played on the Stillington ground, with games consisting of 24 six ball overs, weather and light permitting. The competition was supported by a broad range of clubs from Senior League at one end of the spectrum to small village sides such as Oulston and Evening League sides such as L.N.E.R. Motors at the other. As a result a handicap system was used that saw the smallest clubs receiving a 30 run start, reducing to 20 or 10 for the bigger clubs with the best starting off "scratch". The success of the competition is evident from the number of teams who came back year after year to play, much of this being down to the efforts of Dennis North who always made visitors welcome, did the bulk of the work on the ground, ran the bar afterwards and also found time to play. Dennis happily is still going strong but sadly the Cup is no longer played for; having gone the way of so many others it came to an end in 2009.

Stillington also ran the Norman Wood Memorial Trophy, which was donated by Norman Wood, a long time player and chairman of the club. He and his brother Cecil, who captained them to win the Myers & Burnell Cup in 1964, were part of the family business of Thomas Wood & Sons Builders who were responsible for much of the development of the Clubhouse over the years. The competition ran for 30 years from 1975, the last senior side to win being Newburgh Priory. It was then used a junior cup for local under 11's for two years before finally ending in 2007.

The Midgley Cup			
year	WINNERS	year	WINNERS
1951	Crayke	1981	Thirsk
1952	Oulston	1982	Osbaldwick
1953	Oulston	1983	Thirsk
1954	Sheriff Hutton Bridge	1984	Osbaldwick
1955	Sheriff Hutton Bridge	1985	Crayke
1956	Bishop Wilton	1986	Dunnington
1957	Sheriff Hutton Bridge	1987	Civil Service
1958	L.N.E.R. Motors	1988	Dunnington
1959	Huntington W.M.C.	1989	Crayke
1960	L.N.E.R. Motors	1990	Sheriff Hutton Bridge
1961	Crayke	1991	Civil Service
1962	Nawton	1992	Duncombe Park
1963	Huby	1993	Duncombe Park
1964	Stillington	1994	Civil Service
1965	Nawton	1995	Crayke
1966	Rowntrees	1996	Crayke
1967	Rowntrees	1997	Easingwold
1968	Sheriff Hutton Bridge	1998	Duncombe Park
1969	Huntington W.M.C.	1999	Civil Service
1970	Sheriff Hutton Bridge	2000	Duncombe Park
1971	Sheriff Hutton Bridge	2001	Duncombe Park
1972	Crayke	2002	Duncombe Park
1973	Dunnington	2003	Heworth
1974	Huntington W.M.C.	2004	Easingwold
1975	Stillington	2005	Sessay
1976	Easingwold	2006	Sessay
1977	Huntington W.M.C.	2007	Heworth
1978	Alne	2008	Sessay
1979	Sheriff Hutton Bridge	2009	Sessay
1980	Huby		

The Norman Wood Memorial Trophy			
year	WINNERS	year	WINNERS
1975	Sessay	1992	Rowntrees
1976	Sessay	1993	Not known
1977	Thirsk Athletic CC	1994	Rowntrees
1978	Sessay	1995	Huby
1979	Thirsk	1996	Crayke
1980	Thirsk	1997	Not known
1981	Thirsk	1998	Stillington
1982	Thirsk	1999	Huby
1983	Thirsk	2000	Stillington
1984	Thirsk	2001	Thirsk
1985	Not known	2002	Stillington
1986	Not known	2003	Stillington
1987	Crayke	2004	Stillington
1988	Not known	2005	Newburgh Priory
1989	Crayke	2006	Alne under 11's
1990	Hovingham	2007	Easingwold under 11's
1991	Rowntrees		

The Doctor Riddolls Trophy

The Doctor Riddolls Trophy had its origins in the "Flaxton Civil Defence Cricket Tournament 1941", a wooden shield thought to be donated by New Earswick C.C. president and local G.P. Dr. Riddolls. It started in 1941 and ran through the War years, being open to teams within the Flaxton Rural District Council area. As the name suggests it was aimed at teams belonging to various branches of Civil Defence but also included local village teams, increasingly so after 1945. The competition was organised by the New Earswick club and the finals were played on the New Earswick ground, which at that time was next to the Joseph Rowntree School. After the War Dr.Riddolls donated a solid silver cup which replaced the shield in 1949, the Cup being engraved "The Dr. A.W. RIDDOLLS Cricket Trophy". From 1949 the early rounds were played as 18 eight ball over games on the competing clubs' grounds, with semi-finals and final being played at New Earswick. Semi-finals were 18 eight ball overs per side, while the final was 40 six ball overs per side on a Sunday afternoon. One new ball was provided for each of the semi-finals and the final, thus lending a subtle twist to the toss, the winning captain having to decide whether to bat and have a used ball to bowl with in the second innings or have use of the new ball and bat second. As with most of the competitions interest began to wane and in the late 1970's it became a predominantly second team cup finally folding in 2001

year	WINNERS	year	WINNERS
The Dr Riddolls Cup			
1941	Heworth Police XI	1972	Dunnington
1942	National Fire Service	1973	Heworth
1943	Casualty Service	1974	Acomb & Dunnington
1944	F.Company 6 North Riding Home Guard	1975	Stockton & Hopgrove
1945	Not known	1976	Sheriff Hutton
1946	Not known	1977	Sheriff Hutton
1947	Sheriff Hutton CC	1978	Stockton & Hopgrove
1948	Burnholme CC in final winner not known	1979	Crayke
1949	Stockton & Hopgrove	1980	Crayke
1950	New Earswick	1981	Acomb 2nd XI
1951	Stockton & Hopgrove	1982	Acomb 2nd XI
1952	New Earswick	1983	Not known
1953	Burnholme	1984	New Earswick 1st XI
1954	Haxby	1985	Not known
1955	Sheriff Hutton Bridge	1986	Not known
1956	New Earswick 1st XI	1987	Crayke
1957	Huntington W.M.C. & New Earswick 1st XI	1988	Woodhouse Grange 2nd XI
1958	Huntington W.M.C.	1989	New Earswick 1st XI
1959	New Earswick 1st XI	1990	Woodhouse Grange 2nd XI
1960	Heworth 1st XI	1991	Woodhouse Grange 2nd XI
1961	Heworth 1st XI	1992	Woodhouse Grange 2nd XI
1962	Sheriff Hutton	1993	Not known
1963	Heworth 1st XI	1994	Heworth 2nd XI
1964	Sheriff Hutton Bridge	1995	Heslington
1965	Sheriff Hutton	1996	Heworth 2nd XI
1966	Rowntrees	1997	Heworth 2nd XI
1967	Sheriff Hutton Bridge	1998	Stillington
1968	New Earswick 1st XI	1999	Heworth 2nd XI
1969	Huntington W.M.C.	2000	Heslington
1970	York Railway Institute	2001	Not known (Dringhouses 2nd XI
1971	Heworth		were runners-up)
Years in Blue the Flaxton Shield			
Years in Black the Dr.Riddolls Cup			

172

The Major Pearson Cup

The Major Pearson Cup was run by Easingwold C.C. The trophy which was donated in 1927 by Major Stanley Pearson, is solid silver and engraved as follows; "Easingwold and District Knock-out Cricket Competition for Village Teams". Not surprisingly, it soon became known simply as the Major Pearson Cup and was last competed for in 2008.

The Major Pearson					
year	WINNERS	year	WINNERS	year	WINNERS
1927	Hawkhills	1955	Crayke	1983	Crayke
1928	Hawkhills	1956	Shipton	1984	Sessay
1929	Easingwold	1957	Sessay	1985	Slingsby
1930	Brandsby	1958	Alne	1986	Crayke
1931	Stillington	1959	Westow	1987	Thirsk
1932	Stillington	1960	Crayke	1988	Easingwold
1933	Easingwold	1961	Sheriff Hutton Bridge	1989	Crayke
1934	Crayke	1962	Sessay	1990	Sessay
1935	Stillington	1963	Sheriff Hutton Bridge	1991	Sessay
1936	Stillington	1964	Crayke	1992	Easingwold
1937	Stillington	1965	Crayke	1993	Easingwold
1938	Terrington	1966	Forresters	1994	Easingwold
1939	Sessay	1967	Crayke	1995	Huntington
1940	Sessay	1968	Easingwold	1996	Sessay
1941	Crayke	1969	Huby	1997	Crayke
1942	Easingwold	1970	Easingwold	1998	Stockton & Hopgrove
1943	Easingwold	1971	Sheriff Hutton Bridge	1999	Sessay
1944	Kilburn	1972	Easingwold	2000	Crayke
1945	Easingwold	1973	Sheriff Hutton	2001	Crayke
1946	Terrington	1974	Easingwold	2002	Crayke
1947	Thornton le Clay	1975	Easingwold	2003	Easingwold
1948	Nawton Grange	1976	Huby	2004	Huby
1949	Aldwark	1977	Sheriff Hutton Bridge	2005	Easingwold
1950	Easingwold	1978	Easingwold	2006	Easingwold
1951	Crayke	1979	Crayke	2007	Huby
1952	Alne	1980	Crayke	2008	Sessay
1953	Sheriff Hutton Bridge	1981	Crayke		
1954	Easingwold	1982	Sessay		

The Canon Hedley Trophy

The Canon Hedley Trophy began in 1969 and has been played for every year since. The competition is for teams in the area south-east of York, the final being played on the Yorkshire Gentlemen's ground at Escrick Park. Teams must comprise players born or living in the Parish in which the club is situated, although as it has become harder to turn out eligible teams the organisers have allowed parishes to merge in an effort to keep the competition alive.

The Canon Hedley Trophy					
year	WINNERS	year	WINNERS	year	WINNERS
1969	East Cottingwith	1986	Ellerton	2003	Wheldrake
1970	Escrick Park	1987	Ellerton	2004	Bielby
1971	Escrick Park	1988	Wilberfoss	2005	Wheldrake
1972	Escrick Park	1989	Not known	2006	Bielby
1973	Escrick Park	1990	Wilberfoss	2007	Elvington
1974	Wistow	1991	Elvington	2008	Melbourne
1975	Elvington	1992	Wilberfoss	2009	Elvington
1976	Melbourne	1993	Not known	2010	Wheldrake
1977	East Cottingwith	1994	Not known	2011	Elvington
1978	Elvington	1995	Wilberfoss	2012	Wheldrake
1979	Elvington	1996	Wilberfoss	2013	Wheldrake
1980	Not known	1997	Escrick Park	2014	Escrick Park
1981	Cliffe	1998	Escrick Park	2015	Bishop Wilton
1982	Melbourne	1999	Escrick Park	2016	Barmby Moor
1983	Thornton	2000	Cliffe	2017	Bubwith
1984	Not known	2001	Cliffe	2018	Bishop Wilton
1985	Wheldrake	2002	Escrick Park		

The Wilson-Todd Challenge Cup

Established in 1897 after W.H. Wilson-Todd, MP for Howdenshire, donated a beautifully decorated silver cup, which, as the inscription states was "For competition amongst the Cricket Clubs in the Parliamentary Division of Howdenshire". The Cup was competed for by Clubs in the Pocklington League and had a unique format. Ties were played over two nights, one on each of the opposing Club's grounds. The first night, normally a Tuesday, was a game of 24 six ball overs per side and the score was carried over to the Thursday of the same week, when an identical game was played at the other Club's ground, the total of the scores deciding the winner. Teams had to remain unchanged for

174

both games. Originally the final was 35 overs per side played on a Saturday afternoon, but by the early 1960's the final was also played over two nights with the aggregate score deciding the result. By the 1980's all ties including the final were played on a single night, each game consisting of 20 six ball overs per side. It has been competed for continuously since 1897 and is one of the oldest local cup competitions in the country, although it is also on the brink of extinction. 2018 saw Bubwith and Bishop Wilton as the only two participants and it may well soon disappear to leave the Canon Hedley as the sole survivor of a once thriving tradition.

	The Wilson-Todd Challenge Cup				
year	WINNERS	CAPTAIN	year	WINNERS	CAPTAIN
1897	Pocklington	J.Robson	1975	Burythorpe	Tom Foxton
1898	Barmby Moor	A.Sidall	1976	East Cottingwith	Nigel Room
1899	No records		1977	East Cottingwith	Nigel Room
to	No records		1978	Leavening	Geoffrey Day
1935	No records		1979	East Cottingwith	Gordon Houseman
1936	Shiptonthorpe	R.Hardy	1980	Ellerton	Ken Tattersall
1937	Pocklington Y.M.	R.J.Preece	1981	Thixendale	Harry Boyes
1938	Pocklington Co-op	N.Hindwell	1982	Market Weighton	Alan Whitelam
1939	Allison's Sports Club	A.J.Camplin	1983	Barmby Moor	Alan Melling
1940	Allerthorpe	G.Brown	1984	Burythorpe	Geoffrey Milner
1941	Kirby-Underdale	J.Allison	1985	Not known	
1942	Everingham	J.C.Wilkinson	1986	Middleton	Clive Soanes
1943	Not known		1987	East Cottingwith	Geoff Room
1944	Fridaythorpe	E.Sowersby	1988	Thornton	Stuart Craven
1945	Millington	Don Nesom	1989	Not known	
1946	Melbourne	Stanley Wilkinson	1990	Thixendale	Eric Wall
1947	Bugthorpe	F.Smith	1991	North Dalton	Martin Duffy
1948	Barmby Moor	George Brown	1992	East Cottingwith	Richard Lazenby
1949	Millington	John Frank	1993	Wilberfoss	Geoff Room
1950	North Cliffe	Ronald S.Craven	1994	North Dalton	Tony Hara
1951	North Cliffe	Ronald S.Craven	1995	North Dalton	Tony Hara
1952	Wiberfoss	Harry Hindwell	1996	Ellerton	Neil Tattersall
1953	Bishop Wilton	Gordon Foster	1997	Middleton	A.R.Maltas
1954	Bishop Wilton	Gordon Foster	1998	Warter	Richard A.Cooper
1955	Bishop Wilton	Alfred Sleightholme	1999	Black Horse	Jamie Mitchell
1956	Dunnington	Jim Burniston	2000	Warter	Richard A.Cooper
1957	Bishop Wilton	Alfred Sleightholme	2001	Warter	Paul G.Youngman
1958	Thornton	Ronald Hayton	2002	Ellerton	Charlie Cameron
1959	Dunnington	Jim Burniston	2003	Ellerton	Neil Jackson
1960	Barmby Moor	George Brown	2004	Ellerton	Charlie Cameron
1961	Bishop Wilton	Joe Sleightholme	2005	North Dalton	Matthew R.Clarkson
1962	Not known		2006	Woodhouse Grange	Stuart Craven
1963	Bishop Wilton	Harry Ward	2007	Ellerton	Charlie Cameron
1964	Bishop Wilton	Harry Ward	2008	Woodhouse Grange	Stuart Craven
1965	Bishop Wilton	Harry Ward	2009	Woodhouse Grange	Stuart Craven
1966	Bishop Wilton	Harry Ward	2010	Woodhouse Grange	Stuart Craven
1967	Thornton	Kenneth Hayton	2011	North Dalton	Ricky Woodmansey
1968	Thornton	Kenneth Hayton	2012	North Dalton	Ricky Woodmansey
1969	Wilberfoss	Alec Smith	2013	Woodhouse Grange	Stuart Craven
1970	North Dalton	John A.Conner	2014	Bishop Wilton	Dave Blake
1971	Middleton	Barry Snowdon	2015	Woodhouse Grange	Chris Bilton
1972	East Cottingwith	Nigel Room	2016	Market Weighton	AidenMorrell & James Beevers
1973	Thornton	Stuart Craven	2017	Bubwith	Harry Collins & Simon Houlder
1974	North Dalton	John A.Conner	2018	Bubwith	Harry Collins

The Annual Cricketers' Ball

Beginning in 1953 Woodhouse Grange Cricket Club organised an annual Cricketers' Ball, to be held in the De Grey Rooms, at the end of each season. Invitations were sent to clubs in the York area requesting that they brought along any trophies won by the club during the season, which were put on display for the evening. The local press covered the event and usually published a photo showing the successful clubs and their trophies, many of which feature in this book. Below are photos from four of these events along with details of players and trophies where known, I would be delighted to hear from anyone who can fill in the blanks or has pictures from other years.

1958

CRICKETERS' BALL. YORK ASSEMBLY ROOMS. 7.11.58

From left to right; Maurice Woodliffe (S.H.B.), Roy Piercy (S.H.B.), Sam Morse (Stillington), Arthur Midgley (Stillington), Unknown, Eddie Oversby (Ripon), Dick Leadley (York R.I.), Unknown, Stan Fawcett (Dringhouses), John Temple (York), Wally Pearson (Stamford Bridge).

1960

From left to right; Unknown (Woodhouse Grange, Acomb Invitation?), Alisdair Swann (Woodhouse Grange, Senior Charity), Unknown (Harrogate, Y.& D.S.L. Champions Trophy), Unknown, Geoff Britton (York R.I. Myers & Burnell), Unknown, Laurie Thompson (Dringhouses, Sawkill Cup), Unknown, Brian Gray (Alliance, Saturday League Champions Cup), Jim Burniston (Dunnington, Junior Charity), Sam Morse (Stillington), Andy Bulmer (York Ramblers, holding the Midgley Cup won by L.N.E.R. Motors), John Brett (York R.I.).

1961

From left to right; Unknown, Geoff Limbert (Dringhouses, Junior Charity), Alf Patrick (Dringhouses, Y.& D.S.L. Reserve Division Champions), Albert Pattison (S.H.B., the Major Pearson),Eddie Oversby (Ripon, Y.& D.S.L. Champions Trophy), Geoff Wood (Alne, Saturday League Champions Cup), Unknown, Terry Precious (Heworth, Y.& D.S.L. Div.II Champions Trophy, Dr.Riddolls Cup & Senior Charity), R. Thompson?, Nigel Fowler (Woodhouse Grange), John Bradley (York R.I., Myers & Burnell and Acomb Invitation),Tony Temple (York), Unknown, Derek Little.

Back row; Unknown,Unknown,Pete Braithwaite? (Cawood, Myers & Burnell), Unknown (Stillington, Y.& D.S.L. Division II Champions Trophy), Unknown (Ripon, Y.&D.S.L. Champions Trophy),Peter Taylor (York R.I., Acomb Invitation).

Front row; Albert Pattison (Sheriff Hutton Bridge, Y.& D.S.L. Reserve Division B), Unknown, Nigel Fowler (Pocklington Nomads, Sawkill Cup), Francis Golton (Kelfield, Junior Charity), Alidair Swann (Woodhouse Grange, Senior Charity), Brian Wilson (Dringhouses).

Appendix one

The agreement loaning the original Myers & Burnell Cup to the York
Education Committee

ted   19th day of April, 1929.

THE YORK RAMBLERS' CRICKET CLUB

and

THE YORK EDUCATION COMMITTEE.

A G R E E M E N T

as to the YORK RAMBLERS' CRICKET CUP.

Dated   19th April, 1929.

THE YORK RAMBLERS' CRICKET CLUB

and

THE YORK EDUCATION COMMITTEE.

A G R E E M E N T

as to the YORK RAMBLERS' CRICKET CUP.

179

The York Ramblers' Cricket Club having offered to lend a
Cup (The Myers-Burnell Cricket Cup which by virtue of that
Club having won it three times and in accordance with the
rules then governing the competition for the said Cup
became the absolute property of the said Club in August
One thousand nine hundred and twenty eight) to the York
Education Committee for competition amongst the schoolboys
of York with a view to promoting the game of cricket amongst
the schoolboys of York and the offer having been accepted
the following stipulations have been mutually agreed upon:-

1. That the Cup be known as "The York Ramblers' Cup" and
   competed for annually as such by the York Elementary
   Schools.

2. That the said Cup remain the property of the said
   Club at present in existence.

3. That the President of the said Club be asked to
   present the said Cup to the winning team each season.

4. That the said York Education Committee be responsible
   for the running of the aforesaid competition in its
   entirety and such Committee shall have full control
   of the said Cup from season to season.

5. That the said Club insure the said Cup each year.

6. That the said Committee be responsible for the
   safe custody of the said Cup so long as it remains
   in possession of the said Committee.

Signed................................ For and on behalf of the
                                       York Ramblers' Cricket
Signed................................ Club.

Signed................................ For and on behalf of the
                                       York Education Committee.
Signed................................

180

Appendix two

Winners of the York Ramblers Cup	
1929	Knavesmire Higher Grade Boys
1930	Knavesmire Higher Grade Boys
1931	Tang Hall Senior Boys
1932	Knavesmire Higher Grade Boys
1933	Fulford School
1934	Priory Street Higher Grade
1935	St.George's Boys School
1936	Poppleton Road Senior School
1937	Fulford School
1938	Priory Street Higher Grade
1939	Park Grove Senior School
1940	Poppleton Road Senior School
1941	Poppleton Road Senior School
1942	Not competed for
1943	Manor Higher Grade
1944	Poppleton Road Senior School
1945	Scarcrot Road Modern School
1946	The Canon A.R.Lee Modern School
1947	Manor Secondary Modern School
1948	Poppleton Road Secondary School
1949	Scarcroft Secondary Modern School
1950	Beckfield County Modern
1951	No shield
1952	Manor
1953	Manor / Park Grove
1954	No shield
1955	Manor
1956	Scarcroft Secondary Modern School
1957	Acomb
1958	Canon A.R.Lee Modern School
1959	No shield
1960	No shield
1961	Ashfield
1962	Derwent
1963	Joseph Rowntree
1964	St. John's

Manor and Park Grove are both engraved on the shield for 1953, presumably the final was tied or not played for some reason. The blank years simply have no shield on the base, the reason for which is unknown.

Appendix three

Finally I thought I would list my all time Myers & Burnell XI, against which the reader might like to pit their own all stars team. I have restricted myself to "home grown" club cricketers and not picked any overseas or professional players and only players who appeared regularly in the Myers & Burnell were considered, the team in batting order is as follows;

1/ Alf Aveyard (Clifton Hospital)

2/ Des Wyrill (Sheriff Hutton Bridge)

3/ Robbie Marchant (York R.I.)

4/ Dick Sykes (Acomb) (Captain)

5/ John Flintoff (Sessay)

6/ Brian Shirley (Sheriff Hutton Bridge) (Wicketkeeper)

7/ Henry Dalton (Osbaldwick)

8/ Geoff Skilbeck (Easingwold)

9/ Tony Stilgoe (Dringhouses)

10/ Ernie Stubbs (Tadcaster)

11/ Ken Skilbeck (Easingwold)

12th man John Hunter (Clifton Alliance)

Reserve wicketkeeper Paul Miles (Heworth)

My selection is biased toward players who I have either played against or seen play on many occasions. The three exceptions, Alf Aveyard, Henry Dalton and Ernie Stubbs all of whom were before my time, have records in the competition which I feel cannot be ignored in any era, while the remainder will be well known to most readers. The team bats to at least number nine and Ken might well say number eleven!

The last five in the order share more than 450 Myers & Burnell wickets between them, the top five can also bowl and my wicketkeeper as well as being the best I have ever seen in club cricket, was a superb batsman in his own right and a decent bowler in his youth. My 12th man can bat and bowl and was one of the best fielders in local cricket. My reserve keeper may thump me next time we meet for not picking him, but it was a very close call and Billy Carter, Mike Burdett, Dave Rippon and Dave Russell were also candidates. In addition I have left out Dave Simpson, Paul Mosey, Stuart Craven and Dave Taylor, amongst many other great batsmen. I have had to leave out even more top bowlers, Tony Moore, Colin Minton, Noel Hare, Tony Haines, Trevor Walton and Pete Machin being among those I considered.

I would be happy to receive suggestions for alternative XI's and publish them in the second edition should it ever come about.